Learning in Organizations

Learning in Organizations focuses on the issues of diversity in the context of organizational learning. It examines those diversities present in organizations among learners and contexts both within and between organizations. In order for learning to be effective and efficient these diversities must be acknowledged and addressed in the learning design process.

The authors identify the challenges that diversities present and demonstrate how to organize and implement learning in the workplace. They show that there are no generic solutions to these issues and offer context-specific solutions to the dilemmas and issues that diversities present. This is essential reading for all those studying human-resource management and development and anyone involved in learning in organizations.

Peter J. Smith is a senior lecturer in the Faculty of Education at Deakin University in Australia. He has a strong practitioner and research interest in industry training, flexible learning and distance education.

Eugene Sadler-Smith is Professor of Management Development and Organizational Behaviour at the University of Surrey, UK. His research interests include cognitive styles and learning styles, intuition in management, continuous professional development, management development and small and medium-sized enterprises (SMEs).

Learning in Organizations
Complexities and diversities

Peter J. Smith and Eugene Sadler-Smith

Routledge
Taylor & Francis Group

LONDON AND NEW YORK

First published 2006
by Routledge
2 Park Square, Milton Park, Abingdon, Oxon OX14 4RN

Simultaneously published in the USA and Canada
by Routledge
270 Madison Ave, New York, NY 10016

Routledge is an imprint of the Taylor & Francis Group

Transferred to Digital Printing 2006

© 2006 Peter J. Smith and Eugene Sadler-Smith

Typeset in Sabon by
Keystroke, Jacaranda Lodge, Wolverhampton

British Library Cataloguing in Publication Data
A catalogue record for this book is available from the British Library

Library of Congress Cataloging in Publication Data
A catalog record for this book has been requested

ISBN 0–415–35603–2 (hbk)
ISBN 0–415–35604–0 (pbk)

Contents

Figures

Tables

Preface

Developing workable and effective human resource development (HRD) policies, plans and practices in organizations is no easy matter. This is unsurprising since it involves those most complex of organisms – human beings – and those most complex of entities – organizations. As training and HRD practitioners in the corporate sector in our previous careers we didn't, on reflection, always have as strong an appreciation of these complexities as we might have had. Both of us, one working in Australia, the other in the UK, tended to see matters in much more 'algorithmic' terms, based on the assumption that if the right process could be identified and implemented efficiently, this would necessarily yield effective outcomes. After all, this is what the various instructional design frameworks in which we based our practice might have led one to believe. We were sometimes proven correct within the confines of specific HRD projects, but at other times we were surprised and sometimes disappointed. We came to realise that professional life as an HRD practitioner in an organization wasn't just about following a process or a 'checklist'. In fact things were often far more complex than they were presented or at first appeared, although oftentimes some stakeholders saw things in simple, process-driven, algorithmic terms. Simplicity was seductive. It also largely ignored diversity. By trying to make things homogeneous, or by filtering our perceptions (seeing things as simple when they were not, or by just ignoring anything that made life too complex) we could more easily deliver the project, meet deadlines, stay within budget and balance competing demands from different stakeholder groups. From this stance we were also more able to communicate with others in the organization who invariably wanted simple answers to straightforward problems, rather than be faced with messy problems that required complex solutions.

Both of us realised, over a period of time, that if learning in organizations was to be understood and managed it needed much more complex conceptualizations, rather than a relentless drive towards simplifying the messy problems that faced us (indeed each of our doctoral theses addressed this very issue in different ways). The reality of effective HRD practice needed to recognise the many dimensions of diversity that are inevitably present when one is concerned with problems relating to the interplay of individuals and the organization. On reflection it was these diversities that made life complicated, but it also made it interesting, rich and challenging.

In the mid-1990s we both moved from the world of practice to the world of research and teaching in higher educational establishments in our respective countries. This gave us both the opportunity to further explore the diversities and complexities that attend learning in organizations. This book is the result of some of those explorations and represents collaborative thinking and research that we have engaged in over a period of years from either side of the globe. The book seeks to elucidate and acknowledge some of the complexities of learning in organizations, and to identify some of the issues that confront HRD practitioners and managers for whom learning is part of their role or everyday practice. In the book we approach this more complex view of the world by outlining in each chapter what some of the diverse influences on HRD practice are, the different ways in which these may be expressed, and what research and practice tells us about these issues. We also provide the reader with some tools for identifying how those diversities and complexities might manifest themselves in their own environment, and how as an HRD practitioner they might go about reflecting on the issues, and 'taming' them sufficiently to work with them. The tools are not checklists; rather they are prompts which may aid an enquiry-based approach to HRD. The book represents our conjectures as academics who were formerly practitioners. Naturally we hope that academic and practitioner audiences alike will enjoy the book and derive both intellectual and practical value from it. The book will have achieved our purpose if it stimulates reflection and a deeper personal understanding of the complex world of HRD practice and research.

Peter J. Smith, Deakin University
Eugene Sadler-Smith, University of Surrey

1 Designing learning in complex environments

Introduction

Learning and the creation of knowledge assets are two keys to individual and organizational effectiveness in the information age. The management of the learning process is inherently a complex activity involving the accommodation and balancing of a whole range of dimensions of individual and contextual variability. Traditional approaches to human resource development (HRD) have attempted to reduce complexity by simplifying the planning, design, implementation and evaluation of HRD. Our assertion is that the time is right for the profession of HRD to acknowledge and embrace, through a process of enquiry and reflection, the complexities, diversities and ambiguities associated with learning in the workplace. Therefore, this book is concerned with assisting those whose responsibility is the planning, implementing and evaluating of workplace-related learning in managing the complexities and diversities that confront them in their strategic and operational learning activities and projects. It is not a critical HRD studies text; it is a practical book that will be of interest to those professionals who may be labelled broadly as 'learning specialists' or 'learning practitioners' and also those concerned with the education, training and professional development of learning professionals. Within an organization this will include instructors, trainers, learning and development advisers, HR managers, training managers and managers more generally as well as those providers of learning and development who are external to an organization such as consultants and lecturers. These individuals are, in their strategic and operational responsibilities, confronted with a highly complex set of variables (for example, individual differences between learners) and their interactions (for example, the impact of organizational context upon learners' motivations). Each organization is, almost by definition, bound to be unique with regard to its learning system since it is within individual organizations that the various issues that we will identify and discuss come together in complex and causally ambiguous ways.

The planning and management of workplace-related learning cannot have one right answer; there can rarely ever be a definitive and prescriptive solution that is generalisable and transferable between contexts. On the other hand it cannot be left to chance. Therefore the individual practitioner has to be able to identify the salient issues in her or his own context and manage these appropriately. The identification of the pertinent issues for each individual depends first upon an understanding of the various dimensions along which the system may vary; and second, the ability to ask pertinent questions through reflection and enquiry in order that the identified dimensions may be understood and better managed. This is the core pursuit of this book: to explore the workplace-learning related dimensions of diversity and some of the questions that a practitioner may ask in order to understand and manage them more effectively.

In shaping our arguments we use various terminologies that are best defined at the outset. By 'learning', for example, we are referring to a longer-term change in the knowledge possessed by an individual, their type and level of skill, or their assumptions, attitudes or values which may lead to their having increased potential to grow, develop and perform in more satisfying and effective ways (Sadler-Smith, 2006). Training is seen as being a focused, specific and instrumental means by which a predetermined task-related learning need may be met. 'Development' is an increase over the longer term of the capacity that an individual has to live a more effective and fulfilling professional and personal life as a result of the acquisition of knowledge, skills and attitudes (Sadler-Smith, 2006). Human resource development (HRD) is defined as 'a wide range of interacting, integrating processes aimed at developing greater purpose and meaning, higher levels of performance and achievement and greater capacity for responding to an ever-changing environment leading to more effective individuals, teams and organizations' (Davis and Mink, 1992: 201). In each of these areas, particular individuals have certain tasks and responsibilities – it is these individuals whom we refer to as 'practitioners' and it is they and the practitioners of the future who are the primary audience for this book.

Complex environments

Learning practitioners operate in complex environments. The internal environment of the workplace itself may vary in terms of the physical space for learning and this may include the factory floor, the classroom, the meeting room, the office and so forth. These environments may be real, but increasingly they have also a virtual element to them with the advent of the internet and intranets. The environments may vary also in terms of who occupies them and what their interests and agendas are; for example, the new recruit straight from school or college may have a different level of engagement with learning than does an older worker coming up to retirement; a fast-tracked manager may have a different agenda and motives from a part-time peripheral worker; general managers may have different priorities and interests to serve than do HRD managers; senior managers may have shareholder value to the fore in their mind and hence may operate from a different set of assumptions than do other stakeholders. These differences may manifest themselves in a variety of ways: in different motivations, different needs, different conceptions of learning, different sets of beliefs and values – they each will see HRD differently.

The internal environment may also be complex in terms of the various organizational and operational issues that structure the day-to-day functioning of the business. The people and technology issues are a rich source of complexity and diversity and they themselves may interact to compound the richness and variety that confronts the learning practitioner. The social characteristics of work groups are also an important element of the complexity of the learning environment and the learning practitioner increasingly has to conceive of learning and working as being in some senses inextricably linked, and this itself presents challenges if learning is to be managed more effectively.

The external environment for learning may also vary in terms of its physical space and may include the university lecture hall, the conference floor and the premises of a supplier or competitor or customer. The external environment within which the business itself operates may be subject to external forces from political, economic, social, technological and legal influences on its strategy and operations. These external forces are often cited as a source of uncertainty and pressure which means that organizations constantly need to be agile in the face of technological developments, market pressures, economic and demographic forces and so forth. Hence, the environments in which learning practitioners operate are complex, and cause-and-effect relationships are not always simple and linear. The practitioner needs tools and techniques that acknowledge these complexities and uncertainties and allow him or her to be comfortable in addressing complex, uncertain and sometimes ambiguous sets of circumstances.

Learning and competitive advantage

Organizations in the 21st century face a variety of challenges. From an internal perspective, whilst many organizations are or have been subjected to 'downsizing' and the implementation of flatter management structures there are increased performance expectations on the part of customers, managers and shareholders. In addition, employees are central to quality enhancement and the shift in the structure of the economy has meant that there often is now a high premium placed upon knowledge work and knowledge workers. From an external perspective organizations generally have faced the deregulation of their markets, accelerating pace of technological change, increased regionalisation and globalisation of business marketplaces and demographic changes in population structures. These issues are widely documented and discussed in this book.

As a result of these pressures organizations are constantly seeking difficult-to-imitate ways of configuring their resources, structures and processes. The skilful adaptation of the organization to the complexities of local conditions in ways that are also aligned to the strategic needs and goals of the business may mean that competitors may be unable to respond in a like way and hence an organization is able to differentiate itself from the competition. In this respect learning is a key attribute of competent and successful organizations, and the ability of the individuals and the organization itself to acquire new knowledge and skills and the capability to learn is a core competence of an organization.

Learning and its knowledge and skill outcomes provide benefits to customers and shareholders. The competence at the level of the organization to train and develop the workforce is a complex and company-specific, and hence competitively unique, resource. Moreover, the competence of learning represents an opportunity for future growth and development through the creation of new knowledge and a capability to create new knowledge. Prahalad and Hamel (1990) defined a core competence in terms of a number of characteristics including the attributes of providing benefits to customers, not being product-specific or an asset in the accounting sense, competitive uniqueness and forward-looking in the sense that it represents a gateway to the future. Hence in this sense the capability to manage learning and development in an effective manner may be seen as a core competence that may confer non-imitability and hence competitive advantage upon the organization. The knowledge and knowledge-creating processes that HRD may leverage are an intangible resource that competitors may find difficult to reverse engineer and hence make up a competence upon which an organization can build a lasting competitive advantage (Garcia and Vano, 2002). If the ability to differentiate oneself from one's competitors is a means of achieving competitive advantage, the question then arises of how may HRD be configured in such a way as to enable this to happen.

One answer to this question is by acknowledging, rather than glossing over, the dimensions of diversity that exist in each situation and by attempting to manage these dimensions in productive ways. This requires an approach to learning and development in organizations that:

1   designs HRD practices around the diversities that will inevitably exist in any organization;
2   rather than trying to iron out these differences (and provide a one-size-fits-all solution), managers should attempt to use the diversities as strength and as a source of differentiation.

However, in order to do this it is important that complexity, the situated nature of learning and the processes of enquiry and reflection need to be accommodated into the organization's HRD practices. This calls for an HRD based upon, amongst other things, an acknowledgement and accommodation of the complexities of workplace learning and the dimensions of diversity. The establishment of an HRD in this way configures the process and system uniquely to the organization and therefore has a greater likelihood of being a difficult-to-imitate organizational competence and one that may help to differentiate a firm from its competitors.

Learning design

Learning design proceeds traditionally on the basis of a generic plan–do–check cycle sometimes known as the 'training cycle' or the 'systematic approach'. The number of stages in the process can vary from three to as many as a dozen; a commonly used five-stage version of the cycle might consist of identify, analyse, design, implement and evaluate, and represents a systematic process that is applicable across a whole range of human endeavour. Within this cycle the learning practitioner fulfils a variety of roles (investigator, analyst, designer, implementer and evaluator) on the basis of her or his professional knowledge, skills and expertise. The approach may call for team working, or for some elements of projects to be contracted out to specialists (for example, e-learning designers, specialist consultants and so forth). Most of the variants of the approach have one thing in common: each stage of the process depends on the preceding one.

Each element of the process cannot be in any other position within the sequence, and there are clear parallels with areas such as total quality management and continuous improvement. In a learning and development (L&D) context, the design phase can be evaluated by means of pilot testing and the implementation phase can be evaluated by formative ongoing evaluation. The evaluation becomes a summative activity once the implementation stage is complete, and it is at this point where overall issues can be addressed (by asking questions such as 'Were the objectives achieved?', 'Was there an impact on job performance?' and 'Was there a bottom-line pay-back?'). If the results of the preceding stages are invalid (for example, because of misdiagnosis) the subsequent stages of the process will by definition have limited validity also. This is a core element of HRD practice and one which enables the novice practitioner to begin to understand and manage HRD.

The systematic approach has been the mainstay of HRD and training practice for half a century. The process has an inherent logic and amongst its many strengths is the undeniable fact that it is proven and well tried and tested. One of the drawbacks of the approach is the extent to which it may inadvertently lead to an over-simplification of the complexity of local conditions and the variations at the individual and organizational levels that may exist in any system. Furthermore it represents an attempt to make the planning and management more certain; it aims to reduce ambiguity and complexity. However, a number of authors have argued that the complexity of HRD is perhaps something that is not reducible and may therefore need to be acknowledged and embraced. For example, Vince (2003: 559) noted that HRD practitioners are often searching for certainties in an uncertain world of contradictions. He argued that it might be more useful to search for contradictions as they are in more plentiful supply and made a plea for HRD to get 'more complicated'. One way in which this complexity may be engaged with is by recognising and acknowledging the range of diversity that exists in relation to workplace-related HRD. Hence, we are arguing not that the systematic approach is invalid – indeed on logical grounds it is entirely defensible – but that HRD needs to get more complex through acknowledging and accommodating diversity and thereby enabling an organization to differentiate itself from its competitors through HRD (amongst other things).

Learning design in complex environments

An underlying assumption of this book is that designing learning in a way that acknowledges diversity is one way of leveraging competitive advantage. What are the dimensions of diversity that need to be recognised and which may be understood and managed in order to differentiate an organization? In a system as complex as a business organization there are a multiplicity of dimensions along which it may vary. Our approach has been to select those that we see as being most relevant to the practice of workplace-related learning. The dimensions of diversity that we single out for discussion and analysis in this book are shown in Figure 1.1, together with their interrelationships with each other.

Diversities amongst organizational contexts for HRD

Human, intellectual and social capitals are at the heart of HRD. Therefore it is important to understand these different forms of capital and the ways in which their significance is likely to vary between and within organizations.

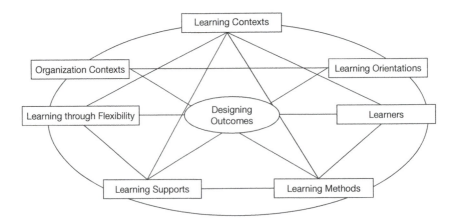

Figure 1.1 Complex and diverse environments

Related to this notion of capital is the concept of knowledge and knowledge workers and the ways in which these are conceptualized within the differing cultures of organizations. The creation of useful knowledge in organizations usually takes place in the context of social relationships and within different forms of networks. The different forms of networks that may be observed are a further means by which the organizational context for learning may vary, and furthermore the ways in which such networks are interpreted and managed is an important aspect of HRD activity within organizations. HRD is an element of human resource management (HRM) and the approach that an organization takes to the management of its human resources is also likely to affect in turn its approaches to HRD. Finally, organizational size is a factor that HRD research has revealed to have a significant impact upon learning and development practices. Therefore it is important that the issue of size is considered as an element of the organizational context in which HRD is situated.

Diversities amongst learning contexts

Learning is sometimes viewed as an individual activity. When we are concerned however with learning in organizations we are, almost by definition, concerned with a process that takes place within a social context and which is based upon or geared towards collaborative actions and behaviours in the workplace. For these reasons work-related learning is in essence the acquisition of knowledge and skills in the midst of action, often as a collective process and geared towards the current task in hand. The socially constructed and task relevance of learning is especially important in adult learning in the workplace where participation with others, and especially those who are more expert than ourselves, is an important means by which individuals may acquire and construct new knowledge. Concepts that are of central importance in this view of learning are the community of practice and the community of learning. But workplaces will vary in terms of the extent to which such communities are present and also in terms of the extent to which individuals are legitimately engaged with these communities. The engagement with such communities is often a naturalistic process. However, activities such as coaching and mentoring are means by which the inclusion or participation of individuals into the community may be managed. It is important therefore that the learning practitioner is able to recognise, understand, interpret and, where possible, influence or manage the learning processes that are associated with such communities of practice.

Diversities in learning orientation

There is a wide range of individuals and groups that may have an interest or stake in learning and its management through HRD systems and processes. To assume a unitary set of interests and motives may not be realistic since the various stakeholders may engage (or not) with HRD for different reasons – not all of which may be commensurate with each other. There are three principal stakeholder groups in this regard: the learners themselves; the managers; and the HRD or learning practitioners (the picture is complicated further since it is possible to be a member of more than one of these groups). From the perspective of the management of workplace-related learning it is important that the attitudes, needs and motives of each of the groups are understood since these are likely to exhibit considerable diversity between and within groups. Hence the learner, the manager and the HRD practitioner will each have their own particular orientation to learning which needs to be understood, acknowledged and, where possible, accommodated in the design and implementation of work-related learning.

Diversities amongst learners

As well as differing in their orientation towards learning in comparison to the other identified stakeholder groups, learners themselves may be categorised into particular groups and will exhibit considerable diversity in terms of a range of dimensions both between the groups and within the groups. For example, there are inter-group diversities in terms of factors such as national culture (a factor that is increasingly relevant as business becomes more global and internationalised) and inter-individual diversities in terms of some tangible factors such as age, but also in terms of psychological variables such as abilities, self-perceptions, cognitive style and learning styles as well as the more tangible matter of learning preferences. All of these are issues that the HRD practitioner needs to be aware of and if possible take account of in the design of learning.

Diversities of learning methods

Against the backcloth of work-related learning being situated in practice, especially when compared to the outmoded perspective of 'learning as training', a different light is shed upon the methods that are available in order to facilitate and promote learning. Concomitantly, there is a very wide range of methods available from which the learning practitioner may choose, and this represents a further dimension of diversity with which he or she may have to contend. The issues of the applicability and utility of the various methods is an important question for the learning practitioner; but again there are few unequivocally right or wrong answers. We are not arguing that any method is superior to any other; we simply present the view that a range of methods are available and there are a number of pertinent questions that may be asked as a precursor to making the choice of one learning method in preference to another.

Diversities in learning supports

It is not enough that learners have the needs, motivations and skills to learn – they need to be supported, both during the learning process itself and in the workplace in order that the newly acquired knowledge and skills may be applied to the job in an effective way. Without this, any investment in HRD is unlikely to yield a worthwhile return. It is necessary therefore to put into place appropriate structures that will support the application to the job of knowledge and skills acquired outside the workplace, but also and equally importantly, the structural and social arrangements that will support learning *in situ*. In order that this may be achieved we argue that there are two issues that must be addressed.

1   There is the issue of learner development (i.e. the development of the individual employee as a self-directed learner who is able not only to acquire the necessary knowledge and skills but is also able to structure her or his own learning within a community of practice). Each individual may vary in his or her preparedness for self-directed and self-structured learning, and this is one of the dimensions of diversity.
2   The second dimension of diversity which we propose in this respect is the degree of support for learning accorded in the workplace and the way in which it is configured vis-à-vis training policies, learning structures and the extent to which the community of practice itself is 'managed' in order to promote learning.

Responding to diversity through flexibility

In order to meet the diverse needs, motivations and preferences of individuals within working and learning contexts (which themselves are likely to vary greatly) it is necessary for the learning practitioner to exercise skill in the blending of methods and approaches. This blending requires careful judgements to be exercised at each stage of an iterative process of analysis, choice and implementation. Moreover, the decision-making task is not complete once implementation has begun since it is necessary and appropriate to not only evaluate the effectiveness of particular blends, but also to monitor their effectiveness on an ongoing basis (i.e. reflect upon them in action).

The picture that we present is a complicated and complex one; it is one in which the practitioner needs to reflect carefully upon a whole host of issues and make judgements based upon their personal knowledge, skills and experiences. Sometimes these judgements will be rational and explicable, at other times the expertise that the practitioner deploys may be more of an intuitive judgement based upon experience and prior learning (which may have been implicit, the lessons of which might be stored tacitly). Our aim is to aid the acceleration of the professional learning process by highlighting the complex issues that may confront the practitioner and by providing for him or her searching and challenging questions that may be asked in the design of work-related learning activities and which may lead the practitioner to formulate conjectures of their own relating to their local circumstances. Our argument is that choosing to configure the learning activities and system in an organization in a way that acknowledges the various dimensions of diversity that we have chosen to highlight is an important means by which an organization may produce a unique HRD. Through such differentiation we argue that the learning which takes place in the organization may meet the learning and growth needs of a wide range of individuals and also provide a difficult-to-imitate source of competitive advantage for the organization.

2 Diversities in organizational contexts

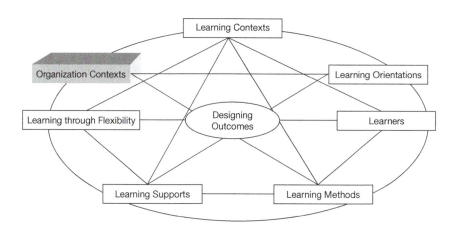

Introduction

Issues of organizational context are widely studied and written about by management and organization researchers; however, these differences are not always acknowledged in the development of models for learning and development and may be overlooked when one is consumed with the detailed aspects of HRD day-to-day practice. In this chapter we intend to examine a selection of organizational contextual issues and provide some suggestions about how they influence the success or otherwise of HRD.

These diversities may be at the inter-organizational level; however, at the same time as acknowledging that organizations vary between each other, we also note that they vary within themselves (i.e. there may be intra-organizational differences). For example, smaller organizations may exhibit less intra-organizational variation simply because they have a more limited range of functions and a smaller number of people and work groups. The larger and more complex an organization becomes, the greater the likelihood that there are substantial variations within it (Pedersen and Sorensen, 1989). As an illustration, the sorts of work culture and work practices that are to be found within the marketing section of a large organization may be different from those that might be found among production workers on the shopfloor, indicating that within a single large organization there can be several sub-cultures (Saffold, 1988) which need to be taken into account in the design and implementation of HRD. The inter- and intra-organizational diversities demand some recognition in HRD strategies, plans and practices. This is important because what might be expected to work in one context may not work in others.

In this chapter we aim to unpack some of the differences that can exist between organizations and within them. We will focus our attention most particularly on concepts of human, intellectual and social capital; on aspects of management and organizational culture; diversity in labour and learning networks; diversity in human resource management strategies; and the issue of organizational size. At the end of this chapter we have included some questions that may help in analysing HRD issues within organizations from the point of view of an HRD practitioner. The questions are designed to assist practitioners in the process of identifying salient issues related to diversity of context, intentions and opportunities in a way that will inform the choice of HRD strategies, plans and practices.

Forms of capital

HRD is concerned with the development of the knowledge and skill assets of the workforce. Although the term 'capital' is most often used in organizations to indicate the various financial, plant and equipment resources available to the organization, there are, from an HRD viewpoint, other equally important forms of capital which represent the less tangible and not-so-easy-to-quantify assets that an organization has at its disposal. In this respect Mayo (2000) drew our attention to the distinction between tangible assets and intangible assets, and offered the simple view that tangible assets plus intangible assets make up the market value of an organization. He also suggested that distinctions may be drawn between customer capital (e.g. contracts, relationships, image, etc.), organizational capital (e.g. systems, methodologies, databases, culture, etc.) and human capital (e.g. individual competence and experience, knowledge, etc.). To this we could add the tangible aspects of intellectual capital (inventions, patents and so forth), and also social capital (see below) which runs as a thread through the customer, organizational and human forms of capital (after Mayo, 2000):

> Market value ≈ Financial capital + Intangible assets (customer capital; organizational capital; human capital; social capital) + Tangible intellectual assets

From an HRD perspective the most significant of these are human capital, including the intellectual capital component, and social capital. A human capital perspective is concerned with the development of the human resources within an organization as a source of competitive advantage. To this extent it is based upon the resource-based view of the firm in which managers 'look inside' for 'rare, valuable and costly-to-imitate resources, and then exploit these resources through their organization' (Barney, 1999: 139). Whilst acknowledging this perspective Boxall and Purcell (2003) argued that it is necessary to go beyond this basic point and examine what it is that can be of exceptional value to a firm (in its human resource base) and how these resources may be developed. In their view firms have two related ways in which this may be achieved:

- by recruiting and retaining outstanding employees;
- through what they term an 'organizational process advantage' which capitalises upon the 'historically evolved, socially complex and causally ambiguous processes' which are difficult to imitate (2003: 86).

Hence human capital and the associated organizational processes are mutually reinforcing in Boxall and Purcell's view; to this extent the learning of an organization's employees (both the content of the learning and the learning process itself) is a rare, valuable and costly-to-imitate form of capital.

Human and intellectual capital

'Human capital' refers to an organization's human resources, including the knowledge and know-how which resides in its people, routines and procedures and which can be converted in various ways to add value to the business (Despres and Chauvel, 2000: 70). From an HR/HRD perspective it is usually conceived of as including individuals' knowledge and skills and their capacity to work that enables them to be engaged with the activities associated with their job role. Accordingly, an investment in human capital is an expenditure that strengthens or increases the stock of human capital that an organization has at its disposal; a return on that investment is the extra value that is derived from that investment. Such investments in human capital can be formal education and training activities that increase the stock of human capital, or the informal derivation of knowledge and skills from others who share them with us. Spender (2000: 150) offered another dimension to this when he described human capital as the knowledge, skill and 'the self-reflexive ability to identify and find sources for the knowledge and skills they do not possess'. This might be referred to as initiative, creativity, entrepreneurship or, from an HRD perspective, a learning process advantage, and may include attributes of the employee such as self-directedness. Whilst some focus upon the notion of human capital as a private 'good' that attaches to individuals, it is just as valid to consider the collective individual human capital within an organization as representing the stock of know-how available to the entire organization. Similarly, the collective learning process (or organizational learning) may be part of the organizational process advantage referred to above.

Organizations are likely to have differing views about the value of human capital, and there will be a diversity of attitudes in terms of the extent to which human capital is recognised as an asset of the organization. For example, Stewart (1997) related an experience of a small engineering firm in the United States that was developing its business strategies to recover from the recession of 1990–1. The management of the company recognised that it needed to lower production costs in order to survive, but that it also needed to position itself for the expected economic recovery. As would be expected, the firm examined the possibilities of purchasing new plant and equipment but was concerned that at a time of a business downturn the strategy represented a financial commitment that they were not in a good position to make. They also recognised that at a time when employees were not as busy as they would be in a time of economic buoyancy, another strategy at their disposal would be to invest in their human capital and increase the skills of their workforce, and to reorganize the way that people worked to increase their capacity to work. The latter paid off for them, to the extent that Stewart reported an annual productivity growth of 20 per cent over a five-year period, enabling the firm to double its production with the same number of employees. With economic recovery, a fuller order book, and resulting increased sales and revenue, the company was subsequently able to afford the plant and equipment upgrades as well. The firm had recognised the potential value of human capital investments to its well-being. Not all firms may be of a similar mind.

Whilst the potential diversities in organizations' responses may be attributable to the attitudes, values and beliefs of managers and other employees, it may also be a diversity driven by circumstance. For example, in a 'low-skill' organization where the knowledge and skills required of the workforce are limited, and the major productivity engine is plant, investment in human capital may not have been seen as an appropriate response. However, these diversities not only exist between organizations but can also exist within the same organization, where the circumstances and human capital requirements and opportunities may differ between functions within the same firm. In a large supermarket chain, for example, the sorts of value placed on human capital among the marketing or legal personnel may be quite different from the value placed on the human capital available from the checkout operators where the skill set required is more limited, and staff replacement easier and less costly to achieve.

Johnes (1993) drew an important distinction between general and specific human capital. By 'general' human capital he is referring to skills and knowledge that can be used by the individual wherever he or she is employed, whilst 'specific' human capital refers to skills and knowledge that can be deployed largely to the benefit of the current employer. Diversity is likely to exist within organizations in terms of the degree of attention paid to the generic and specific forms of human capital. Calder and McCollum (1998) made the point that general human capital development may be least likely to occur at lower staff levels where the development focus is more likely to be on job-specific skills. They use an example of two supermarket chains in the UK where one firm restricted its interest to job-specific competency training for store employees, while the other firm encouraged staff to develop, along with job-specific skills, a broader (more general) set of skills that enabled the acquisition of a National Vocational Qualification (NVQ) which provided individuals with a portability of human capital in the external labour market (Calder and McCollum, 1998: 41).

We ought briefly to re-visit the 'general' versus 'specific' distinction proposed by Johnes (1993). There are forms of skills and knowledge that are dispositional (Billett, 1996a), describing an individual's manner and attitudes towards their work and the way they carry that work out. Those dispositional skills are clearly very general and are transported across employment contexts, however different the tasks in the various forms of employment may be. But there are also skills and knowledge that can be transported to similar forms of employment, but that are nevertheless fairly specific – such as the technical skills and knowledge possessed by an individual. Whilst an individual is employed in a specific role, the role-specific skill and knowledge set will be drawn upon, but it may be of limited value in employment in another field. At the same time, the individual also has skills and knowledge that are very context-specific in the way a particular employer organizes and processes their functions. While other employers will have equivalent systems in place, they will not be the same, such that the knowledge and skill that is very organization-specific may not be transferable. In other words, we suggest that there are forms of human capital that are transferable across employment contexts, and there are more specific skills and knowledge that are transferable to a new employer where the nature of the tasks is similar; finally there are very specific forms of human capital that are organization-unique and that have no direct value to a different employer. Hence, the knowledge and skill aspects of human capital may exist along a continuum from the quite general to the highly specific.

More recently there has been interest in the related concept of intellectual capital. Stewart (1997) provided a succinct definition: 'intellectual capital is intellectual material – knowledge, information, intellectual property, experience – that can be put to use to create wealth' (Stewart, 1997: x). From a knowledge management (KM) perspective Despres and Chauvel (2000: 70), in an adaptation of Edvinsson's work, framed intellectual assets as a product of the firm's human resources which in turn may generate intellectual property (IP) (which is the intellectual assets of the firms for which legal protection has been obtained). A 'softer' perspective is offered by Nahapiet and Ghosal (1998: 245) when they describe intellectual capital as the knowledge and knowing capability of a social collective (for example, an organization, an intellectual community or a professional practice). The parallel with the concept of human capital (the acquired knowledge, skills and capabilities [Nahapiet and Ghosal, 1998]) may be readily apparent: the knowledge components of human capital are included in the concept of intellectual capital; at the same time, intellectual capital includes some other more tangible creations of humans, such as inventions, documents, patents, processes and so on (Harvey and Lusch, 1999; Sveiby, 1997). Garavan, Morley, Gunnigle and Collins (2001) provided a useful summary of the conceptualizations of intellectual and human capital and make the useful observation that the conceptualizations and definitions that they review make a distinction between 'thinking' assets (i.e. people) and 'non-thinking' assets (e.g. operating procedures, processes, patents) (Garavan *et al.*, 2001: 49).

Every organization has its stock of intellectual capital but, of course, there is considerable diversity in the amount of such capital, its level of sophistication and complexity, how it is organized, and the value placed upon it. Diversity also exists in the ways in which an organization uses its existing intellectual capital to leverage new intellectual capital for its competitive purposes. Brooking (1996: 153) examined quite extensively the drivers in organizations that extend what she called the 'intellectual capital asset base'. She argued that one aspect of diversity among organizations is the 'youthfulness' and 'energy' of the employees; she suggested that younger people are more likely to create an environment of greater excitement and innovation. While there may be some validity in the link she suggested between youthfulness, energy and innovation, it would be an unfortunate conclusion to draw that older workers do not (or cannot) bring fresh ideas and innovations to the workplace. The demographic problems faced by many nations (for example, lower birth rates, expanded and more inclusive higher education systems, ageing populations and so forth) means that the potential offered by the intellectual capital of the entire workforce irrespective of age needs to be part of an organization's HRD strategy and plans.

It is the connection that Brooking made between innovation and development of intellectual capital that we suggest is more important and useful, where the point is made that where employees 'constantly look to their leaders for new ideas . . . they are not contributing to the growth and life of a company' (1996: 154). She suggested that such things as divergent and generative thinking, conceptualizing and defining problems, evaluating ideas and planning action and implementing new ideas are the keys to developing an innovative environment and the leveraging of new intellectual capital. How well organizations are able to engender and manage those processes, and how much they value them are matters that vary considerably between them but are likely to be important potential sources of competitive advantages for many of them.

Nahapiet and Ghosal (1998: 249) argue that creation of intellectual capital involves the processes of combination (putting together previously unconnected elements or recombining things in different ways) and exchange (since combination depends upon exchanges between knowledge holders), and that combination and exchange depends upon three conditions being met:

- The existence of the opportunity for combination or exchange (for example, accessibility and the new opportunities afforded by the internet and intranets);
- The expectation on the part of the various knowledge holders of the creation of value through the processes of combination and exchange (in other words it must be perceived as being valuable and worthwhile);
- There must be the will or the motivation to engage (i.e. it will be worth each individual's while, as well as being worthwhile).

HRD's contribution to the creation and management of intellectual capital must therefore take into account the physical and social arrangements for exchange and combination and must also attempt to ensure that there are necessary expectations and motivations on the part of knowledge holders in order to secure their engagement.

Social capital

'Social capital' refers to the relationships between people that exist within a social structure. Among these relationships there are such things as trust, shared values and social norms, and mutual understandings (Cohen and Prusack, 2001). While human capital can be described as the stock of skills and knowledge held by individuals and by groups, social capital is the relationships that exist between them. These relationships are powerful in 'greasing the wheels' – in making things happen more easily than they may otherwise do, because of the relationships and the trust that exists between the actors. François (2002) has written extensively on the role that social capital can play in the economic development of nations and of organizations. Nahapiet and Ghosal summarised the central proposition of social capital theory as being that networks of relationships constitute a valuable resource for the conduct of social affairs; they define it as 'the sum of the actual and potential resources embedded within, available through, and derived from the network of relationships possessed by an individual or a social unit' (1998: 243). Moreover they conceptualize social capital as having three facets:

- structural: the impersonal configuration of linkages or overall pattern of connections between people or units ('who you reach and how you reach them');
- relational: the personal relationships (such as respect and friendship, norms and sanctions, obligations and expectations) and the assets created and leveraged through such relationships;

- cognitive: the shared representations, interpretations and systems of meanings amongst the parties (for example language and codes); it is this aspect of social capital that comes closest to the intellectual capital of the social group (see above).

The conscious development and maintenance of social networks is an important facilitator amongst groups. As we have noted above, social capital itself may have different dimensions in itself, which adds a further level of complexity to our discussions. The importance placed on developing and maintaining social capital represents a source of diversity both within organizations and between them. As we discuss management and organizational culture in the next section of this chapter, it will become increasingly evident that social capital and the way in which it relates to intellectual capital and collective learning is an important component in HRD policies, plans and practices as well as in informal learning processes in organizations. With regard to collective learning, for example, as Nahapiet and Ghosal noted, social capital may not always be a beneficial asset since the shared norms and mutual identification may reinforce established ways of behaving and performing.

Management, organizational culture, knowledge and learning

In our consideration of management and organizational culture we do not propose to give a comprehensive review of these two areas, rather we prefer to highlight some of the salient issues regarding the impact that diversities in management's perceptions and organizational culture may have upon HRD processes within organizations. An important issue in all of this is how management views and values HRD. The extent to which managers, and especially senior managers and directors, 'buy into' the significance of learning and development is a key determinant of the strategic impact of HRD. Whilst many writers, for example Bartlett and Ghosal (1993), have argued that learning and HRD are crucial contributors to enterprise performance and growth, well-being, and overall competitiveness; this view is not universally held. Within an investment conceptualization of HRD resources are dedicated to the development of human, intellectual and social capital and are seen as part of a strategic approach to organizational capacity building. This indicates an alliance between business strategy and HRD strategy that many writers (e.g. Boxall, 1996) have argued is essential to effective HRD. At the same time, though, there still exists a conceptualization of HRD as a cost only – a burden that has to be borne in order to provide people with the skills necessary to carry out their work. There is also evidence (e.g. Smith, Wakefield and Robertson, 2001) that it is not uncommon for organizations to take an investment view of HRD among its professional and managerial staff, but a cost burden view when it comes to their operator and lower-level staff. This attitude may be related to the human resource management strategy consciously put in place by an organization, consistent with our earlier discussion of the utilisation, innovation and accumulation strategies. However, the same diversity can come from some much less strategic positions such as a belief that some groups of employees are in less need of HRD or less capable of providing a return from it, a habit because 'that's the way things are done around here', or a failure to understand the significance of knowledge and skill development for a range of jobs beyond those that are technical, managerial or professional. As Snell and Dean (1992) suggested, in the conclusion of their review of relevant research in the area, there are trends in organizations to develop the skills of workers to become knowledge workers since in a knowledge era there is much more to the execution of quality and productive work than physical effort or manual skill.

Senge's 1990 book *The Fifth Discipline* and others at the time did much to promulgate the idea of the 'learning organization', defined as a company where people are encouraged to extend their knowledge, understanding and capacities to achieve the results they want, where new ideas and new thinking are nurtured and where collaborative learning and working are encouraged. Important to the concept of the learning organization is the idea that people at all levels are encouraged to develop their capacities and contributions, and that the organization continually searches for ways to achieve this end. The suggestion was made by Snell and Dean (1992) that HRD needs to recognise the knowledge component of a much broader range of occupations as part of its HRD planning processes. It is also important to realise that this more complex HRD planning is not the maintenance of a sophisticated machine, but a much more complex and ever-moving mosaic of interdependent and unpredictable events.

In the following paragraphs we draw on the contribution one of us (P.S.) made to an Australian National Training Authority project in 2003 (see <http://flexiblelearning.net.au/projects/pdfuture.htm>). Tymon and Stumpf (2003) were identified as writing of knowledge workers as those who 'make their living by accessing, creating, and using information in ways that add value to an enterprise and its stakeholders' (p. 12). They suggested that the characteristics which are the most valuable ones among knowledge workers are likely to include the speed with which they can learn and share knowledge and skill, ability to access relevant information and differentiate it from less relevant information, and a high degree of adaptive problem-solving ability with respect to technology and people. According to Tymon and Stumpf these characteristics differentiate knowledge workers from other expert workers. The latter are characterized by a seemingly automatic selection and execution of choices, judgements, skills and actions (Dreyfus, 1982). The rapid accessing and acquisition of new knowledge, the recognition of its relevance, and the need to share it for the benefit of other individuals and the organization are amongst the characteristics of knowledge workers.

The importance of social capital becomes even more salient in the context of this discussion since successful knowledge-work performance is likely to be much more social and relational than propositional and procedural. To share knowledge in a meaningful way, and to have it accepted by and influence the behaviour of others, requires the development and maintenance of social relationships. It is the adept use of such relationships that will enable the knowledge worker to contribute to the development of intellectual and human capital and, in turn, to organizational capacity building. The socially situated nature of much adult and workplace learning amplifies the significance of the various types of learning networks that employees may be part of and of social capital with its structural, relational and cognitive components.

Breaking out of the confines of the individually focused acquisition and storage of knowledge which typifies an individualized conception of learning is often a considerable challenge for some individuals, and also for organizations which may need to unlock and effectively use knowledge assets in a shared way. For organizations this means the development of a culture that rewards the surfacing, sharing and codifying of knowledge and an emphasis on building capacity of knowledge workers, other individuals and the organization. As Jurie (2000: 265) puts it, 'Organizations which hamper or stunt the free development of their members or constituents . . . limit their own effectiveness.' Jurie also makes the point that effective organizations see themselves from a standpoint of their relationship to society. In this context, these organizations see the individuals who work within them as more than a means to achieving a particular purpose, but also as adding to those purposes. Indeed in McLean and McLean's (2001: 4) definition of HRD the wider societal role is evident: '[HRD is] any process or activity that, either initially or over the long term, has the potential to develop adults' work-based knowledge, expertise, productivity and satisfaction, whether for personal or group/team gain or for the benefit of an organization, community, nation, or ultimately the whole of humanity.'

Returning to the issue of knowledge workers, in New's (1996: 45–7) competency model, the knowledge worker requires competency at each of three categories of competence:

1   Job-specific competencies are the attributes required to carry out a specific job successfully.
2   General management competencies are the ways in which a person interacts with other people in the organization.
3   Corporate-specific competencies are the means by which a person adjusts his or her way of working in order to operate within the culture of an organization.

At the job-specific level, as Tymon and Stumpf argued, the knowledge worker requires the requisite knowledge base. But to be effective, the knowledge worker also requires competency at the general level and must be able to interact with people in ways that disseminate the knowledge and enable it to be understood and used by others. Additionally, New's corporate-specific competencies are important for the knowledge worker to understand, use, and be effective in the culture of the particular organization. As New argued, an organization's competence and capacity becomes a function of how well individuals can acquire and deploy the three levels of competency he identifies. In turn an organization's competence and the competence of individuals within it are related to how well the organization recognises the importance of each of these three categories of competence and encourages their development and operation.

It might be easy to value knowledge workers more highly than other groups in the workforce (and in a sense privilege their contribution), and also to think in didactic terms of the knowledge that they create as being transmitted on a one-way basis to the rest of the workforce. However, in modern, information-rich and integrated organizations it is unlikely that successful knowledge workers are able to operate purely in transmitting mode and, as Stebbins and Shani (1995) suggested, the mode of involvement of a knowledge worker is far more likely to be participative, where there is recognition that knowledge workers identify, select, share and deploy knowledge that is derived from the knowledge sets of others whose primary role may not be knowledge-based. Recognising this, organizational capacity building is enhanced where knowledge workers and others are provided with the culture and the opportunity for non-hierarchical organizational structures and relationships, and for forums which provide opportunity for knowledge sharing (Stebbins and Shani, 1995).

At this point we will briefly return again to Tymon and Stumpf (2003) and their characterization of knowledge workers as people who 'make their living by accessing, creating, and using information in ways that add value to and enterprise and its stakeholders' (p. 12). We would question this definition and suggest that it is too narrow. Our view is that there is a case to argue that becoming a knowledge worker is strongly related to the attitudes, the 'mind-set' and the behaviour of individuals. For example, there are likely to be individuals who, perhaps because of a particular set of dispositions, are generous in sharing their knowledge at whatever level in the organization they might occupy, and whatever their function might be. These are people who 'know' something and recognise the benefit to others of such knowing and who will be forthcoming in sharing knowledge with others. Indeed, their primary function may not be at all associated with accessing information, creating and using information at all – it may be that for personal or dispositional reasons they are generous with, and good at, sharing the information that they acquire through carrying out their primary tasks. The social capital notions of networking, relationships and trust come to the fore here in relation to the contribution that such individuals make to the general development of human and intellectual capital in their organization. The diversity issue here is how well valued those people may be, how well recognised they are, and whether or not they are encouraged to share their knowledge. As several writers (e.g. Calder and McCollum, 1998; Smith, Wakefield and Robertson, 2001) have observed, such sharing activities might even be viewed as 'time wasting' and in conflict with the efficient maintenance of production schedules.

Finally, there is a connection to be explored between an organizational culture that encourages and values knowledge workers' contributions to capacity building, and the learning network theory developed by Poell, Chivers, Van der Krogt and Wildesmeersch (2000) in the Netherlands. Poell and his associates have been examining the forms of labour networks that exist within organizations, and to which individuals variously belong, and the forms of co-related learning networks. There is opportunity to extend the concept of learning networks in organizations as a vehicle through which to foster the participative culture that enhances the utility of knowledge workers in general organizational capacity building.

Labour and learning networks

The development and application of Learning Network Theory (LNT) by workers such as Poell and van der Krogt represents a useful framework to explore the dynamics that operate within an organization, as well as the diversities that exist between and within organizations. Van der Krogt (1998) drew on Mintzberg's (1989) ideas to identify a number of theoretical types of labour networks, namely entrepreneurial work, 'machine-bureaucratic' work, 'adhocratic' group work and professional work. Entrepreneurial work is not complex but it is broad in its content and characterized by contractual relationships between people, and a liberal work climate. Poell *et al.* (2000) suggested that entrepreneurial work is found in small organizations, in the self-supporting units within larger organizations, and where individual employees have 'their own shop' (Poell *et al.*, 2000: 39). Machine-bureaucratic work is characterized by work that has very established processes and practices that are largely management designed and determined, that are regulated, and fairly narrow in scope and repetitive. The work is carried out as a function of the collective work relationships between individuals. Adhocratic work is normally found in complex, problem-solving environments where there may be a project focus. Groups of people come together to focus on a problem, and once that problem is resolved, the actors become involved in another group focusing on a different project or problem. Teams are most usually autonomous and multidisciplinary, bringing together the skills required for the focus at the time. Finally, professional work is highly complex and specialised and the dominant influence here is the professional associations that exist outside the organization.

The learning networks identified in LNT are, of course, central to the theory. Four theoretical types of learning network are identified: liberal, vertical, horizontal and external. The liberal learning network within an organization operates within implicit organizational learning policies, and is characterized by employees identifying their own learning needs, how to meet and service those needs, and then managing their own learning to achieve the outcomes required. A vertical learning network is characterized by learning needs identified by management, programmes designed by training or HRD staff, and then the programmes delivered to employees. With the horizontal learning network programmes of learning develop organically, such that there are no pre-designed programmes, but these develop and evolve as the learning proceeds towards goals that may remain stable, or may also evolve as the learning proceeds. Groups are the dominant entity within this form of network. The external learning network is normally driven by professional associations outside the organization, where identified learning policies and learning needs are a function of new developments within the broader profession.

An important component of the thinking behind LNT is that any given individual, or group of individuals, is likely to be involved in more than one form of learning network at any given time. Additionally, organizations may be quite diverse in terms of the form of labour networks and learning networks that most characterize them. For example, a repetitive production company may be most characterized by a vertical network, where the aim of management is to increase productivity and, perhaps, quality. The major interest here is likely to be on the development of job-specific competencies so that individuals become more skilled at the specific and predictable tasks that they carry out. However, at the same time that this vertical network may be the dominant one, individuals are likely to also engage in self-identification of some of the knowledge that they need and may pursue this through a network that appears to be more liberal and informal in its nature, insofar as they learn from other more expert workers on a basis of individual request. For example, a software development company might be more likely to favour a liberal or horizontal network for learning among employees, but certain forms of learning (e.g. safety procedures) may be organized and delivered on a more vertical network basis. Groups of employees within a large organization are likely to be characterized by different forms of learning networks. An example here might be a supermarket chain where the checkout operators may be more subject to a vertical network, while their colleagues in, say, the marketing department, may work within a more liberal or horizontal network.

Learning network theory and the related labour network theory both provide useful frameworks for exploring inter-organizational diversities as well as those diversities that occur within organizations. The sorts of training and HRD policies that are developed and implemented within an organization are likely to be a function of how the organization sees itself and its workforce in terms of the four sets of orientations developed by Poell *et al.* (2000) and Van der Krogt (1998), and how it sees the various groupings of employees within. At the same time, the LNT forms a useful framework for identifying potentially dysfunctional and misplaced HRD orientations within the organization. Going back to our discussion of knowledge workers and the learning organization, it may be the case that managers should identify where there may be vertical networks that do not need to be such but instead could be better developed towards a liberal or horizontal network orientation.

Human resource management strategy

Dowling and Schuler (1990) explored the link between competitive strategies with human resource management strategies of utilisation, facilitation (also sometimes called the 'innovation strategy') and accumulation. These categories of HRM strategy, as identified by Dowling and Schuler, form a useful framework for exploring diversity within and between organizations. A utilisation strategy, in its association with the cost reduction strategy, indicates that what is required is employees to be hired who can 'hit the ground running' as far as is possible. Within this 'buy-in' approach employees would be recruited, as much as is possible, with the requisite skills already developed so that they can begin productive work as soon as possible, and incur low HRD costs. The utilisation strategy is normally associated with work that is predictable, repetitive and reasonably limited in its scope. An example here might be the supermarket checkout operator where company requirements are mainly associated with a pleasant manner with customers, ability to keep product and customers moving efficiently through the checkout, and ability to operate the cash register in an accurate way. There often is a plentiful supply of labour and high turnover which makes the utilisation strategy a comfortable one.

An innovation strategy is often associated with businesses that are subject to rapid and even unpredictable market or technological change. Employees need to be creative and to be able to identify and solve problems as they present themselves unexpectedly, unpredictably and sometimes frequently. Uncertainty is one of the hallmarks of the employee's work and the nature of the business, but skills and knowledge are required in order to build competitiveness through new product or service design and delivery, and the ongoing enhancement of those products and services. An example is to be found in high technology companies, such as those that develop and sell computer games software. The market and its tastes move quickly and sometimes unpredictably (subject to the expectations of an increasingly sophisticated market). Once users have mastered the game in one form, the game needs to be developed further to raise the challenge and level of skill required for mastery of a new version. The skills possessed by successful employees become highly prized, as does the imagination required to conceptualize and operationalize the game and its software. Training and skills development need constant attention, and successful employees are not at all easy to develop or to replace.

The HRM accumulation strategy is most commonly associated with the quality enhancement business strategy. Competitiveness here is not so much the result of new products, but the result of continuous improvement in the quality of existing products to meet increasing market requirements for quality, and to ensure that competitor products do not develop a reputation for quality and reliability that is superior to that of one's own product line. The work is fairly predictable and repetitive, but subject to incremental change in processes. What is important here is the retention of employees and the continuous development of their skills to enable competitive productivity and quality outcomes. An example here might be a manufacturing company where the product line is generally not subject to discontinuous change, but quality enhancement of the product is necessary such that customer satisfaction and warranty claims are reduced. Skilled employees are valued and continually trained to meet increasing productivity and quality requirements, and become increasingly difficult to replace as their level of skill accumulates.

This framework is a useful lens through which to explore forms of diversity between organizations, but is also useful to explore diversity within the same organization. For example, a utilisation strategy might apply to checkout operators, while an innovation strategy may apply more to the marketing personnel. The legal or finance staff, though, are more likely to be associated with an accumulation strategy since much of their work relies on an understanding of company processes and precedents, and the fairly predictable evolution of those processes to achieve higher quality and reliability. The HRD strategy and policies of the organization need to be cognisant of these differences and adjusted accordingly.

Organizational size

One very obvious dimension of inter-organizational diversity is size. Large organizations have at their disposal resources and opportunities that may be more difficult to find amongst smaller organizations, and also are likely to have structures and processes that are more complex. Additionally, small organizations may be more likely to be influenced by particular key individuals (such as the owner or general manager), while the influence of any individual in a large organization is tempered by the influence of a greater number of others.

Small businesses are less likely than large businesses to have the HRD capability, expertise and resources necessary to develop and implement systematic learning strategies (Sadler-Smith and Lean, 2003). For that reason they may face greater obstacles in the continuous development of the workforce's knowledge and skills. Gibb (1999), drawing on Australian research (Industry Task Force on Leadership and Management Skills, 1995; Baker and Wooden, 1995) summarised a number of barriers faced by small business in implementing and sustaining training and development:

- the features of training: cost, relevance and availability of externally offered training programmes;
- the features of the workforce: employment is often part-time, staff turnover is high, owner/managers are often characterized by a low level of formal qualifications;
- the features of the small business itself: focus on short time horizons, need for high-level skills may not be there, fear of trained staff being poached, a desire to contain costs, lack of training capability within the business.

The issue of lack of internal training capability was shown by Baker and Wooden (1995) to be a major driver in a small business seeking training from external providers. However, that brings with it the need to release staff to undertake HRD in a context of limited staff availability and low opportunity to be released from the workplace to engage in learning and development activities. It also places the business in the position of accepting the content and process of training as it is delivered by an external provider, rather than being more closely aligned to the precise needs of the business itself. The external off-site nature of the training delivery may also reduce the opportunities for situated learning to occur in the same workplace in which the learner carries out those tasks.

Sadler-Smith, Gardiner, Badger, Chaston and Stubberfield (2000) have developed a number of research-based suggestions to encourage the development of collaborative learning groups that comprise people from a number of small businesses who can network and share issues and resources (in an action-learning-type format). A cornerstone to their framework was the notion of assessment-centre-type workshop based around SWOT (strengths, weaknesses, opportunities, threats) analysis to assist participants to identify their own learning needs and those of their small business while, at the same time, minimising the time people had to spend away from the business or in isolation from other management colleagues within the business.

Although there are disadvantages faced by small businesses in engaging in HRD there are also some advantages. First, a small business is often in a position to respond with agility to changes in skill and knowledge requirements since there are simply fewer people and levels of organization to engage with. Additionally, Smith *et al.* (2001) identified that training in small business, where it does occur on the job in a structured way, is often better supervised and subject to greater interest from colleagues in the workplace. It is arguable (Pedersen and Sorensen, 1989) that small organizations are more likely to have values that are shared much more universally by all employees than is the case with larger organizations and, as O'Regan and Ghobadian (2004) have observed, it is arguably easier to create a sharing culture. Apart from the comparatively 'cosier' environment that can occur in small businesses, the owner or general manager may have a considerable stake in the employees' developing levels of skill that enhance the business and enhance its financial well-being, though this is not always acknowledged.

Within larger businesses MacDonald (1999) noted there is a stronger degree of structure to HRD, with around 42 per cent of employees in his case studies of organizations having some place in the training plan and a formal assessment of skills and knowledge, the latter often forming part of the calculation of remuneration. MacDonald was also able to identify a number of examples of different HRD philosophies that embraced some of the notions of learning network theory. Smith *et al.* (2001) in their research with twelve Australian organizations across a number of business sectors identified considerable interest towards and provision in the conscious development of communities of practice designed to support training outcomes. What was clear from that research was that larger organizations tended to have more formal HRD structures and plans that were developed in considerable detail. Smaller organizations on the other hand were more characterized by informality. Sometimes the informality was a strength in that responsiveness was enhanced, while in some larger organizations the more formal structures mitigated against responsiveness and against the development of more liberal learning networks.

Smith *et al.*'s (2001) research also identified that training infrastructures, in terms of HRD policies, plans and strategies, were better developed in larger organizations, and that training staff were more likely to be available in-house, or on a reliable out-sourced basis. However, there was evidence that these more developed structures and resource bases may not be equally available to all employees across the larger organizations. Working with apprentices, Brooker and Butler (1997) found that training structures to support employees were sometimes poorly developed and that apprentices often gained little value from them. The Smith *et al.* (2001) research observed also that well-developed HRD structures in large organizations often mainly benefited professional and managerial employees, while they afforded less benefit to operator and lower-level staff. They suggested there was the possibility that organizations were making quite different strategic decisions about different employee groups and had different views of them, similarly to the human resource management strategies discussed earlier in this chapter. There seemed also to be a view that lower-level staff did not require as much HRD input, not just because their work was seen as less complex and less crucial to organizational well-being but, paradoxically, because they were just supposed to know their jobs without much more attention to sustained HRD. The same research included several smaller businesses, including one restaurant of about 25 employees. In that business considerable attention was paid to management staff becoming personally involved with the training and skills development of cooking and waiting staff, since the business accepted that it was those people whose work directly interfaced with the customer and who were, then, crucial to the well-being of the business. A small hairdressing salon made the same point in discussion of its attention to training its one apprentice. The owner of that business pointed out that she could hardly ignore someone who worked next to her all day, and neither could she fail to see the quality of the apprentice's work.

It is possible to speculate that one major difference between large and small businesses with regard to HRD is in relation to the human and physical resources that can be deployed towards HRD rather than the mind-sets and culture that may be present within the organization. In an interesting piece of research that compared small businesses of less than 20 staff with larger SMEs (small and medium-sized enterprises) of between 100 and 249 staff, O'Regan and Ghobadian (2004) showed little difference in leadership characteristics, organizational culture, and the activities associated with strategy planning. Their research provided some evidence that, at least among smaller businesses, size has less effect than may have been thought and that the differences between organizations are more likely to be quite individualistic rather than systematically associated with size.

Focus on practice: quantifying the human face of intellectual capital

In developing this next section we have drawn on the important contribution by Mayo (2000) to the thinking around the importance to intellectual capital enhancement through employee development. One of Mayo's prime concerns was the question of how we quantify human capital since the proponents of a 'softer' view of KM (knowledge management) and related notions of intellectual capital may be at a disadvantage in discussions with the financial community since in the latter's eyes non-financial measures may lack credibility. Mayo suggested a number of ways in which the contribution of human capital to 'value' might be assessed in terms of a number of dimensions which are summarised in Table 2.1. A further issue that Mayo highlights is the extent to which it is possible to quantify the proposition of people or activity that is concentrated on a firm's present versus its future; he notes that it may be salutary experience for managers and HRD practitioners to witness perhaps how little time is spent on the future in some organizations. In sum he concluded that the strategic growth in an organization's value must be directly related to a positive change in the factors outlined in the table and also that HRD needs to be managed in a way that focuses upon the development of a firm's intellectual capital. To the latter we might add its social capital since this is likely to be of considerable significance in the social learning processes that characterize much of the informal and incidental learning that occurs in the workplace.

Table 2.1 Dimensions of intellectual capital

Dimension	Attributes
Individual employee's capability	The ability to do ('can do')
	Employee's personal capabilities (current versus needed; behavioural and interpersonal; prioritised in terms of their criticality for success, etc.)
	Employee's professional and technical know-how
	Employee's experience (previous experiences, personal interests, etc.)
	Network and range of employee's personal contacts (internal and external; who they can call on for help and guidance, etc.)
	Values and attitudes that influence employee's actions
Individual motivation	The 'will to do'
	Goodness of the match between employee and the nature of the work
	Individual needs and aspirations
	Morale indices (e.g. employee satisfaction, commitment, etc.)
Leadership	Team productivity and performance
	360-degree feedback
	High-performance behaviours, future leadership needs
Organizational climate	How are people and teams valued?
	What is the general attitude towards mistakes?
	Are experimentation and the use of initiative encouraged?
	Are the resources made available to support development?
	Is knowledge shared or jealously guarded?
Work group effectiveness	Are the members of work groups mutually supportive?
	Does the group take time and trouble to share their continuously developing knowledge with others?
	Do certain groups or individuals within groups have a 'liability value'?

Source: adapted from Mayo, 2000: 527–31.

Identifying diversity: questions for situational analysis

This chapter has been something of a snapshot of the complexities that lie behind the beguilingly innocent term 'organizational context'. In this final section of the chapter we aim to provide a systematic way of thinking about the diversities and complexities that lie within 'organization context', and a focus that enables them to be brought under a little more control when making decisions about HRD strategy, plans or activities. The questions are intended to foster enquiry, reflection and analysis as a precursor to any HRD project or activity.

Who is the target group?

1 Is the target group the whole organization?
2 Is the target a number of people scattered throughout the organization?
3 Is the target group a quite specific group of employees within the organization?
4 What are the implications of this for the extent to which and the ways in which the target group will engage in learning?

Which type of capital is it most important to develop?

1 What is the relative significance of human and intellectual capital, or social capital in the organization?
2 How do you differentiate between these in the organization?
3 How do these various forms of capital relate to the learning needs of the various target groups and the whole organization?
4 Is a single HRD process appropriate, or will you have to develop several responses to achieve the necessary outcome?

Management and organizational culture

1 Is management supportive of HRD?
2 Does the organization view HRD as investment for the future or as a cost to be borne in developing specific immediately required skills and knowledge?
3 What is the need and opportunity for developing a sharing culture through the HRD process, starting to build towards a learning organization and a knowledge worker mind set?
4 To what extent is it feasible to make learning in the organization a continuous and collaborative process?

Labour and learning networks

1 What forms of labour networks exist in the organization?
2 What sorts of learning networks exist in the organization?
3 Are there dominant forms of labour network and learning network?
4 Are these forms appropriate or is there opportunity to shift from one form of network towards another?

Organizational size and resources

1 What in-house resources does the company have at its disposal?
2 How can these resources be best deployed to facilitate learning?
3 Will resources from outside the organization need to be sought?
4 What will be the impact on production and work schedules of any HRD activity?

3   Diversities in learning contexts

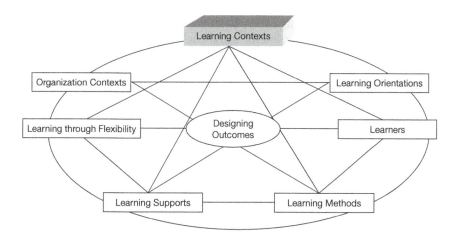

Introduction

As was noted in the previous chapter, there are considerable diversities between organizations and within organizations, in the value that is placed upon learning, and upon the outcomes that are expected from human resource development (HRD). At one extreme some organizations see learning as central to their development, to their well-being and, ultimately, to their survival. At the other there are organizations that see learning as instrumental, where the learning needs to result in tangible and readily usable knowledge that can be very directly tied to efficiency and product or service quality. In the latter scenario what are deemed important to be learned are those things that increase task efficiency.

The readiness for organizations to effectively embrace training and HRD can be related to these aspects of diversity. In an organization that sees HRD as contributing to the development of the various forms of capital (human and intellectual, and social) and where learning is viewed as part of a legitimate and necessary empowerment of individuals, a different set of

HRD policies, processes and evaluative mechanisms are likely to be found when compared to an organization that views learning as a necessary means to the end of efficiency in a range of prescribed tasks. Of course, these diversities are not just to be found between different organizations, but are to be found also within the same organization, as discussed in the previous chapter.

In this chapter we discuss the various aspects of the diversity of contexts for learning that exist among individuals and groups in organizations, and how these different contexts can result in some different opportunities as well as barriers for effective HRD. To commence our discussion we will spend some time discussing the socio-cultural contexts that may be used to characterize organizational learning environments. From there we will move on to discuss some of the concepts important to an understanding of various approaches to the management of HRD including work-based learning, communities of practice and communities of learning, and coaching and mentoring. Finally the chapter will discuss some forms of open and closed learning contexts as they are to be found within organizations, including a consideration of the contexts for learning that result where work is carried out at multiple locations or in single locations.

Socio-cultural contexts of learning in the workplace

Although it is possible to view learning as an individualistic activity which engages a person in the acquisition of skills and knowledge (indeed this has been and continues to be the focus of some learning theories) as Alfred (2002) has observed, learning is a more complex activity than this view might lead us to believe. Learning takes place within social and cultural contexts that 'determine what and how we know and learn' (Alfred, 2002: 5). This perspective on learning demands an understanding and acknowledgement of the social and cultural milieu in which the learning takes place, as well as of the social relationships and experiences of the learner. Workplaces form a rich and varied set of contexts that need to be considered as a whole when we try to think about and understand learning in the workplace. Indeed, acknowledgement of these socio-cultural contexts for learning provides opportunities for leveraging the social and cognitive attributes of those contexts in order to attempt to create more powerful learning environments that make use of all of the resources and relationships (human and physical) that are available in workplaces. Exemplifying this increased potential power, Raelin (2000) defined work-based learning in terms of a process characterized by being:

- acquired in the midst of action;
- appropriate to the task at hand;
- a collective activity;

- a process that of itself enables participants to question the underlying assumptions of their actions.

Smith (2003b) drew attention to the view of the constructivist school of learning, where the central idea is that learners construct knowledge from the circumstances in which they experience that knowledge (von Glaserfield, 1987). The construction is viewed as a process of interpretation which is reinforced by past and ongoing experiences. Individuals make sense of knowledge in an interpretative way such that, as Rogoff (1995) argued, the appropriation of knowledge is not just the internalization of externally derived stimuli but rather the individual's active construction of those stimuli. In this context, communication is viewed as a dynamic two-way process in which meanings emerge in the space between the learner and a more expert other. Pea (1993) proposed that meaning negotiation and appropriation are integral to this process, whereby initial interpretative construction of knowledge is idiosyncratic. It is through social mediation that the construction becomes more congruent and communicable. This mediation may involve the learner in joint problem solving and the construction of knowledge is progressively realised cooperatively. Consequently, individuals collaboratively construct a common grounding of beliefs, meanings and understandings that they share in activity (Pea, 1993) through a culture, or community, of practice (Lave and Wenger, 1991). Through this process of meaning negotiation individuals appropriate their understanding. Although other less socio-culturally influenced learning methods, such as observing and listening, provide important guidance, they may not be able to provide access to knowledge which is less visible.

Coupled with the acknowledgement of the socio-cultural contexts for learning is the notion of situated learning. Situated learning is learning that takes place in the same situation in which the knowledge is deployed (Billett, 2001), such that the skills and knowledge are acquired in authentic settings of use. As such, the socio-cultural contexts for learning are more often than not similar to those of practice, as distinct from classroom-based learning where the learning is removed from the contexts of practice (Resnick, 1987). There is increasing recognition in learning theory of reciprocity between knowing and doing (Brown, Collins and Duguid, 1989). Sadler-Smith and Smith (2001) contended that HRD in general, and work-based learning in particular, should be inherently practice-based. Barab and Duffy (2000: 26) expressed the issue thus: 'In general, situative perspectives suggest a reformulation of learning in which practice is not conceived of as independent of learning and in which meaning is not conceived of as separate from the practices and contexts within which it was negotiated.' A socio-cultural approach to workplace learning does not negate the importance of cognition, but it adds to it and acknowledges the complexity of those aspects of the process that are beyond the characterization of knowledge as a purely individual activity.

Billett (1996a, 1998) has written extensively on the compatibility between cognitive and socio-cultural contributions to adult learning in the workplace. In his exploration of the notions of situated learning and situated cognition to describe learning that takes place within a culture of practice, and where the knowledge is deployed in the same context as the learning, Billett suggested that transferable knowledge is developed through participation in socio-culturally rich and authentic learning experiences that are guided by experts who play a mentoring role in relation to the learner. Similarly, Lave and Wenger (1991) have argued that situated learning in a culture of practice enables the expert to provide a legitimisation of new knowledge acquired by the learner. This legitimisation is crucial to the development of knowledge and understanding through the recognition of the learning and the assurance that an acknowledgement by an expert may provide. Lave and Wenger have suggested the concept of 'situated activity' where the situatedness is not just the physical surrounds but includes the negotiated character of meaning within the context, and the engaged, or problem-solving, nature of learning activity for the individuals involved. As Smith (2003b) observed, it is these conceptual developments that Lave and Wenger suggested that are the most important consequences of situated activity. Their concept of situated learning is more than learning *in situ*, or learning by doing, and involves their concept of 'legitimate peripheral participation' (where the learner has a place in the culture of practice, but not as yet a central place) to describe participation in social practice that includes learning as an integral part.

Billett (1996a, 1998) has provided a comprehensive set of arguments to show that the cognitive structures that are the result of internally processed information and memory are developed in social circumstances. These arguments are important in drawing the distinction between other learning theories that concentrated on the processes internal to the individual with little regard for the circumstances of learning, and more recent theories that recognise and explore the socio-cultural contexts within which the learning occurs. Billett (1996a) identified and discussed six areas of complementarity between the cognitive literature and the socio-cultural contexts for learning literature. For example, in accepting that skills required to develop expertise can be developed away from socio-cultural settings in simulated environments such as classrooms and workshops, Billett suggested that the effective and accurate deployment of this expertise to problem-solving within workplaces is developed through the influence that socio-cultural learning has on providing for recognition of when those skills are to be deployed and how. Similarly, it is the need to solve problems in the socio-cultural setting of a workplace that further develops cognitively derived knowledge and skill. In that way the learning includes situated knowledge relating to the skill required and its effective deployment in particular social circumstances. Similarly, Billett argued that transfer of knowledge from an already known situation to a new set of circumstances is not only the product of internal memory mechanisms, but is related to the conditions in which the knowledge is to be transferred (see also Robins, 1998). The presence of the relevant situational cues is crucial to the application of new knowledge in the workplace (see: Rouillier and Goldstein, 1997). Billett also suggested that the development of knowledge and understanding is influenced by perceptions of the value that will be assigned to that knowledge when it is deployed in a socio-cultural setting. Put in another way, the likelihood of an individual developing further an already held set of knowledge is likely to be enhanced where there is a belief that the knowledge will be useful to others, and is recognised as useful. It is these goal-directed activities that result in learners constructing and accessing relevant cognitive structures for deployment in the workplace, and for their potential modification in the socio-cultural environment of the workplace.

Cunningham, on the basis of his experience with adult learners in the workplace, observed that participation with groups of other learners or more expert others is particularly appropriate for adult learners. He also suggested that workplace learning is best facilitated when the knowledge is constructed through the use of workplace problems as a basis for learning; and that adult learners need opportunity to reflect on, and articulate, their personal learning experiences and to direct their own learning process. Writing from a perspective of experience in practice, rather than a theoretical one, Cunningham (1998) preferred a social interaction conceptualization when he described workplace learning as:

> An infinitely large set of informal interactions which take place when one person is trying to help another person. It is one of the most pervasive and successful functions performed by people at all levels of every workplace and accounts in considerable measure for people's success in their organization.
>
> (Cunningham, 1998: 6)

These observations afforded by Cunningham emphasise the importance of the human interaction through processes such as coaching and mentoring in workplace learning, and see the essence of workplace learning in the interaction between a more expert and a less expert worker.

Concepts of workplace learning

A set of ideas useful in understanding diversity in workplace learning contexts are those associated with the forms of knowledge that learners pursue within workplaces. Billett (1993) summarised the differences between three forms, or domains, of knowledge: propositional (knowledge about), procedural (knowledge how) and dispositional knowledge (values and attitudes). Using a similar conceptualization, but adding a notion of the deployment of strategic knowledge to unfamiliar situations, Mansfield (1991) developed the Job Competence Model which encompassed four aspects of competence:

- task or technical skills;
- task management skills (planning, decision making, prioritisation);
- contingency management skills (management of the unexpected, events beyond the scope of routine instructions);
- role and environment skills (understanding, working in and using the physical, organizational and cultural environment).

Both Billett and Mansfield have been able to explore workplace learning in terms of the forms of knowledge or skill that represent the outcomes. The value in these conceptualizations of different forms of workplace knowledge lies in the resultant opportunity to identify and separate out in more detail the various tasks associated with the acquisition of workplace knowledge, and to develop appropriate ways of developing the knowledge in each domain.

Starting with a simpler dichotomy of workplace knowledge, adapted from Anderson (1982), Billett and Rose (1996) discussed the distinction between conceptual knowledge (knowing 'that') and procedural knowledge (knowing 'how'). They then linked these two forms to the earlier identification of three forms of workplace knowledge (see Billett, 1993) to suggest that both conceptual and procedural knowledge are used in everyday practice to organize activities and to secure goals, with conceptual knowledge being used to provide the facts and propositions drawn upon to formulate goals and secure those goals.

A different conceptualization of forms of knowledge in the workplace is provided by Mezirow (1991), who also described three forms of workplace learning (instrumental, dialogic and self-reflective):

- Instrumental learning focuses on learning aimed at skill development and improving productivity.
- Dialogic learning involves learning about the individual's organization and their place in it.
- Self-reflective learning is described as learning which promotes an understanding of oneself in the workplace and provokes questions about one's identity and the need for self-change; it involves a transformation of the way a person looks at the self and relationships.

These three domains of learning are integrated when the learner achieves a critically reflective state in which he or she is sensitive to why things are being done in a particular way, and is critically reflective before accepting 'given' solutions to problems or methods of practice. Mezirow conceptualizes transformative learning as development through challenging old assumptions and creating new meanings that are 'more inclusive, integrative, discriminating and open to alternative points of view' (Mezirow, 1991: 224). Similar to Mezirow's three forms of workplace learning is the framework of Gott (1989) who, focusing most particularly on apprentices, argued that the knowledge required for 'real-world tasks' involves the following:

- procedural knowledge, which is 'how to do it' knowledge;
- declarative (domain) knowledge of the object, system or device;
- strategic knowledge of how to decide what to do and when (which is analogous to an executive control mechanism).

Failing to recognise the different forms of knowledge to be developed in workplaces can result not just in inappropriate training and assessment methods, but can also result in tensions. Robertson (1996), for example, observed that tension can develop where there is a less clear understanding and recognition for the different forms of knowledge. In his research he noted that it was not unusual for young trainees to be expected to accept without question or criticism what they were shown and told by trainers and supervisors. However, at the same time, they were expected to have an understanding of processes to a level that would enable them to suggest new and different ways in which processes could be carried out and improved. It appears that workplace trainers in Robertson's research preferred the development of propositional and procedural knowledge by a passive recipient learner on the one hand, while expecting reflective learning to have occurred with dispositional and strategic knowledge outcomes. Clearly therefore when designing and implementing HRD it is important to be clear about the nature of the learning that it is anticipated will take place and of any potential contradictions or tensions between these and the underlying forms of knowledge. As with other models of learning design, such as those of Gagne and Briggs (1974), we are advocating that practitioners pay especial attention to the nature and type of learning that needs to be facilitated. Our approach differs from theirs in that we are advocating that cognisance is taken both of the form of learning and the context in which it will take place.

Smith (2003b) has developed a summary of the different conceptualizations of workplace knowledge. In his model he offered a four-domain taxonomy of workplace learning that included propositional, procedural and dispositional knowledge, as identified by Billett, but identifying as a fourth domain the strategic knowledge identified by Gott. Smith then used this taxonomy to link the four forms of knowledge to the development of workplace expertise, using Dreyfus's (1982) model as a framework. Dreyfus (1982) described the five stages of skill development as follows:

- Stage 1, novice, characterized by limited, inflexible, rule-governed behaviour;
- Stage 2, advanced beginner, where, in addition to the set of rules, the learner begins to learn some of the important situational aspects of the task, but may not be able to differentiate the importance of these features;
- Stage 3, competent, where the learner sees actions in terms of goals and plans, based on the selection of important features of the situation, and which are used to guide action;

- Stage 4, proficient, where the best plan of action is selected seemingly unconsciously, and where situations are summed up quickly and plans selected;
- Stage 5, expert, where the performer acts intuitively from a deep understanding of the situation, appears to not be aware of the rules and features, and performance is fluid, flexible and highly proficient.

In the progression of a learner from the level of novice through to expert, it is likely that there is also a progression from passive receipt of training information to a more reflective and involved stance (Ericsson and Charness, 1994; Farmer, Buckmaster and LeGrand, 1992). Since knowledge is often appropriated through demonstration and discussion that focuses on 'rules', the construction of the procedural knowledge may be via the assistance of a mentor or guide. Elements of this knowledge may also be developed in off-job learning; however, as the learner moves from the simple rule-driven level of the novice through to more advanced levels of skill and competence the need for discussion, analysis and critical evaluation with a mentor, coach or expert other becomes more and more critical. The dialogue between the parties can be expected to focus more strongly on the strategic or contextual deployment of knowledge, on judgement, and on the development of dispositional skills. It is through these middle stages of the Dreyfus model that deeper understanding develops, and the strategic deployment of learned skill is enhanced, together with judgement that enables the learner to move away from the originally 'taught' and 'followed' sets of rules.

At the higher levels of the Dreyfus (1982) classification, where there is more demand for the intellectual dimensions of the skill to be understood, it is likely that the need for a mentor or coach decreases as knowledge becomes more internalized and is more integrated and complete. Gott's (1989) conceptualization suggested that experts are able to coordinate the three sources of skill (i.e. procedural knowledge, declarative knowledge and strategic knowledge) and that the progression is a development in these three aspects from a partial to a complete state. Evans (1994) concluded that the progression of this skill acquisition relies on the efficient presentation of instructional information in training and learning resources. It is also important that the trainer, coach, mentor or facilitator provides feedback to enable progression in the expectations of the learner and that monitoring processes or indicators are used that approximate expert performance.

Communities of learning and communities of practice

Communities of practice and communities of learning are both important concepts within the context of a socio-cultural interpretation of learning. The understanding of them is an important aspect of professional knowledge and skill, especially if attempts are to be made to intervene in and manage the learning processes therein.

Communities of learning

Mitchell and Sackney (2000) argue that a community of learning is a highly complex entity, but that its characteristics do not go uncontested. They point to 'the plethora of meanings given to the idea of community' (Mitchell and Sackney, 2000: 7) that indicate that we must be careful about what we mean if we are to avoid considerable confusion. Eraut (2002) has observed that a learning community can take several forms:

- First, he identifies an 'ecological' form that comprises people who live close by each other, or who work in the same organization, and goes on to question whether such communities provide equal access across all members, and also raises the question of who gets access to what kinds of knowledge.
- Second, he identifies that a learning community can be a political entity, such as an occupational group or religious group, each of which is interested in acquiring the resources for learning for its members. Within an organization this might mean that the needs of some learning communities are placed above the needs of others.
- Third, he identifies an ideological definition that tries to maximise participation within a democratic culture of inclusiveness, sharing and interdependency.

Tosey (1999) argued this slightly differently when he made a distinction between the more general idea of a 'learning community', and the more specific idea of a 'peer learning community', where the participants are characterized by a greater equality and set of common interests. The peer learning community idea is important from our perspective since it is communities of peers that provide the most likely opportunities for workplace learning, and furthermore it is these that most typically characterize the liberal and horizontal learning networks suggested by Poell, Chivers, Van der Krogt and Wildesmeersch (2000). Tosey suggested that a peer learning community has a number of distinctive characteristics:

- Personal development: peer communities of learning have the capability to develop a number of aspects of knowledge and are successful when they provide not just for development of procedural and propositional knowledge to do with the tasks of work, but they also serve to enhance dispositional and strategic knowledge through the necessary interaction with others.
- Community interaction: it is through interacting and experiencing common events that the community is created (Tosey, 1999). Attention is paid to the development of group psychosocial processes which develop group norms and forms of mutual supportiveness and assistance.
- Facilitation: effective peer-learning communities include a process of facilitation in order to bring together the resources that each member

has to offer so that these may be more effectively utilised and shared across the group. Furthermore, Tosey (1999) suggested that although there are skills that are necessary among facilitators, each member has a potential to facilitate, and that multiple facilitation is a community characteristic to be pursued and prized.

- Formal interdependence: a community of learning has capability to enable shared identification of learning goals and learning outcomes, mutual assistance towards the achievement of these, the monitoring of progress towards achievement, and even assessment of that achievement. This does not mean that all learning outcomes are the same for each group member, but it does mean that identification of learning outcomes for any one individual can be assisted by others in the community, as can progress towards them (Tosey, 1999). This differentiation among the members in terms of learning intents and outcomes is important, and the warning of Mitchell and Sackney (2000) that learning communities can reduce diversity between members is salient here.
- Boundary management: the peer learning community has boundaries in terms of its foci. It is important that these be managed carefully to avoid the community broadening into areas that shift it away from its foci (Tosey, 1999). Of course, broadening may legitimately occur, and even be necessary, but that broadening needs to be managed rather than just allowed to happen in an ad hoc way.

There is a relationship between the development of communities of learning and learning: communities can be an important vehicle through which a learning network can develop and enhance its efficacy. An issue here is whether a community of learners is something that happens naturalistically within a workplace, or whether there is a place for managing the process in a proactive manner. Our view here is that, although there will be naturally occurring communities, in much the same way as there are 'naturally' occurring learning networks, there is a strong case for developing them as a deliberate aspect of HRD (although deliberately developed learning communities may not be so easily characterized as 'peer' in Tosey's terms, or 'ideal' in Eraut's terms). Developing the focus of a learning community within a broader HRD strategy is, in our view, important both in terms of bringing together the people who can benefit from each other, and whose interactions will benefit the organization.

Smith's (1997) research with wool-scouring plants revealed a need for learner support by mentors working in conjunction with learning materials and training sessions to ensure that positive feedback was given to employees who lacked confidence as learners, and revealed that learners were sufficiently engaged with the learning process to enhance development of propositional and procedural knowledge, together with dispositional and strategic knowledge. The solution to this set of challenges was to develop sets of learning communities, where learners were each associated with an in-house mentor, and with a learning facilitator who was drawn from an external training provider. Working together, the community was able to establish learning needs, identify useful resources, and collectively determine the ways that they would go about developing the required knowledge to encourage progress through some of the stages of expertise acquisition.

Poell and Van der Krogt (2002) have extended their work on learning networks to an analysis of how these networks influence the development of individual learning and development programmes. A central idea in this work is an emphasis on the network of actors who form learning groups and create learning programmes with each other (Poell and Van der Krogt, 2002: 286). The actors include workers, managers, HRD personnel and employee and professional associations, including trade unions where relevant. These groups, or communities, can organize learning programmes in a large number of quite diverse ways and, over a period of time, develop into learning structures that represent the place at which new learning for individuals or groups start. Poell and Van der Krogt suggest that there are three major influences on the content and organization of learning programmes, including the context of the work and the learning structure, the views and other characteristics of the individuals in the learning group, and the actual process of learning programme creation by the learning group. Also identified in the Poell and Van der Krogt paper are three phases that attend learning sequence of a learning community: the orientation phase where the idea is developed to a learning contract; the learning phase itself; and a continuation phase where the learning is placed in a context of individual learning pathways, or leads to the development of further learning programmes. These phases are differently played out in each of the liberal, vertical, horizontal and external learning networks identified by Poell and Van der Krogt in their learning network theory to show that the process of learning programme creation is strongly, but not exclusively, related to the context within which it occurs. Action learning sets (see Chapter 6) may also be considered to be a form of inter- and intra-organizational learning network.

Communities of practice

The work of Lave and Wenger has been an important theoretical contribution to the development of the notion of communities of practice (CoP) and legitimate peripheral participation (LPP), and in researching the characteristics and efficacies of these communities for learning in the workplace. Wenger, McDermott and Snyder (2002) define communities of practice as:

> Groups of people who share a concern, a set of problems, or a passion about a topic, and who deepen their knowledge and expertise in this area by interacting on an ongoing basis.
>
> (Wenger, McDermott and Snyder, 2002: 4)

In workplace environments these may be communities of people who work together consistently every day in the same place, or they may be people who only interact on an occasional basis to share common problems and discuss issues of common concern. These communities are often a quite natural part of workplaces, with people being together through the nature of their work, or discovering each other and beginning to interact on a sustained basis. A definition of communities of practice that is more limited to the workplace was provided by Roth (1998: 10) in suggesting that these communities are characterized by 'the common tasks members engage in and the associated practices and resources, unquestioned background assumptions, common sense, and mundane reason they share'. This description of a community of practice is more easily recognised as being the one most often found occurring in workplaces among people who work regularly together, and has a parallel in Eraut's (2002) notion of the ecological community of learning. To that extent, it is a less broad definition than that of Wenger *et al.*, having parallels with each of Eraut's identifications of community.

As Wenger *et al.* (2002) argued, the 'health' of a community of practice is strongly related to its voluntary nature, and on 'the emergence of internal leadership' (Wenger *et al.*, 2002: 12). However, having said that, rather than just relying on naturally occurring groups of people who work together, or who have common interests, communities of practice can be developed and nurtured or, as Wenger *et al.* put it, cultivated. Apart from the capacity to develop individual members and provide a sense of belongingness and confidence, cultivating communities of practice also provides opportunity for the organization to identify individuals who have common sets of issues, and who are not aware of each other, and connect them together through the means of a community of practice. It is in this way that a community of practice differs from a community of learning. The latter is developed with the intent of identifying and achieving learning outcomes, while the former is a community based around these common interests and concerns and, while it will result in learning, the intent in a workplace is more likely to be associated with matters of common operational concern or practice. The learning is an outcome of those common concerns and practices, rather than an outcome necessarily intended through design.

Communities of practice may operate over a long period of time, as would be the case among a stable group of people who work together, or they may come together only for a short period of time as a common interest is temporarily shared by a group. Wenger *et al.* have identified seven principles associated with cultivating communities of practice, designed to ensure that they can evolve, that they have access to perspectives that are outside the community and that bring new thinking and new ideas and that they embrace different levels of participation whereby some members are quite central to the community while others have a more peripheral role.

On the other hand communities of practice can, as was noted in our discussion of social capital, be dysfunctional, and Wenger *et al.* (2002) explored these possibilities in some detail. Individual members or groups within the community can develop a sense of ownership and control which will reduce the effectiveness of the community, and the important sense of belongingness. Communities can become self-satisfied and no longer strive to evolve and enhance practice, but to protect what is already there. As Reynolds (1998) has argued, communities can be normative and can develop conformity rather than challenge, developing a disparaging mind-set towards those who are outside the community. Additionally, but by no means unrelated, since most people in workplaces probably belong to more than one community of practice, there can be discordance in the expectations or operations of those different communities that make it difficult for members to comfortably operate within multiple communities. The community in this sense is an embodiment of the social capital that exists in the workplace.

Developing and maintaining communities of practice is a clear challenge to small organizations where there may be limited numbers of staff who do similar work. This challenge is particularly relevant to very small businesses where there may be virtually no opportunity for participation in a wider community of practice. There have been several attempts to address this issue in effective ways. For example, working with small businesses in a regional environment in Australia, Southern (1996) also recognised the constraints on small businesses where there may only be one worker dealing with a large set of functions within the business, such that access within the organization to an expert 'other', or the development of a community among a number of others was either not available or was very limited. Southern developed a network among local small businesses that enabled people to participate in a community of practice that extended across a number of these small businesses, and he then facilitated the commencement of regular contact and meetings between participants. An interesting component of Southern's model was his recognition that a number of businesses in the network he formed were actually in competition with each other, such that there would be understandable discomfort among them. Integral to his model was the encouragement of people to join a community of practice where participants faced similar issues in their work and their practice, but where no two members of the community were employed in organizations in competition with each other. This is a variant of the notion of the action learning set as first proposed by Revans (1982).

Coaching and mentoring

A further set of issues that needs some discussion in this chapter is related to coaching and mentoring. These processes, with their varying degrees of formality, are important because they involve a learner in the workplace in association with another more expert or more experienced worker who has a role to play in the development of the learner's knowledge and skill and learning-related social interactions and relationships. The approach is a very common, even usual, learning method in smaller organizations that may not have the employee numbers to develop effective communities of learning or communities of practice. Mentors and coaches are often identified in a formal way by the organization and given a definite training and development role in association with a specific learner, or group of learners. On the other hand, they also may be identified by the learner in an informal way on a basis of a friendship relationship, or someone who is admired and has commitment and patience to assist. This distinction between a mentor who is appointed in a formal sense, and an informal mentor was recognised and developed by Willis and Dodgson (1986), writing in the context of women in educational workplaces.

Hudson (1999) in writing about the relationship between coaching and mentoring was of the view that a mentor is a person who has 'the inner competence to pass on knowledge and skills through example, inner authority and dialogue' (Hudson, 1999: 6). In his view mentoring is the model for coaching, but Hudson prefers the term 'coach' because of its lower degree of formality (see also Veale and Wachtel, 1996), and its use in more common parlance in association with athletics. A coach is someone who is trusted, who may have a friendship relationship with the learner and who, at the same time, is trained in the guidance of others towards increased competence and confidence. Hudson suggested that a coach within an organization models mastery for others to learn, guides others to higher performance, advocates and criticises, endorses and sponsors others without having control over them, and facilitates professional and organizational development. Specific coaching strategies identified by Hudson include one-on-one coaching, group coaching and systems coaching. This last form of coaching involves working with an organizational unit to develop it and its members in some planned way. Writing in a context of mentoring and coaching as strategies used within Coca-Cola Foods, Veale and Wachtel (1996) have usefully identified different types of coaching that relate not to the style of relationship with the learners, as in Hudson's specific forms of coaching, but rather, to the sorts of activities being pursued. They identify coaching being used at Coca-Cola for purposes of modelling, instructing, enhancing performance, problem solving and inspiration, and support.

Not all writers see the relationship between the terms 'coaching' and 'mentoring' in the same way as Hudson. For example, Parsloe and Wray (2000) dedicated some discussion to this issue and provided a summary of various definitions of the terms that have been proposed by different writers. A conclusion that can be drawn from the Parsloe and Wray discussion may be that coaching focuses more on the development of specific skills that are quite measurable in outcome or improvement, while mentoring applies to the broader development of the individual or group. A further distinction is offered by Johnson (2001) in terms of a sporting analogy: the coach is usually 'off-the-court', helps the learner to 'play' but is not in the team; a mentor is someone who is 'on-the-court' and can help the learner develop her or his game from within. As Johnson also noted, a mentor may have power within the organization and sponsor the protégé into opportunities and the role may be taken on spontaneously or as a part of a formal system. The different types of coaching and mentoring are all compatible; they simply serve different functions and are usually provided by different individuals.

The notions of cognitive apprenticeship are relevant here in a discussion of coaching and mentoring. As a major contributor to the development of the notion of cognitive apprenticeship Collins (1997) advocated that a complex modern society and workplace necessitates that learners be taught to learn through cognitive apprenticeship (Collins, Brown and Newman, 1989). Cognitive apprenticeship, Collins argued, has a number of features that lend themselves to deployment among workplace learners:

- Authenticity: material to be learned is embedded in tasks and settings that reflect the uses of these competencies in the real world;
- Interweaving: learners go back and forth between a focus of accomplishing tasks and a focus of gaining particular competencies;
- Articulation: learners articulate their thinking and what they have learned;
- Reflection: learners reflect and compare performance with others';
- Learning cycle: learning occurs through repeated cycles of planning, doing, reflecting;
- Multimedia: each medium is used to do what it does best.

Collins argued that a cognitive apprenticeship is an effective way to develop learning strategies among learners, since robust knowledge has to be both situated and un-situated, and that 'powerful abstractions are needed to organize the knowledge, but those abstractions must be grounded in real situations. Much of the expert's learning is working out the mappings between situations and abstractions' (Collins, 1997: 9). In Collins's view of goal-based learning in the workplace, learners are given the tasks they need to learn, and the scaffolding that they need to carry out these tasks. Farmer, Buckmaster and LeGrand (1992) suggested that experts provide scaffolds for early learning by novices, gradually decreasing the assistance as learners construct their own knowledge base. This gradual withdrawal of expert-provided scaffolding is consistent with Dreyfus's (1982) postulated five stages of skills development, from novice through to expert, and the progression of the learner from dependence on the expert to independent learning and knowledge construction. Carefully sequenced learning activities are required to develop the integration and generalization of knowledge and skill, and are sensitive to the needs of the learner as they change through increasingly competent performance. Under the conditions of successive approximations of skill development and the strategic deployment of these skills to the workplace, learners begin to construct the goals and sequences of actions that are most efficient in understanding and solving a workplace problem. Although strategic knowledge is sometimes overlooked in HRD (Glaser *et al.*, 1985; Soloway, 1986), learners need strategic knowledge for formulating, evaluating and choosing courses of action. In this 'meta' sense (i.e. beyond the learning content per se) the understanding and management of one's own learning processes are significant.

Open and closed learning contexts

So far in this chapter we have been concerned with examining those learning contexts which take place outside of training rooms or classrooms, and that we characterize as 'open' environments in that the learning is largely situated in the broader workplace, and largely makes use of the resources that are available within that context. (Note that we are using the term 'open' in a different sense from that of 'open learning' as it is often used in the discussions of distance and flexible learning methods.) However, a considerable amount of learning within workplaces is conducted in the formal context of a training room or classroom, and is planned and facilitator-led or instructor-led. In terms of learning network theory, it would be reasonable to suggest that these forms of training are more closely related to the vertical network than they may be to other networks, but these more controlled learning contexts have legitimacy and relevance in all learning network environments. Participation in more formally constructed and delivered learning programmes can be the result of deliberate choice in any form of learning network.

Although it may be that classroom-based instruction in the workplace is often used as a matter of habit, in response to expectations rather than of conscious deliberation, there are a number of reasons that may impact on this decision. Writing in a context of flexible delivery of training in UK industry, Calder and McCollum (1998) have made the point that controlled and planned absence from the workplace to attend a training course is often seen as more legitimate, while participation in workplace-embedded learning activities can sometimes be seen as less legitimate, less valuable, and even as 'time out'. Evans (2001) has made the same observation in his work with small enterprises in rural parts of Australia. Also, the requirement for a group to assemble to focus on, discuss and share the learning that they are undertaking in an environment away from the workplace and its attendant demands of production and so on, can be a valuable experience. The networking and potential development of a community of learners associated with these sorts of group learning experiences can be important outcomes that are seen as highly desirable. Additionally, from time to time the learning outcomes are such that all employees are seen as needing them, for example to satisfy operational, health and safety, or legal reasons, so there is a strong argument for a common, consistent and controlled learning experience. Induction programmes for new staff would also normally include classroom components as an efficient way for them to meet new colleagues and managers, to be familiarised with organizational policies and processes, to establish for themselves some other contacts in the organization on a face-to-face basis and to get an initial feel for the climate of the organization. In Sadler-Smith and Smith (2001) we suggested that formally presented HRD, such as 'taught courses', provides opportunity for critical reflection and the exchange of ideas with others, while Keeling, Jones, Botterill and Gray (1998) have pointed out that some jobs demand the understanding of considerable theoretical knowledge best derived through formal taught courses. It is important that off-job methods and on-job methods are not polarised and seen as either–or choices. Each has much to offer; the skill in the design of HRD lies in the blending of the different approaches.

Training and development programmes that we would view as less open, and more controlled, would be characterized by prior organization of curriculum and teaching delivery methods, and to take place in an instructor-led or instructor-facilitated teaching context, and to be held in a particular place at a particular time. Participants would be expected to attend that location at the appointed time. McKavanagh (1996) has compared classroom-based training with workplace learning on dimensions of support, clarity, independence, collaboration and innovation. His research has shown that, for HRD purposes, workplace-based learning appears to be more clearly defined in terms of outcome and application, more collaborative, and more independent. At the same time, workplace learning was generally less supportive of the learner and characterized by less independence.

On other important matters such as time and cost, several writers (e.g. Calder and McCollum, 1998) have observed that there is some reluctance on the part of organizations to release staff to formal training sessions since there is a loss of productivity while staff are absent. This is an important issue for organizations in general but especially so in smaller firms where there may be no other person with the skill and knowledge to undertake the tasks of the absent learner (Sadler-Smith, Down and Lean, 2000; Evans, 2001). For organizations with geographically dispersed staff there are other costs associated with travel to the training site, and possibly accommodation costs, all of which need to be added to the costs of worker downtime.

The negatively perceived, and particularly the cost-related, elements of classroom-based training and development have led to a movement towards flexible delivery, where a number of training methods, such as on-the-job, resource-based and online, delivery techniques are used to substitute for face-to-face classroom instruction or, at least, to minimise it. We explore these methods later in this book, but some comment is warranted here. The interest in the use of distance education training methods as part of flexible delivery, and as a cost-efficient form of HRD, has increased over the past few years in response to new forms of technology that are becoming more widely available – most notably the potential of online learning. Although possibly attractive to management when perceived as a more cost-efficient form of

HRD, there is evidence that training delivery methods based only around the use by learners of independent learning-resource-based learning materials may not be so popular among workers and their managers. Sadler-Smith, Down and Lean speculated that flexible modes of training may be more enthusiastically embraced by 'converted and privileged groups (such as managers)' (2000: 475) than among employees themselves, although Guglielmino (2001) has argued that among managers in European organi-zations there is an overwhelming preference for trainer-supported learning over independent learning. There is similar evidence from Australia (Smith, 2000a, b, c; Twyford, 1999) among vocational learners, together with the sobering observations of Cornford and Beven (1999) that 'Leaving learners, particularly novices, to piece together a picture of the complex workplace environment without guidance is more likely to result in incorrect and fragmented understandings' (Cornford and Beven, 1999: 28).

Although there is considerable value in independent learning through resource-based learning as a delivery method for HRD, considerable care needs to be given in the choice and application of those methods. We deal in greater detail with these issues in a subsequent chapter but observe here that, given the recognised importance of socio-cultural contexts for learning in the workplace that we have discussed in the current chapter, the concerns shown in research to have been expressed both by learners and managers need to be taken into account in designing those forms of HRD. We suggest that resource-based HRD methods are a valuable element of the learning context but may not be suitable for the full range of diversity of learners and contexts that HRD practitioners and managers more generally need to meet the needs of. What we can conclude is that off-job classroom-based learning, although having some features that may not be seen as totally desirable when viewed from a socio-cultural or situated perspective, most definitely do have a role to play as part of a blend to meet the complex needs that are likely to exist across a diversity of learning contexts.

Focus on practice: creating communities of practice at Eli Lilly and Company

Plaskoff (2003) has contributed an important paper focusing on creating a community culture at Eli Lilly, and we have drawn strongly on that work in this section. Innovation projects are often organized upon a project team basis. This has the advantage of bringing together different specialists and focusing their attentions on a specific task or outcome. One of the problems that the Eli Lilly Company encountered with this approach was the lack of cross-team or inter-team learning. Plaskoff described an approach taken in the Eli Lilly Company which not only aimed to establish a community of practice which resulted in that community thriving on a different value set than that of the whole organization and in doing so functioning as an instrument of change for the whole organization. The focus of the activity was the scientific communications community (referred to here as the SCC) which is responsible for developing material for submission to regulatory agencies and publication in technical journals. The project had a number of stages:

- A core group was established to design the community charter. This core team was educated about the nature and ethos of CoPs (for example in this case as a safe haven for experimentation, risk-taking and hence learning). The issue of voluntary participation and distributed leadership was played-up and the role of performance management down-played.
- Pre-launch planning: the SCC was inclusive rather than restrictive, and contained members from all four of the relevant product groups. Moreover, the SCC developed a metaphor for itself – that of scientific storytellers, which clearly defined that nature of their practice and provided a focus for their activities.
- Ground rules: the SCC set some clear ground rules for those managers who were part of their CoP; for example, participation as practitioners not as supervisors, allowing others to lead and drive, remaining in the community only so long as they follow the ground rules. Furthermore, SCC activity was not part of performance review since intrinsic motivation was seen as a crucial reason for engagement with the CoP. Feedback was included and seen as useful, but this was usually in private.
- Launch: the CoP extended the metaphor at a formal launch (the SCC Solar System) and a community space was established through which people could participate in the community electronically.

The CoP had at the time of writing 14 core members and 150 subscribers to community space. It is a place for the organization to 'test ideas, gather input and guidance on organizational direction, and a source of new practices' (2003: 19). The CoP gave voice and had a coaching and mentoring role. In the coaching members were reminded that they best understand practice in the everyday life of the community, and through open and critical discussion of scientific practice. Plaskoff offered his experiences with Eli Lilly as evidence that a CoP can be facilitated and managed and that it can positively influence change in the organization and foster cohesiveness and performance.

Identifying diversities amongst learning contexts: questions for situational analysis

This chapter has explored the complexities that lie behind the learning context of HRD. In this final section of this chapter we offer a systematic way of thinking about the diversities that lie within the different learning contexts that may exist within and between organizations. The questions are intended to foster enquiry, reflection and analysis as a precursor to any HRD project or activity.

Socio-cultural contexts for learning

1 Within your own organizational context, what are the opportunities for developing learning within a socio-cultural context?
2 What may be the constraints on your organization, in terms of its culture, the relationships between people and organizational support for more socially constructed forms of workplace learning?
3 What might you need to develop within your organization to benefit from the learning that can accrue from the socio-cultural relationships?
4 Is such an approach likely to be accepted and valued?

Forms of knowledge

1 How are the different forms of knowledge we have discussed important to different parts of your organization?
2 Are there some areas of the organization where dispositional skills, or strategic skills, are more important to develop than in other parts of the organization?
3 In working towards expert knowledge, is your organization generally capable of supporting the sequence from novice to expert that we developed through the work of Dreyfus?
4 What needs to be put in place to develop systematic approaches to the development of expertise?
5 How might it be determined that expertise has been developed?

Communities of learning/communities of practice

1 Where in your organization do you already see effective communities of learning and/or communities of practice?
2 What has led to these communities being effective?
3 Where else do you see opportunity for the development of these communities, and what would you wish to achieve from them?
4 How would your organization go about developing such communities where they are desirable but not yet present?
5 What would be the barriers to that in different parts of your organization?
6 Would peer learning communities be more effective than broader communities in some parts of the organization?
7 Do you see communities that are ineffective, or even counter-productive from the point of view of learning? If so, what characterizes them? Are they salvageable and, if so, how might you achieve that?

Open and closed contexts for learning

1   Does your organization currently conduct traditional classroom-style training? What are the reasons for that, and is that the best way to conduct HRD?
2   Is it possible to develop communities of learning or practice from the networking developed in group learning contexts?
3   What might be the opportunities for shifting the learning contexts more into workplace contexts?
4   What groups of workers in your organization might benefit from resource-based learning approaches?
5   Where the workforce is distributed across shifts or geographically, what are the opportunities for different approaches?

4   Diversities in learning orientation

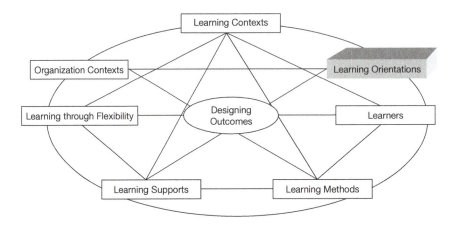

Introduction

In this chapter we will explore the concepts of attitudes, motives and needs as these are seen as central in determining individuals' purposes for engaging in learning and with learning. We define these as three facets of a learning orientation on the basis that all three are necessary and inter-linked prerequisites for engaging in learning. Contemporary questions about learning are inextricably linked with issues of performance since it is the centrepiece of human resource management (HRM) and human resource development (HRD) processes in organizations and organizational life. Learning surpasses performance in that it is a generic capability and is future-oriented. Employees who have a learning orientation are likely to be able to work both smart and hard; employees with a performance orientation are likely to simply work hard (Chalofsky, 2003). Moreover, a learning orientation on the part of the key stakeholders in the process is an essential component of a strategic approach to HRD.

The distinction between engaging in and engaging with learning is an important one: individuals may engage in learning as learners; individuals may also engage with learning as facilitators and contributors to the process (for example in the case of the human resource function) or as managers in the specific sense of managing learning or in the general sense of being a manager (although a manager may also be a learner). This raises two issues. The first is the notion of stakeholders in learning. We identify three principal groups of stakeholders: learners, managers and human resource practitioners. Second, the issue of the organizational context for learning is significant in terms of whether the approach adopted is strategically focused and proactive or whether a more tactical and reactive stance is adopted. The role that each stakeholder plays (or indeed whether they behave as stakeholders at all) may depend upon how human resource development (HRD) relates to the organization and its processes more broadly. Arguably the underlying dimension is in diversity of strategic need, motive and outcome at the organizational level, the extent of the strategic integration of HRD into the business and the way this manifests itself at the level of the individual manager, learner or human resource (HRM or HRD) practitioner. Harrison (2002) identified three levels at which this integration may take place: the level of corporate strategy; the level of business unit objectives; and the operational level. These levels are not mutually exclusive and a major task of integrating strategy, human resource management (HRM) and HRD is configuring the activities at each level in such a way that they mutually support and reinforce each other.

At the level of corporate strategy HRD's intent should be to formulate an HRD mission that supports the corporate goals in a reactive (or 'fit') sense but also to influence and develop strategic thinking within the organization (Harrison, 2002: 91) in a more proactive manner. So, for example, executive development programmes may be provided in response to a need to develop strategic thinking, but this in turn, if successful, may influence strategy itself. Organizational development may require executive development which in turn leads to further organizational development in a virtuous circle (or positive feedback loop). At the business-unit level the intent of HRD activity should, according to a strategic HRD (SHRD) perspective, be to develop HRD policy and practice in a systematic way that supports the needs of the business unit in order that those targets are met that contribute to the corporate strategy (Harrison, 2002). Finally, at the operational level the intent (of an SHRD approach) should be to implement personal development plans for employees that enable them to meet performance and development targets in ways that support the business unit objectives. Our view is that in order to make an impact upon the performance of individuals and the organization in mutually reinforcing ways a strategic approach is necessary; however, in spite of the rhetoric that surrounds it, it is not without its tensions and associated problems.

As well as considering the various stakeholders and the context we will also examine the underlying issues at the individual level which are likely to influence why an employee (be they learner, manager or HR practitioner) engages in learning or with learning. Fundamental in this regard are attitudes, motivations (including expectations) and needs of the individual and how these impact upon the design, planning and implementation of HRD. It is of course impossible to consider issues related to learning at the individual level without also acknowledging the broader human resource issues such as appraisal and reward, especially when one is considering employees' needs and motivations. Broader structural matters are also raised that are relevant to the relationship between the individual and the organization, for example, the psychological contract and organizational power in that they are likely to exercise some influence on learning outcomes (for example, via resource allocation). These discussions are likely to shed further light on our understanding of how and the extent to which each of the stakeholder groups engages in or with learning.

The chapter will begin by taking an overview of the concept of stakeholders; it will propose that there are three key groups and it will consider how these groups relate to each other in a strategic framework. The overall aim of the chapter is to debate how issues of diversity of attitudes, motives and needs may impact upon the practice of HRD in organizations and how any potential tensions and conflicts might be acknowledged, managed and hopefully, in practice, resolved.

Stakeholders in learning

A stakeholder in an organizational process is defined as a person who resources, is involved in or is affected by an organizational process. A stakeholder may be internal to or external to the organization. The internal stakeholders in HRD include the learners, the providers and facilitators of learning (or HRD) and the managers; external stakeholders in HRD are likely to include customers, external providers and facilitators, suppliers, contractors, competitors, and so forth. Stakeholders vary in terms of their level of interest in a particular organizational process (in this case HRD) and the power that they may or may not have in that process. As far as the issues of learning attitudes, motives and needs are concerned, we will focus our attentions on the internal stakeholders and their roles as it is they who are likely to have the highest levels of interest in HRD as an organizational process.

The extent to which the internal stakeholders engage with the process of HRD may also depend upon the context and the degree to which HRD is integrated with broader HRM issues and the organization's strategy. In this sense stakeholders act upon and are also influenced by the organizational process of HRD. Therefore a more accurate definition of an HRD stakeholder is: someone who affects and is affected by the process of HRD. These relationships are further complicated by the fact that the actions of each of the stakeholders may affect the others. Hence the network of relationships between the various stakeholders is a complex one.

The nature of the relationship and the strength of the effects in these linkages may depend upon the way HRD is configured, and a distinction can be drawn between HRD that has a broader strategic focus (SHRD) and that which has a narrow operational and tactical focus (for example as in 'traditional' training). Strategic HRD involves developing people within what might be termed a 'learning culture' as part of an overall HR strategy. HRD processes (for example the identification of needs, the planning and implementation of learning interventions and the evaluation of impact) are in this scenario, aligned (vertically) with the organization's mission. In this virtuous state of affairs HRD may be seen by senior management as a value-adding investment that is essential to the future of the business and in which ownership of and responsibility for HRD is shared between directors, HR specialists, senior managers, line managers, teams and individuals (Harrison, 2002: 80). Ideally, in a situation in which internal stakeholders are part of strategic partnerships furthering the creation of a learning climate, it becomes difficult if not meaningless to separate out the stakeholders in terms of their interest and power in HRD processes. Arguably, the task for an HRD-related organizational development project would be to increase the power over and interest in HRD processes of all of the internal stakeholders to a 'high power-over' and 'high interest-in' combination in our stakeholder analysis and to attempt to maximise mutuality of interest. Understanding the diversity of attitudes, motives and needs amongst the internal stakeholders may be one way to further the development of an organization with respect to the degree of strategic integration of its HRD processes with HRM and strategy.

Relationships (between the stakeholders), responsibilities (for engagement in and with learning), ownership (of the process) set the scene for an effective strategic partnership (McCracken and Wallace, 2000). Within this partnership the individual stakeholders' conception of learning (in terms of attitudes, motives and needs) may determine the way in which individuals engage with learning; this in turn is likely to affect and be affected by cultural and structural issues within the organization.

Table 4.1 Stakeholders in the HRD processes

	Low power in HRD management processes	High power in HRD management processes
Low interest in HRD	Customers Suppliers	Senior managers Line managers
High interest in HRD	External HRD providers Learners	HRD practitioners

Research by McCracken and Wallace (2000) suggested that in deciding whether or not SHRD is an organizational reality as opposed to a management or HR rhetoric it is the strength of the strategic partnerships and especially that between HRD and senior managers which are important. The organization's position on an operationally-focused/strategically-focused continuum is also likely to affect and be affected by the roles taken by HRD practitioners within the organization. This depiction of a continuum emphasises extremes and clearly it is possible to have integration at strategic and operational levels – but in depicting the continuum we are highlighting the significance of the impact that an operations focus or a strategic focus in HRD can have. How an individual conceives of HRD itself and their associated HRD stance or role is likely to be dependent to some extent upon their basic attitudes and beliefs about learning and how they engage in or with the HRD process.

We will now go on to examine the diversity of attitudes, motives and needs of the different internal stakeholders. It should be noted that there are two additional sub-dimensions of diversity in operation here: first, the differences

Table 4.2 Roles of the HRD stakeholders under different conceptualizations of HRD

Internal stakeholder	HRD role	
	Tactical	*Strategic*
Learner	Participation	Identification of training needs Commitment to learning Engagement in learning Feedback and reflection
Senior manager	Planning Resourcing	Championing HRD Resourcing Vertical alignment
Line manager	Control	Learning needs identification Commitment to learning Evaluation of learning transfer
HRD practitioner	Learning needs assessment (i.e. needs identification and analysis) Planning HRD Provision of HRD Evaluation of HRD	Learning needs analysis at the individual, job and organizational levels Facilitation of individual and collective learning Horizontal integration of HRD with HRM Vertical alignment of HRD with business strategy Evaluation and monitoring of HRD

between the various stakeholders and how these inter-stakeholder differences can affect the HRD process; second, differences within specific stakeholder groups and how these intra-stakeholder group variations can also impact upon HRD and how it can be managed. Our ultimate aim is to explore these issues in order that they may be better understood and better managed in order to enhance the effectiveness of the HRD process.

To understand the diversity of attitudes, motives and needs within and between the stakeholders necessarily entails an individual level of analysis. For example, at the simplest level the role of the learner in engaging in learning can be seen to be fourfold, namely to

- take some measure of responsibility for the identification of their learning needs;
- acquire knowledge, skills and attitudes that are relevant to them and their job role;
- apply newly acquired knowledge, skills and attitudes to their job;
- reflect upon the usefulness of the learning to themselves, their job and the organization.

But within this there are likely to be a whole range of diverse attitudes, motives and needs and associated behaviours exhibited at the individual level. We therefore need some way of beginning to understand what factors might influence the extent to which an individual will engage with the HRD process (for example with respect to learning needs identification, the acquisition of new knowledge, skills and attitudes, application to their job role, and giving feedback on the value of the learning).

The learner's orientation

We will consider the orientation of the learner in terms of the three factors that we argue make up a learning orientation (attitudes, motives and needs). The orientation we propose is part of what traditionally has been referred to as a 'person analysis' (Goldstein, 1993), although there are additional dimensions, some of which we will consider in subsequent chapters (for example, learning styles and cognitive styles).

Learners' attitudes

We argue that learners' attitudes towards HRD are an important factor in determining the extent to which they engage in learning. As well as having high face validity there is considerable empirical evidence to support this assertion. Clardy (2000) observed that individuals differ in their orientation to learn on their own and that various measures of self-directed learning are available for assessing this and other motivationally related characteristics. But he argued that orientation to learning is a more situationally dependent opinion or belief and less a fixed personality trait. The implication of Clardy's argument is that the orientation of an individual to learning is a dimension of diversity that is affected by other factors, such as the actions of the other stakeholders and the context; it can therefore to an extent be managed in order to enhance the level of engagement with learning.

The antecedents of employees' attitudes towards skills upgrading were investigated by Lim and Chan (2003) who found that an individual's attitudes towards skills upgrading, their self-efficacy, the perceived usefulness of skills upgrading and long-term orientation were positively related to motivation for skills upgrading. They argued that an individual's attitude cannot be changed overnight and advocates of skills upgrading (such as managers and HR practitioners) must 'preach the long- and short-term benefits and the necessity of skills up-grading to people who are not sufficiently positive about it' (2003: 238). For this to be effective they maintain that these exhortations must be at the right level and that they should fully elucidate the benefits for the individual's and organization's performance.

A different perspective on the notion of attitudes towards learning can be found in the concept of 'curiosity' (Reio and Wiswell, 2000). Epistemic curiosity (Berlyne, 1960) is an information- and knowledge-seeking activity that is aroused when individuals are confronted with information that challenges their knowledge, attitudes or beliefs: they will then be motivated to resolve the resulting conceptual conflict. The idea of epistemic curiosity was extended by Day (1971) who argued that it is an enduring trait – an idea that subsequently received some empirical support (Boyle, 1989). Curiosity is a potentially powerful motivator in HRD, and in self-directed learning in particular (see Long, 1989) and is one that does not appear to diminish with age (see Reio and Wiswell, 2000) – an observation consistent with the personality trait of 'openness to experience' (one of the 'big five' personality trait clusters, Costa and McCrae, 1988). Curiosity about and interest in the job is likely to impact upon engagement in learning because participation in learning can increase knowledge and skills levels, improve performance and elevate feelings of self-worth. Self-curiosity is also likely to be an important factor because it will reveal strengths, weaknesses and interests and the self-realisation of development needs that will result (Noe and Schmitt, 1986: 502).

From a practical point of view the fact that individuals are likely to bring varying levels of curiosity to the HRD process which impact upon their intent to engage in learning suggests that manipulating levels of curiosity is a useful technique in the design of effective learning. From a theoretical perspective curiosity is important when seen as an intrinsic motivator for adult learning and as such lends further support to Knowles's andragogical model (Knowles, Holton and Swanson, 1998) in which he made the claim that internal motivators are potent in fostering learning (Reio and Wiswell, 2000). Noe and Schmitt (1986) argued that investment in HRD might be wasted if employees with low job involvement and lack of career interest are forced to engage in learning, and also that self-assessment of interests, career goals and plans may help to improve the efficiency and effectiveness of HRD.

Another perspective on attitudes to learning (and upon which Knowles drew in his andragogical learning theory) was provided from research by Houle (1961) which explored why adults engage in continuing education. From the analysis of interview data of a small sample he identified three orientations depending upon the individual's conception of the purposes and values of continuing education:

- Goal orientation: continuing education is used for the achievement of clear-cut objectives;
- Activity orientation: continuing education is used to satisfy a need for social contact which was more important to the learners than the content or purpose of the learning activity itself;
- Learning orientation: these individuals seek knowledge for its own sake.

Maurer (2002) described as 'development-oriented' those individuals who are oriented towards learning, have favourable attitudes towards learning, and experience favourable affect during learning activities. For such individuals each challenging situation is viewed as an opportunity to incrementally add to one's capabilities to reduce the discrepancy between 'what I am' (the actual self) and 'what I might be' (the possible self). The wider implications of this are that because development-oriented individuals experience less anxiety and more positive affect during the pursuit of difficult and challenging tasks they are able to adapt to changing work situations, cope with challenge and difficult constraints and pressures and maintain performance through difficult developmental experiences (Maurer, 2002: 25). A high development orientation is likely to manifest itself as persistence through difficult learning material. Moreover, experiences of mastering difficult material may lead to increased self-efficacy (Gist and Mitchell, 1992) and further involvement in learning (a hypothesis consistent with Locke and Latham's (1990b) goal-setting theory). Therefore if the development orientation of an individual can be enhanced through learning experiences that satisfy their needs this may create a positive feedback loop fostering ongoing engagement in learning and may support the aspiration to lifelong learning espoused in much HRD policy and rhetoric. Attitudes to learning are inextricably linked with the concept of learners' motivation and it is to this concept that we now turn our attention.

Learners' motives

It is not enough that learners have the ability to learn (that they 'can do'), they also need the desire to learn (that they 'will do') (Tracey, Hinkin, Tannenbaum and Mathieu, 2001: 7). Even if trainees possess the prerequisite skills needed to learn (the necessary ability), performance will be poor if motivation is low or absent (see Tracey *et al.*, 2001). Indeed Aditya and his colleagues have argued, admittedly from a leadership development perspective that one of the most useful 'formulas' in management is:

Ability + Motivation = Performance

In other words, 'if you want someone to do something they're not doing now you've got to make them able (guidance), make them want to (good feelings). To [us] this is the closest we're likely to get to any universal truth about leadership' (Aditya, House and Kerr, 2000: 155). Most researchers agree that motivation is an internal process that regulates external behaviours which includes both stable and malleable features and that activating or maintaining the 'will-do' aspect of learners' intents is a crucial element of learning design and the HRD process more generally. In failing to address the issue of motivation HRD practitioners and managers run the risk of dismissing it as a subjective choice or failing in the disposition of the learner (Hardré, 2003). These issues are to some extent encompassed by the notion of attitudes to learning discussed previously: however, we feel that by considering the notion of motives we have greater explanatory power in our framework over and above that provided by attitudes alone since it addresses issue of behaviours and cognitions explicitly and the ways in which these manifest themselves in the learning situation. Without understanding why an individual may or may not have reasons to engage in learning, HRD practitioners may overlook one of their key leverage points for adding value in the HRD process.

Motivation is from the Latin *movere* meaning 'to move' and is a concept that is helpful when trying to understand what moves individuals to engage in learning. It can benefit practitioners' understanding of how to manage the learning process in organizations. Psychologists define motivation as a process through which goal-directed behaviour is initiated, energised, directed and maintained (Huczynski and Buchanan, 2001). Learning cannot take place unless individuals are motivated to learn, and so for example since attendance at a training course (for instance) is not the same as participation, or engagement, in learning, it is important to understand the psychological bases of human motivation. As one might expect, motivation has been shown to be an important influence upon training performance (Tracey, Hinkin, Tannenbaum and Mathieu, 2001) and is one of the factors that Noe (1986) argued determines the extent to which an employee is trainable. In Noe's model motivation is seen to comprise three facets:

- energiser: providing enthusiasm for the learning;
- director: guides and directs learning;
- maintainer: promotes application of newly acquired knowledge and skills.

Within this model trainability is defined thus:

Trainability = *f* {ability; motivation (energiser; director; maintainer); environmental favourability}

Given the potential that an understanding of the role that motivation plays in determining employees' orientations to learning presents for leveraging enhanced performance, it is perhaps surprising that motivation has not been well-researched in HRD *per se* (Naquin and Holton, 2003). Theories of motivation are derived from mainstream research in organizational psychology but nonetheless the concepts, frameworks and empirical findings are highly relevant and translatable to the HRD context. Motivation to learn is frequently cited as being one of the most important determinants of learning outcomes and participation in HRD (Bartlett, 2001; Noe and Wilk, 1993; Tharenou, 1997). Moreover, highly motivated individuals are also more likely to apply the skills they developed in learning to their job (Cannon-Bowers, Salas, Tannenbaum and Mathieu, 1993). Motivation theories may be divided into two broad groups, content theories (i.e. 'we can attribute a similar set of motives to all individuals') and process theories (i.e. 'the individual has a cognitive decision-making role in setting ends and means'), each of which provides for variability in individuals' learning intents.

Content theories

Content theories of motivation attempt to understand and explain the 'baggage' of needs that it is assumed we all bring with us. These theories include the seminal contributions to the organizational behaviour literature by Douglas McGregor, Abraham Maslow and Clayton Alderfer.

McGREGOR'S THEORY X AND THEORY Y:

Early attempts at understanding motivation in an organizational context were made in the 1950s and 1960s by McGregor who argued that many companies in the USA appeared to treat their employees as if they were 'work-shy' and therefore needed constant direction, monitoring and control (McGregor, 1967). Underpinning this interpretation was what McGregor termed 'Theory X' with its precepts that the average person inherently dislikes work, that people must be directed to work and that they wish to avoid responsibility. McGregor asserted that by managing in accordance with these precepts there would be a knock-on effect on the ways employees behaved – they would act in a Theory X way. On the other hand, managers operating according to Theory Y precepts work on the assumptions that work is as natural as rest to people, they will exercise self-direction and self-control and they enjoy responsibility. If employees were managed in a

Theory Y way they would respond by reciprocating accordingly (Torrington, Hall and Taylor, 2002). McGregor's ideas are now somewhat dated and more elaborate theories of motivation have subsequently been developed; however, at the core of his model is that of the Theory Y 'complex man' who possesses a bundle of social and self-actualizing needs, and who under the right conditions can show high levels of responsible behaviour and self-direction (Fincham and Rhodes, 1999: 137). The concept of the complex employee is therefore significant in a number of contemporary HRD issues such as empowerment in learning, responsibility for identification of one's own learning needs and the capacity to be self-directed in learning, which are all predicated in a sense on a Theory Y assumption and, it may be argued, inform at least to some extent SHRD thinking.

MASLOW'S HIERARCHY OF NEEDS

One of the most widely used content theories of motivation is the hierarchy of needs comprising biological/physiological, safety, affiliation, esteem, knowing and understanding, aesthetics, transcendence, freedom of enquiry and expression and self-actualization, as posited by Maslow (1954). One of the key assumptions from an HRD perspective of Maslow's theory is that any need is not an effective motivator until the lower needs are satisfied. We have an innate desire to ascend the hierarchy to meet higher order needs (such as self-esteem and self-actualization) and self-actualization cannot be satisfied since the 'peak experiences' associated with it stimulate the need for more such experiences (Huckzynski and Buchanan, 2001). Content theories assume that we can attribute similar sets of needs to all individuals. If this is the case it begs questions such as 'What light can it shed upon the diversity of intents amongst learners?', 'Which aspects of our "baggage" of needs could learning in a work context address?' and 'How can planned HRD address the needs in a progressive fashion?'. For example, need for esteem may be satisfied by achieving the respect of others through enhanced achievement, reputation, prestige, recognition, attention and appreciation. The ability to perform in a competent manner, to be knowledgeable about one's job, to be a source of knowledge for others, to have attained a certain level of skill or attained a qualification might represent self-esteem needs that engagement in learning could address. Similarly, learning may address curiosity about knowledge and understanding, aesthetics and ways of achieving one's full potential through 'peak' experiences. So by following the logic of the progression hypothesis of Maslow's framework it would be important that organizations provide opportunities for employees to meet their higher-order needs through learning and development on a continuing (not to say lifelong) basis.

ALDERFER'S ERG THEORY

There are similar implications from Alderfer's existence-relatedness growth (ERG) theory where individuals are assumed to possess self-esteem and self-actualization needs (Alderfer, 1972). Although on the face of it there are overlaps, Alderfer's theory differs from Maslow's in that he argued that individuals will regress to the lower level if they experience frustration in satisfying a higher-level need (a regression hypothesis). From an HRD perspective this could be helpful in explaining why individuals may withdraw from satisfying higher-level growth needs; if they are frustrated in their attempts to learn, develop and grow they may regress or withdraw.

Table 4.3 Summary of content theories of motivation

Maslow	Alderfer	Herzberg
Self-actualization	Existence: physiological and safety needs	Motivators (content): achievement; advancement; growth; recognition; responsibility; the work itself
Freedom of expression		
Transcendence	Relatedness: affiliation and esteem needs	
Aesthetics	Growth: self-actualization and self-esteem needs	
Knowing and understanding		Hygienes (context): pay; company policy; supervision; status; security; working conditions
Esteem		
Affiliation		
Safety		
Physiological		

Some of these theories have been criticised on a number of grounds including culture-boundedness (in the case of Maslow), lack of empirical support (see Fincham and Rhodes, 1999) and bias in research methods employed (as in Herzberg's two-factor theory). One of the practical difficulties is the assumption that all individuals possess these needs; this may not concur with our own experiences in the workplace or classroom where people with apparently similar needs will embrace learning with very different degrees of enthusiasm and varying levels of motivation. This raises the important question of whether it really is the case that we have a predetermined set of motives or if there is more individual variability (Huckzynski and Buchanan, 2001). If the latter is the case an explanation is needed that accounts for the conscious decisions that individuals make with respect to which motives they choose to address and how they do so. Process theories go beyond content theories in providing additional explanatory power for some of these issues.

Process theories

Process theories of motivation attempt to explain the role that an individual's cognitions (including their awareness of the risks involved, their expectations) play in determining how behaviour is initiated, re-directed and terminated (McKenna, 1994: 83). Goal setting, expectancy and equity theories are helpful in understanding learners' motives in the HRD process.

GOAL SETTING

A goal is defined in the learning context as a desirable level of achievement. Goal setting theory has a number of underlying assumptions (see Latham, 2004):

- individuals who are given complex and challenging goals perform better than those given no goals or simple and unchallenging ones;
- goals are more effective in eliciting performance when they are specific rather than vague;
- to maintain or enhance an individual's self-efficacy the goal should be commensurate with the individual's ability to successfully accomplish the goal;
- participation in goal setting can enhance performance: the individual has to accept the goal that has been set;
- for goal setting to be effective individuals need to be aware of the extent to which they are achieving the goal.

Goal setting theory has some clear-cut applications in the management of learning. For example, learning targets should be clear, challenging and achievable; ideally they should have been agreed with learners; and facilitators should give feedback on the extent to which targets are likely to be met. The degree of challenge presented by a goal and the commensurability with the learners' abilities to achieve it are aspects of an individual's learning orientation that should be accommodated in the HRD process. Furthermore, learners should be seen as participative stakeholders who are able to assume some responsibility for their engagement in HRD. Moreover, goal setting theory suggests that it is advisable to have a diversity of learning goals suited to individuals' circumstances if motivation is to be maximised, and also that complex goals may need to be broken down into sub-goals.

EXPECTANCY

An important aspect of motivation is the way in which individual choice appears to be exercised in terms of which needs are important and how they are satisfied. Expectancy theory says that in order for an individual to make an effort in a task he or she must believe that exerting the effort will increase the probability of getting the desired reward. The theory was developed by

Vroom (1964) and has three elements: (a) valence: the value (positive, negative or neutral) that an individual attaches to an outcome; (b) instrumentality: the perceived likelihood that the performance will lead to reward; (c) expectancy: the perceived likelihood that effort will lead to performance (measured from zero to one). Learners will be more motivated to perform well in HRD if they perceive (Noe, 1986) that:

- high effort will lead to high performance in HRD;
- high performance in HRD will lead to high job performance;
- high job performance is instrumental in obtaining desired outcomes and avoiding undesirable outcomes.

Clearly there are a multitude of permutations on the values that the parameters can take: the important point of the theory is that it attempts to explain how individuals' perceptions (in this case their subjective probabilities) and conscious decisions can influence their motivations and result in individual differences in motivations to engage in learning. Studies have suggested learners' beliefs that they can learn the material presented in a training programme and that desirable outcomes, such as promotion or salary increase, will result from learning, are important antecedents of motivation to learn (see Noe, 1986). Noe and Schmitt's (1986) exploration of the relationship between pre-training motivation (effort–performance expectancies, performance outcome expectancies and motivation to learn) and learning found that motivation was positively related to learning performance and also that learning was related to job performance. The results demonstrate the importance of motivation in predicting learning.

One practical implication of the expectancy model when used to explain learning orientations in HRD is the significance that perceptions (subjective probabilities) can have upon motivation to learn. This suggests that the attitudes and values an individual brings with them to the learning situation can be crucial in deciding the extent to which they will engage in learning. It means that it may often be necessary to try to convince individuals of the value of learning in order to motivate them sufficiently to engage with it. The HRD process should be managed in such a way that the anticipated links between performance, effort and reward are made explicit. Expectancy theory also predicts that the perceptions and values which individuals bring to the learning situation are likely to be diverse, may exert an influence over their motivations, and that these factors (and the way in which they interact) should be taken into account in the management of learning.

SELF-EFFICACY

Related to the notion of expectancy and goal setting is the concept of self-efficacy (the belief on the part of an individual that she or he can perform a specific task), and whilst it is not a content theory of motivation per se, it is nevertheless highly relevant. When there is stronger perceived self-efficacy the individual will set higher goals and have firmer commitment to those goals. Goals provide a sense of purpose and direction because individuals seek self-satisfaction by fulfilling goals. Self-efficacy therefore is an important part of the motivation process (Locke and Latham, 1990a, 1990b). If individuals believe they possess the capacity for learning it is more likely that they will make the extra effort required to acquire new knowledge and skills. A positive relationship has been observed between pre-training self-efficacy and pre-training motivation and also between pre-training motivation and outcome measures (reactions to training and application-based knowledge) (Tracey *et al.*, 2001). From a learning design point of view, as well as setting long-range goals with explicit sub-goals (Goldstein, 1993), it is also important that individuals have the opportunity to pursue goals that are commensurate with their perceived capacity to fulfil these goals.

EQUITY

Social comparisons and perceptions of fairness can exert an influence over whether or not individuals put effort into an activity (such as engaging in HRD). The comparisons that are made with one's peers can lead to the view of fair or unfair treatment and lead to actions in an attempt to resolve any perceived unfairness. Equity theory proposes that the greater the perceived inequity the greater the tension and the higher the motivation to act. Individuals examine their inputs to a process and what the outputs achieved and compare them with the inputs and outputs of others: equity is perceived to have been achieved when these factors are in balance. Strategies for reducing inequity include altering the inputs (effort) or outputs (reward) of self or trying to influence these in others, comparing with a different other (than in the original comparison), rationalizing the inequity or exiting the organization (see Table 4.4).

Equity theory predicts that the comparisons that individuals make between themselves and others is likely to be a strong influence over their actions in relation to initiating, maintaining or terminating their engagement in the HRD process. These comparisons are likely to manifest a very diverse array of perceptions and interpretations which need to be managed carefully if learners' engagement in the process is to be managed sensitively.

There are other dimensions of motivation beyond content and process, for example the distinction between intrinsic and extrinsic motivation has particular utility for HRD (Hardré, 2003: 62) and the distinction is summarised in Table 4.6. Intrinsic motivation promotes higher-quality learning, better task performance and greater creativity, whereas extrinsic motivation does not facilitate valued outcomes (Knowles, 1990). The andragogical learning model (Knowles, 1990) is predicated on the assumption that adults are motivated towards learning that helps them solve problems in their lives and that the internal need is a more potent motivator than is an external pay-off

Table 4.4 Examples of equity theory in action

Office worker Jane found out that as part of her Personal Development Plan agreed with their manager her colleague Kerry has been given the opportunity to undertake a part-time Master of Business Administration (MBA) degree with all fees and expenses paid and some study leave as well. Jane has not and is not best pleased; she sees this as unfair. Her strategies for reducing this perceived inequity might be:

1 I will persuade our manager to let me do a part-time MBA (alter outcomes).
2 I'm not going to work as hard now as Kerry does (alter inputs).
3 I will persuade the manager to send Kerry on a time management course instead of an MBA (alter the comparison person's outcomes).
4 I will leave all the hard work to Kerry now – she's trained for it (alter the comparison person's inputs).
5 Oh well, David is not doing the MBA (compare with someone else).
6 After all Kerry is gifted and able and needs to be groomed for an executive position (rationalize the inequity).
7 I'm going to leave this company at the earliest opportunity (leave).

Source: adapted from Huckzynski and Buchanan (2001: 246).

Table 4.5 An HRD causal chain in equity theory

Stage	Thoughts and actions
Perception of inequity	You've been offered a place on that training course even though I do the difficult jobs around here.
Experience of tension	That is unfair.
Motivation to resolve	I'm not standing for this.
Action to resolve	I'll ask the manager if I can have a place on the course, or get you to do more of the difficult work around here.
Equity restored	My efforts and the reward I get from being trained are now comparable with yours.

Source: adapted from Huckzynski and Buchanan (2001: 247).

Table 4.6 Intrinsic and extrinsic motivation

Intrinsic motivation	Extrinsic motivation
Internalized	Externalized
Self-owned	Other-owned
High quality	Low quality
More stable	Less stable
Challenge seeking	Challenge avoidance
Risk taking	Easy success

Source: adapted from Hardré (2003).

(for example, salary increase) (Knowles, Holton and Swanson, 1998: 149). This is explained by Wlodowski (1985) as being the result of adults wanting to be successful in learning, having a choice in learning, learning something they value and in experiencing learning as pleasurable.

Chalofsky (2003) argued that a deeper and more comprehensive understanding of intrinsic motivation is beginning to emerge with renewed interest in Maslow's higher levels and the work of the psychologist Csikszentmihalyi (2003) and his concept of 'flow'. Flow is described as a particular kind of experience in which people's performance seems effortless with a sense of fun, mastery and potential for growth of the self. It encompasses the concepts of need and self-esteem in the context of work that is intrinsically meaningful to the curious learner and can become an expression of the inner self and connects with emerging notions of spirituality (in a non-religious sense) in the workplace. Chalofsky argued that:

> Meaningful work isn't just about the meaning of the paid work we perform; it's about the way we live our lives. It's the alignment of purpose, values, relationships and activities that we pursue in life.
>
> (2003: 58)

Putting emerging issues of the meaningfulness of work to one side for the moment and returning to performance enhancement, the concern so far has been with motivation to engage in learning *per se*; however, arguably learning in the workplace is only a means to an end, the ultimate goal being, at least from a management perspective, to improve performance. A higher-level dimension of 'motivation to improve work through learning' has been posited by Naquin and Holton (2003). They argued that the performance improvement process does not begin or end with learning but also involves the employees' willingness to transfer newly acquired knowledge or skill to the job. Therefore, in a development of an 'equation' originally put forward by Noe, they proposed that:

Motivation to improve work through learning $= f$ (motivation to engage in HRD; motivation to transfer learning to job)

They provided initial construct validation evidence for this higher-order construct through confirmatory factor analysis of a single factor model with 247 participants and claimed that this provided empirical evidence that motivation cannot be thought of as just motivation to learn or to train but has to include both. One practical implication is that pre-training interventions designed to address both facets of motivation may be warranted rather than an exclusive focus on motivation to engage in HRD.

The use of objectives, as specifications of outcomes, is commensurate with theories of motivation and performance, for example in goal setting theory a goal is defined as a desirable level of achievement and, as noted above, the theory is based on a number precepts (see Lathan, 2004): (1) individuals who are given complex and challenging goals perform better than those given no goals or simple and unchallenging ones; (2) goals are more effective in eliciting performance when they are specific rather than vague; (3) to maintain or enhance an individual's self-efficacy the goal should be commensurate with the individual's ability to successfully accomplish the goal; (4) participation in goal setting can enhance performance: the individual has to accept the goal that has been set; (5) for goal setting to be effective individuals need to be aware of the extent to which they are achieving the goal. The implications of goal setting theory for learning are that learning targets should be clear, challenging and achievable: ideally they should have been agreed with learners, and facilitators should give feedback on the extent to which targets are likely to be met.

Learners' needs

Individual employees may also vary in terms of the learning needs that they have and which may be satisfied through HRD. A simple distinction may be drawn between learning needs that aim to enhance job performance in the short term (typically met by a short sharp solution, such as a training course or some performance coaching on the job) and those that articulate a need to enhance personal and career development in the longer term.

In the former case the need is often predicated upon the assumption of some actual or potential deficit in job or task performance. The need is the gap between the current levels of performance and that which is desired either now or at some point in time in the immediate future. A gap in performance may be identified by means of some metric or other which draws managers' attention to the performance deficit (for example a rise in customer complaints, a fall in productivity, etc.), by requests for training by the employee or their manager or as a result of the outcome of a formal assessment process (such as performance appraisal or 360-degree feedback). The need itself will often indicate the desired learning outcome. HRD which is provided under these circumstances aims to fulfil a performance remediation, maintenance of performance or a performance enhancement function. Off-job learning must be supported at the workplace (through supervisor encouragement, opportunity to practice and so forth) if it is to transfer effectively to the job situation and yield a return on investment.

As well as short-term job performance enhancement, learners' needs might also encompass longer-term personal and career development issues. Again performance appraisal or 360-degree feedback may be ways by which the need is identified, or an employee may be singled out to be fast-tracked within an organization as part of an HR or succession plan. In any case the needs may be articulated in a variety of ways, for example as a personal development plan (PDP). A PDP might consist of a specification of an individual's development objectives, the link between these objectives and the business plan, the HR plan and their personal development need along with the proposed developmental actions with specified timescales and a recording and monitoring of LandD activities (both formal and informal) engaged in to support the plan (see Woodall and Winstanley, 1998: 147–148). PDPs are important in our discussion of learners' needs (Floodgate and Nixon, 1994: 43) because they provide a means of:

- Encouraging individual responsibility for learning;
- Supporting workplace-based learning more explicitly and overtly;
- Highlighting the role and opportunities for managers to be involved in HRD through needs identification, providing coaching for employees and so forth;
- Translating learning needs into meaningful and measurable action plans.

The manager's orientation

In order for HRD to be implemented effectively in organizations, and certainly at the level of SHRD, there has to be a commitment from managers to learning as a necessary prerequisite for effective HRD (Smith and Dowling, 2001). Unfortunately, financial short-termism may mean that managers all too often look for immediate gains from any investment, including HRD, rather than taking a view of HRD as an activity that builds the longer-term capacity of the firm to compete more effectively.

Smith and Dowling (2001) conducted a qualitative study of HRD in a number of manufacturing companies in Australia in an attempt to explore the relationship between the extent of HRD provided and managerial attitudes to HRD. The overwhelming attitude towards training in the firms studied was one of looking for an immediate gain from 'short sharp' training programmes. There were, however, significant inter- and intra-firm differences. For example, at IBM the attitude amongst managers was that structured shopfloor training to all staff was critical to the firm's performance in overseas markets and they were committed to its being carried out properly for all employees. Other organizations had what Smith and Dowling referred to as a 'lower but emerging commitment' (2001: 163). They also noted a difference between the effusive rhetoric of the benefits of HRD that senior managers espoused compared with a more sceptical attitude towards training amongst middle and junior managers, for whom training was only of value if it had immediate tangible results. This research revealed a diversity in attitudes towards HRD between managers: not surprisingly senior managers tended to take a broader and more future-oriented view, whereas lower-level managers were more concerned with the direct effect that HRD would have on the targets by which they were measured (for example, quality and output). There is an important practical implication here: it is often the case that the middle and junior managers are the ones charged with managing the impact of employees being released from their work in order to undertake off-job HRD; therefore the attitude of this group as to whether or not employees should be 'released' to participate in HRD may be coloured by the operational pressures that they may be under. Smith and Dowling argued that:

> analyses of firm training that do not pay attention to the fissures and fractures in management attitudes towards training risk grossly over-simplifying the critical role of managers in the implementation of training programmes.
>
> (2001: 164)

The diversity of attitudes amongst managers may cause an implementation failure as HRD 'disappears down the gap' between the attitudes and values towards HRD espoused by senior managers and the more day-to-day concerns of managers on the shopfloor. Managers' attitudes are also important because of the effect that they may have upon learners' perceptions. Learners' perceptions of managerial attitudes and support for learning may affect their engagement in learning and their performance. Hardré (2003: 67) argued that it is important for managers and HRD practitioners to recognise that learners' and managers' perceptions may be quite different, and if they are different it is the learners' perceptions that are likely to influence learning and performance. Managers should not assume that what motivates themselves to engage in or with learning is the same as what motivates employees to engage in learning. The unitarist assumption that often underpins HRM and HRD practices should always be scrutinised critically.

One of the main challenges facing organizations and their managers in trying to shape or manage attitudes to learning relates to the changed nature of the employment contract. In many organizations long-term contracts are no longer able to be offered and movement between jobs may be horizontal rather than the traditional upward trajectory. In these changed circumstances not only the wider organizational contract but the HRD 'clause' of that contract has to be based upon mutuality of interest. 'Mutuality' in this sense refers to the enhanced employability the employer can offer to the employee and for which he or she can receive in return some benefit to the organization. This mutuality may be based upon diverse intents; the success of the relationship depends upon those diverse intents being reconciled to the benefit of both parties. The traditional or idealised image of the pattern or sequence of work roles is that of the upward trajectory via promotions or changed job roles to some appropriate or ceiling level. However, the modern reality of organizational life may be characterized by redundancies, short-term contracts and part-time working. The nature of the developmental dimension of many job roles is one of extension within the job, lateral moves and portfolio working. Within this context the purposes of HRD might be seen as to meet current and future needs of the

Table 4.7 The old and new psychological contracts

Psychological contract	Employee intent	Employer intent
Old	Give employer one's loyalty	Give employee security
	Commit to organization	Guarantee future career
	Maintain adequate performance	Look after employee
New	Engage in continuous learning	Maximise chances of employability via HRD
	Keep pace with change via HRD	Give the employee tools to keep pace with change
	Manage one's own career via PDPs	Engage with employee's career development plans
	Maximise individual performance in support of organizational goals	Care for employee interests to the point of departure from organization

Source: adapted from Torrington, Hall and Taylor (2002: 442).

individual and the organization (including developing employability). The traditional psychological contract in which the employer gives long-term career progression and the employee gives loyalty, commitment and performance is no longer viable in many workplaces. In a world in which many organizations have become flatter and leaner, it may no longer be possible to offer long-term progression and hence the change from long-term organizational careers to 'portfolio careers' or 'boundaryless careers' (Arthur, 1994). Table 4.7 summarises what each of the stakeholders can contribute under the new psychological contract in an attempt to satisfy some of the interests of both parties.

The HRD practitioner's orientation

One of the principal intents of the HRD practitioner must be to add value to the business by achieving outcomes (Harrison, 2002: 23):

- that increase the organization's capability to reach its goals or to set new and original goals;
- in ways that mean in the long run their value will offset the costs incurred in their implementation.

As far as their role is concerned, arguably the prime aim of the HRD practitioner should be to align HRD policies, plans and practices with the business goals, and connect HRD activity with corresponding HRM activity (such as selection, reward and appraisal) to achieve horizontal integration in order that HRD and HRM are mutually supportive and to provide effective and efficient HRD. Perhaps beyond the remit of the HRD practitioner and in the domain of senior managers, directors or the executive is the next level of intent, namely that of strategic alignment of the HRM strategy and goals with those of the business (Harrison, 2002: 65). Nevertheless the dual intent of ensuring business-led HRD (aimed at the achievement of current business goals) and strategically aligned HRD (responsive to the needs raised by the organization's longer term goals and 'built to last') should be a fundamental element of the strategic partnership between HRD and senior managers (Harrison, 2002).

The traditional training and development role was operationally focused (and usually emphasised off-job learning), but an important dimension of the HRD practitioner's orientation is the extent to which their activities are strategically focused. It should be noted that the strategic and operational (or tactical) foci are not mutually exclusive; on the contrary they may be seen as mutually reinforcing. Arguably the ideal orientation of the effective HRD practitioner is upon strategic and operational HRD activities.

The intent (strategic and/or operational) pursued by the HRD practitioner determines the way in which they are likely to engage with learning and this manifests itself in the role they play in the HRD process. Over two decades ago research in the UK examined the roles taken by training and development staff in industry (Pettigrew, Jones and Reason, 1982). In this research, four contrasting roles (excluding the training manager) were identified:

1   Passive provider: adopts a 'sit-back-and-wait' attitude in the hope that internal clients will come forward and then provides training aimed at maintenance and improvement but not major change. In modern organizations this role is an anachronism and is likely to be untenable except where internal clients are obliged to use the organization's own training function;
2   Provider: concerned with the maintenance and improvement of performance but without major change. This is a traditional role which is no doubt still to be found in some situations;
3   Role in transition: in between the roles of provider and change agent, no longer content to provide courses but desires to have more proactive and influential role. This is likely to be the most common role for the HRD practitioner since it does not occupy the fully fledged change agent role (which may be unnecessary and undesirable in some organizational contexts);
4   Change agent: main concern is organizational development and complex issues of cultural change. The effective execution of such a role depends upon a receptive organizational culture which is attuned to change.

Other research on the same theme in the UK in the 1980s by Bennett and Leduchowicz (1983) suggested that trainers may occupy one of four roles: caretaker, educator, evangelist and innovator (based upon the two dimensions of a traditionalist versus an interventionist orientation, and maintenance versus a change orientation). Bennett and Leduchowicz noted some polarisation of roles along the diagonal of this typology corresponding to the continuum that is implicit in the Pettigrew *et al.* framework (from passive provider to change agent) and corresponds to the tactical/strategic distinction offered earlier. What is not clear is the extent to which today there is in fact a polarisation along a tactical–strategic dimension. As was argued above it is conceptually feasible and practically viable to have both strategic and operational (or tactical facets) to one's HRD role orientation (indeed to do so is portrayed here as desirable). These various aspects of the role are encompassed in a number of nationally or institutionally agreed standards for the HRD profession (for example the American Society for Training and Development (ASTD) model and the UK's national occupational standard). Our argument is that as far as trying to describe, understand and manage HRD in organizations is concerned the notion of a strategic orientation is an important one both in terms of the descriptive and explanatory power that it provides and also in terms of its prescriptive utility (given that a strategic approach to HRD is deemed to be highly desirable). Some of the relationships between the various factors explored in the chapter are shown in Figure 4.1.

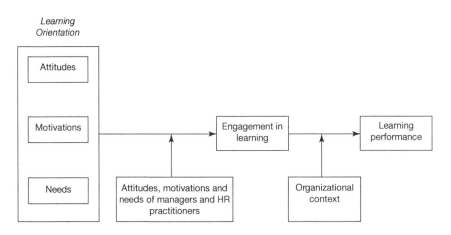

Figure 4.1 Learning orientation, engagement and outcomes

Focus on practice: managing employees' motivation to learn

In this section we have drawn substantially on the work of Traut, Larsen and Feimer (2000). Traut *et al.*'s research was concerned with the relationship between job tenure and motivation and specifically how long-term workers' (i.e. long-tenured) motivation might be managed and secured. It should not be assumed that long-term employees will automatically be motivated to learn and perform, and consequently motivational efforts should be directed at both long-term employees and new recruits. Traut *et al.* conducted survey in a fire department in a state in the central USA (*N* = 123). The findings revealed that even after controlling for the effect of job level the most satisfied employees are those with the fewest years' service (contradicting the assumption that job satisfaction increases with tenure). The HRD-relevant implications of this research are that:

- Employees must know their jobs, how they relate to other jobs and other employees' jobs and how their jobs contribute to the overall goals of the organization.
- Employees with an 'organizational history' (and who therefore will be a source of knowledge, skill, experience and expertise) should be consulted in decision making and their contribution should be valued.
- Rewards should be geared towards individuals' development needs, aspirations and trajectories; rewards should be available other than career promotion (especially for those employees for whom promotion is not an aspiration or for whom it is unavailable).
- Employers should distinguish between training (for immediate acquisition of skills for a current job role) and learning (creation of more flexible workers to meet longer term needs and aspirations).
- Team working, cooperation and collective learning should be an expectation and be encouraged and rewarded.
- Opportunities should be created for learning and skills development which go beyond the immediate job role of the employee.
- Mentoring should be used as a developmental tool for the new recruit (as a protégé) and as a recognition for the experienced worker (as a mentor).
- The personal and private life needs of employees should be recognised and acknowledged (for example by the provision of wider development opportunities).
- HRD should recognise different levels of ability, different needs and motivations amongst employees.

Traut *et al.* (2000: 350) contended that the positive effects that such approaches are likely to have on satisfaction and commitment are essential in modern organizations because:

> employee development is not finished when new employees are selected and trained . . . the costs of replacing good experienced workers can be prohibitive, especially in organizations requiring ongoing training and teamwork.

Identifying learning orientations: questions for situational analysis

This chapter has suggested that there are three key stakeholders whose orientations to learning must to be taken into account in the management of HRD. The three stakeholder groups are learners themselves, managers (including line managers) and HRD practitioners. Each has a different motive for engaging (or not) with learning and development and if HRD is to be managed effectively it is important that these various diversities are recognised, acknowledged and if possible accommodated. In this final section of the chapter we offer a series of issues that may be worthy of consideration and that may act as prompts or aides-memoire for enquiry, reflection and dialogue.

General

1   Who are the key stakeholders in HRD in the organization?
2   What are the different agendas of the different stakeholder groups?
3   What are the power relations and power differentials between the respective groups?
4   To what extent are their interests mutual?

The learners

1   Who are the learners and what are their attitudes towards HRD?
2   To what extent do the learners exhibit curiosity and self-direction?
3   Can curiosity be manipulated in order to manage the level of engagement in HRD?
4   To what extent are the learners likely to be oriented towards learning and development through intrinsic or extrinsic motivational factors?
5   Are learners' abilities and motivations commensurate with the level of performance that is desired?
6   What are the learners' needs (in terms of the necessary knowledge and skill but also in terms of the human needs that HRD might satisfy)?
7   How might goals be managed and manipulated in order to foster engagement in effective learning?
8   To what extent do the learners possess self-efficacy?
9   Do expectancy and equity exert any influence over the extent to which individuals will engage in learning?
10 To what extent are learners likely to engage in learning for the sake of performance improvement and/or personal career-development purposes?

The manager

1   What is the manager's likely role in HRD?
2   What is the manager's attitude towards HRD?
3   Will managers support employees engaging in HRD; will they support the application of learning in the workplace post-HRD?
4   What is the nature of the employment/psychological contract and how might this affect learners' and managers' attitudes towards and engagement with HRD?

The HRD practitioner

1   To what extent are HRD practitioners and the HRD function aligned to a strategic approach to HRD?
2   To what extent are HRD practitioners and the HRD function aligned to a tactical approach to HRD?
3   To what extent does HRD support the goals of the business?
4   To what extent do HRD practitioners integrate their activities with those of mainstream HRM?
5   What role do HRD practitioners see themselves as fulfilling in the organization?
6   To what extent are HRD practitioners' roles commensurate with the strategic direction of the organization?

5 Diversities amongst learners

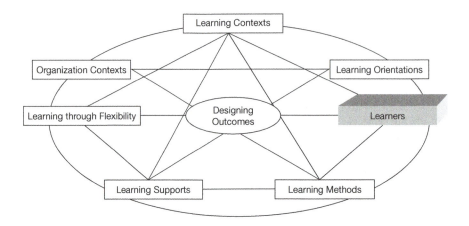

Introduction

Learners can exhibit a wide range of diversities both at the individual level and at the group level. These diversities may manifest themselves in terms of the ways in which they engage in learning and thinking (i.e. the process) and how effective a particular learning experience or situation has been for a particular individual (i.e. the outcomes). These diversities are often readily apparent to teachers, trainers and HRD practitioners in learning situations and introduce further aspects of complexity into HRD practice. The diversities may be as a result of differences in a large number of variables including the learners' backgrounds, abilities, styles and preferences. In this chapter we aim to examine some of the diversities that may exist between learners both as individuals and as members of a group. In our discussion of diversity in this context we note that there are individual diversities and group diversities, but we should be mindful of any tendency to stereotype individuals or groups:

- Individual diversities (within group differences): these are the inter-personal differences between one individual and the next. There should always be the recognition that every member of a group is an individual with their own unique characteristics which may affect the learning process and its outcomes.

- Group diversities (between group differences): these are collective differences between groups of individuals, and likewise, there should always be the recognition that these are underlain by the differences between the individuals that make up those groups.

Both types of difference may affect not only the individual learning process (e.g. due to differences in cognition) but also the social interactions between individuals (and hence collective learning). Typecasting, or stereotyping, may follow from any erroneous perception that the group's characteristics are present in some homogeneous way across all of the individuals within the group. Similarly, we also have to remember that all individuals belong to more than one identifiable group, such that an individual may belong to an age group, an occupational group and so forth. Hence there is a kaleidoscope of possible differences within and between groups. Stereotyping occurs if we assume that the characteristics of the group pertain to the individuals in the group; to do so may lead to erroneous assumptions about any given individual. Whilst there is value and utility in identifying common group features, it cannot be emphasised too strongly that these common features have to be tested against the individual differences that occur between the people who make up the group.

In this chapter we will first discuss group characteristics and identify in particular those HRD-relevant dimensions of diversity that may exist at the group level in terms of the variables of national culture and age, since these are amongst the group diversities that are most likely to be encountered in organizational settings. In focusing upon HRD-relevant issues we have chosen not to explore the issues of gender and ethnicity in any depth as there is already an extensive published literature (see for example Halford and Leonard, 2001). Second, we will discuss the diversities that may be encountered between individual learners that might affect learning, including such factors as abilities and preferences, and styles and strategies of learning and thinking.

Group-level diversities

The aspect of group-level diversity that will be considered here is that of national culture. The notion of culture is a slippery one, and by no means uncontested. The term is used in many different contexts and to describe some quite different aspects of groupings of people. Culture is a term applied to a commonly held set of beliefs, values and behaviours. For example, it is used to refer to people from the same country (a national culture), from the same workplace (an organizational culture), or from the same occupation (a particular professional culture) (Parsons, 1951). Kuper, in discussing the concept and the contestation around the various notions of culture, suggested that there is at least some agreement that 'culture is here essentially a matter of ideas and values, a collective cast of mind' (1999: 227).

We acknowledge the many other forms of 'culture' that exist; from our standpoint, however, national culture is of importance in examining the HRD-related diversities that may exist amongst learners in a multicultural and global business environment. Two models of national culture will be examined and the HRD implications of the differences that they imply will be explored. The two models are those of Hofstede (1984, 1986, 2001) and Trompenaars and Hampden-Turner (1997).

Arguably the pre-eminent theorist in the area of cultural difference is Geert Hofstede who developed a highly influential model of cultural difference and its consequences. Hofstede's interests were in the underlying dimensions of difference between cultures. He identified four dimensions:

1   *Individualism–collectivism*: the extent to which individuals take care of themselves and their immediate family versus the extent to which individuals will work together for the collective good.
2   *Power-distance*: this is a concept proposed by Hofstede to describe the 'extent to which the less powerful persons in a society accept inequality in power and accept it as normal' (Hofstede, 1986: 307).
3   *Uncertainty avoidance* is the extent to which people in any given culture feel comfortable with situations that are unclear and/or unstructured.
4   *Masculinity-versus-femininity*: this dimension describes the degree to which a culture is characterized by different roles and expectations between the sexes.

Cluster analysis of a large dataset revealed an eight-category typology (high or low on each of the four dimensions) into which a country could be placed. For example, the UK is high on individualism and low on uncertainty avoidance; Australia is high on masculinity and individualism and low on power distance. Hofstede (1986) explored the relationships between these different cultural orientations, as expressed through the various dimensions, and their implications in learning and instructional settings, yielding some quite specific advice for practitioners. In his later work he further explored their consequences within organizational processes and cultures (Hofstede, 2001).

Hofstede pointed towards behaviours and practices that are acceptable within different cultural settings and those that are not, and also pointed out a number of differences in the area of teaching and learning. Building upon and applying this work, Yamauchi (1998) summarised some of the implications of Hofstede's arguments for learning thus:

- Changing the goal and reward structures to be more compatible with learners' home cultures can influence attention and engagement.
- Learning discourses can be individualistically oriented or collectively oriented. Learners from collectivist cultures may not want to cause conflict by 'appearing smarter or in other ways superior to others in the group' (Yamauchi, 1998: 190).
- Similarly, attempts to maintain the group's harmony may mean that individuals from collectivist cultures may hold back criticism and emotions such as anger or frustration.
- Learners with a collectivistic orientation may prefer goals that are more group-oriented and may perform better in situations where such goals are emphasised.
- If an individualistic system is in place learners from a collectivistic culture may modify rules and processes so that they can work towards collective goals.

The other dimensions of Hofstede's framework may also have important effects in terms of: (a) the influence they may exert upon power relations in the learning environment (and the extent to which individuals feel justified in challenging the teacher or other authority figure) and (b) the extent to which uncertainty and ambiguity in the situation are tolerated and affect the learning process. For example, learners from particular cultural groups may be more comfortable with ambiguity (for example, there being no single correct answer or right way) than are others. These issues need to be recognised and where possible accommodated in interactions with learners, in order either to reduce ambiguity or to make the reasons for any such ambiguities apparent and acceptable to the learners.

In their discussion of national cultures, Trompenaars and Hampden-Turner (1997) made a distinction between what they called the 'explicit products' of culture and the norms and values of a culture which are less identifiable to the casual observer. The explicit products of a culture are the things that we see fairly readily, such as the language, fashions, architecture, and so forth. They suggested that the norms and values of a culture, and its explicit products, derive from the basic assumptions held by a cultural group. The basic assumptions of a culture are related to matters of survival and vary as a function of the characteristics of the environment within which the culture developed. According to Trompenaars and Hampden-Turner 'norms are the mutual sense a group has of what is "right" and "wrong"' whilst values 'determine the definition of "good" and "bad"' and are related to shared ideals (1997: 21–2). Using Talcott Parsons' (1951) definitions of the ways in which people relate to each other, Trompenaars and Hampden-Turner (1997: 29) discussed a number of dimensions that differentiate cultures and that have some relevance for HRD practice.

UNIVERSALISM–PARTICULARISM

Universalism is characterized by a belief that rules and standards are universal in that they apply to everyone in the same way, while a particularist cultural orientation takes account of particular circumstance. Hence, a tension can arise in multicultural settings where universalists believe that everybody should be treated in the same way, while particularists believe that it is right to treat people with whom we have an emotional relationship (for example, friendship, family, etc.) differently. A source of tension may derive from what a universalist culture believes is 'right' since this can be quite different from what a particularist culture believes to be right. Research by Trompenaars and Hampden-Turner (1997) suggested that much of western Europe (and many of the English-speaking countries) are more likely characterized by universalism, while southern Europe, Asia and South America tend more towards particularism. There is also a suggestion that within particularist cultures, where relationships rather than rules and policies are more important, commitment between employer and employee tends to be greater.

National cultural diversity may have some influence upon the development of HRD policy and practice. For example, universalist policies determined by a head office may have less purchase across the organization in a particularist culture where considerations of local issues, relationships and people have considerable importance. The expectation that HRD policies and practices will be enacted uniformly across an organization located in a particularist cultural environment may be unrealistic. This aspect of culture therefore may have some moderating effect upon the extent to which HRD strategies and policies translate into local practice and the ways in which they are received.

COMMUNITARIANISM–INDIVIDUALISM

Communitarianism is characterized by the strong sense of importance placed on the needs of the group, while individualism emphasises the needs of individuals. Tension here may accrue from some members of a multicultural work group believing that individual interests should be secondary to the interests of the group, whilst others might believe that their value to the group is as an individual who contributes to the group 'as and if they wish' (Trompenaars and Hampden-Turner, 1997: 9). The geographical distribution of individualism is similar to that of universalism, whilst that of communitarianism is similar to particularism. The importance placed on individual effort, and the celebration and reward of that individual effort, may have less meaning in communitarian cultures.

These issues may have a significant impact upon the way HRD is perceived, organized and enacted in organizational settings. In an individualistic culture HRD might take an approach focused on individual development needs (e.g. in personal development plans, PDPs), with any progression towards those needs being rewarded on an individual basis (e.g. in individual performance review). Within a communitarian setting, there may be a greater expectation that these needs and the ways in which they are addressed might be focused around a group of employees (e.g. a project team) and with rewards being shared. For organizations whose HRD and reward systems are based around an individualist orientation, this may represent a difficult challenge to address. Similarly, the view taken of and importance accorded to team learning or collective learning may be influenced by this dimension of national culture. The value placed upon the sharing of information and knowledge may be more closely aligned with the communitarian culture than it is with the individualist culture.

NEUTRAL–EMOTIONAL

Individuals from a neutral background retain a detachment and objectivity in their dealings with others to the extent that emotion is seldom displayed, for example in business dealings. Emotional cultures on the other hand are more accepting of displays of humour, anger, excitement and so forth. In a neutral culture these emotional expressions can be seen as inappropriate, confrontational and even threatening. On the other hand a lack of emotional display can be confusing to a person from an emotional culture, as well as possibly engendering the feeling that there is lack of interest or emotional coldness. Research by Trompenaars and Hampden-Turner suggested that China and Britain tend to be more neutral than those countries where there is a strong southern European influence (including some South American and some Asian countries). There are some interesting further distinctions within this dimension. For example, it is suggested that Americans 'tend to exhibit emotion, yet separate it from "objective" and "rational" decisions' (Trompenaars and Hampden-Turner, 1997: 73).

There are implications for HRD; for example, delivering training in a neutral culture may be frustrating for individuals who expect openness and emotional display. On the other hand, such displays in a neutral culture may be seen as quite inappropriate. The level of emotional expression and emotional engagement may have an important bearing upon the dynamics of a group training situation. Group learning facilitators need to be aware of the potential role that this aspect of national culture may exert, especially in those situations where individual learners are from a diverse range of cultural backgrounds or where the facilitator and the group members are from different cultural backgrounds.

SPECIFIC–DIFFUSE

In a specific culture, the relationship of one person to another is seen as specific to a particular context; the expectations that individuals have of each other are defined only within that context. On the other hand, in a diffuse culture the relationships are perceived more broadly such that the relationship an individual has with another individual in one context has influence in another context (Trompenaars and Hampden-Turner, 1997). One potential tension here is that in a specific culture one individual may have only certain limited rights in what he or she can expect others to do, and can only expect instructions and opinions related to the formal role of say manager or supervisor, to be taken notice of and acted upon. In a diffuse culture an individual's power relationship may be extended such that a supervisor's or manager's opinions on broader matters may be seen as more important and valuable through the fact that the person has a power relationship over others.

Developing an understanding of this difference in a multicultural work environment is important for HRD since it is possible, for example, for a supervisor from a specific culture who is working in a diffuse culture to offer an opinion or knowledge that is given a more privileged status than the opinion or knowledge of a more junior person who is actually much more expert. This may also exert some influence upon the role and remit of a trainer or facilitator and the extent to which their influence may be legitimately extended (for example from the training room to the shopfloor, or vice versa in the case of the manager or supervisor).

Trompenaars and Hampden-Turner explored the consequences that these differing cultural orientations can have within different business environments, and illustrated the tensions that can result. They also explored a vast array of nations and their location on each of these fundamental dimensions of cultural difference. While the focus of their book is on national cultures their arguments can be used as a basis to analyse differences between the cultures of many different sorts of groups. For example, if we return briefly to our earlier discussion in Chapter 2 of the learning network theory proposed by Poell and his colleagues (Poell, Chivers, Van der Krogt and Wildesmeersch, 2000), we can see how the organizational or work group culture can impact on effective engagement with a network. A liberal network is largely formed around individuals identifying and pursuing the learning objectives and outcomes that each sees as important in contributing to personal and organizational goals, whilst a horizontal network places its emphasis on the needs of the team, or work group. The tension between a group orientation and an individual orientation (communitarianism-versus-individualism) can mean that working in both a liberal and a horizontal network may require different skills and ways of dealing with others and particular individuals may find the one network more comfortable than the other. Attempting to move a highly individual work culture towards a team culture can reveal obstacles and barriers that will need to be worked through with care over some time. The implementation of a team culture in an otherwise individual culture may prove more difficult than expected. Likewise, the development of a team culture in an environment where some members see the display of emotion as a legitimate form of expression in dealing with each other (others may see those displays as 'improper' and 'unprofessional') will provide another set of issues to be dealt with in the successful implementation of team work.

Yamauchi (1998) argued that in general terms as a result of cultural differences learners come to the learning environment with different expectations about what should occur. These cultural models influence the learners' comfort with and participation in various classroom activities and arrangements. Learners may need to make some adjustments to their expectations of the appropriate behaviours; similarly, trainers or facilitators may also be required to adjust their expectations of what might reasonably be expected. Yamauchi asserted that the cultural compatibility of the learner and the learning environment will be enhanced when teachers and other facilitators make culturally sensitive modifications to classroom structures and change the way they communicate with students. One way to do this is to list the methods, activities and discourses that are typically used or which occur in an HRD setting and then assess the extent to which these may be compatible or not with cultural differences, and also to look at the ways in which they might be adapted to embrace a wider set of expectations and behaviours, thus:

- What learning methods am I planning to use?
- What are my expectations of the learners?
- What might be the learners' expectations of the teaching?
- Are there likely to be any mismatches in expectations?
- Are the mismatches likely to be productive or counter-productive?
- How could counter-productive mismatches be addressed?

Similarly HRD programmes that prepare individuals for working and living in other national cultures must be cognisant of the differences in behaviours and expectations which may be prevalent. Bhawuk and Brislin (2000) reviewed a number of approaches and techniques for cross-cultural training, including the use of:

- lecture methods, which from their review of research they deemed to be largely ineffective in cross cultural training;
- experiential methods, for example using active learning, problem identification and solving, dealing with emotions, people skills and oral and non-verbal communication;
- 'cultural assimilators': tools which employ cases and vignettes for the learner to choose between various plausible behavioural responses;
- self criterion reference method which consists of framing a problem in terms of one's own culture, and then in terms of the host culture and the isolation of self reference criterion when making judgements in the host culture;
- behaviour modification training based upon Bandura's (1977) social learning theory and human modelling techniques using the four steps of

attention, retention, reproduction and incentivisation (motivation) (Bhawuk and Brislin, 2000) of a 'model's' behaviour in a particular setting.

In terms of the methods used for accommodating cultural adjustment Shim and Paprock (2002) found that the strongest relationship was between cultural adjustment and three particular techniques, namely watching visual media about a host country, learning the local language and developing cultural mentors. Thornhill (1993) argued that the two most important implications of differences in national cultures for HRD are, first, the recognition of cultural differences in relation to the content and methods of training and, second the existence of cultural and national differences that may lead to different expectations about the role of the trainer, the interaction between trainee and trainer and the preferred learning methods and styles. With regard to the latter Jaju, Kwak and Zinkhan (2002) found that there were differences across the USA, Korea and India in terms of learning styles as defined by Kolb (1976) (i.e. the four learning style types, namely divergers, convergers, assimilators and accommodators). The US learners preferred reflective observation and concrete experience (i.e. diverger style), whilst learners from India preferred active experimentation and abstract conceptualization (convergers), and the Koreans preferred reflective observation and abstract conceptualization (assimilators). This discussion of individual difference in learning styles highlights the ways in which group differences and individual differences may interact and complicate the picture further. It is to the issue of individual differences per se that we now turn our attention.

Individual diversities

A number of HRD-relevant aspects of individual diversity will be considered here, namely age, ability and various learning/thinking process-related aspects of individual diversity (including styles and strategies of learning and thinking). The latter are especially important since these are the attributes of the individual learner that designers of HRD need to take into account, acknowledge, and try to accommodate, in the learning design process. The assumption is that if learning can be designed in such a way as to acknowledge and accommodate individual differences in styles of learning and thinking (essentially learning styles and cognitive styles), the efficacy of the learning process will be enhanced (note that this need not necessarily imply a matching of learner's styles with learning methods).

Age

The changes that have taken place in many nations and economies towards work being knowledge-driven allied to the increasing automation of production processes has meant that the physical and mental requirements of jobs are changing fundamentally. For example, the majority of tasks no longer require continuing physical strength and this fact together with increasing life-spans and healthier old age means that the notion of age as a limiting factor in employee effectiveness has less purchase nowadays than in previous times.

Tomporowski (2003) argued that ageing is no longer generally associated with physical and mental decline, especially given that older adults are generally better-educated and more affluent than older adults in previous generations. He further argued that, contrary to some popular beliefs, there is little decline in mental abilities with age, at least in the window of age during which employment is generally held. For example, he cited research which indicated that the problem-solving strategies used by older adults are much the same as those used by younger adults. According to the view presented by Tomporowski, in the range of ages during which people are most commonly employed, there seems to be little reason to think that mental abilities change or decline in any important way. Interestingly, however, feelings of self-efficacy may decline in older adults due to their own perception that their skills and abilities have declined (Tomporowski, 2003). This decline in self-efficacy can be exacerbated where older adults are led to believe that they have lost some of their previous skills and abilities. For this reason the discussion of diversities associated with age may be explored through a 'diversity of experience' approach (since by definition older people will have had some experiences to draw upon that younger people have not).

An interesting set of ideas on age differences in the conception of work has been identified and researched by Pillay, Boulton-Lewis and Lankshear (2002). Their underlying interest was to explore how a move from what they have called 'old capitalism' to 'new capitalism' may have changed not only the expectations of HRD specialists, but also changed the demands placed on workers. In summary, they argued that old capitalism was based around the notion that workers sold their labour and their skills to an employer, and that there was a separation of individual self from the labour to be sold (see Sayer, 1983). The new capitalism, they argued, expects employees to 'think critically, reflectively and creatively and invest their heart, mind and body in work' (Pillay *et al.*, 2002: 28). This reflects a shift towards a knowledge economy and the importance of knowledge work. Pillay *et al.* point to research (for example: Handy, 1995; Gee, Hull and Lankshear, 1996) that indicates that younger workers find it easier to adopt newer practices than do older workers, and they further argued that this is due to a conception of work among younger people that embraces the need for integrated knowledge-development to occur within work. Older workers, they suggested, see work and learning as separate entities where work may not even include learning. In their research with older workers (defined as those of over 40 years of age) Pillay *et al.* identify four hierarchical conceptions of work as:

- a job;
- a challenging experience;
- personally empowering;
- structuring one's life.

They suggest that it is in these last two conceptions that the ideas of the new capitalism are to be found; but they also identified that these two conceptions were present only in a minority of the older workers in their sample. The researchers make the point that managers and HRD practitioners often make the assumption that the nexus between learning and work is one that is clearly established and recognised by all workers, but their research would indicate that this is not necessarily the case.

Many of the assumptions which they identify may be seen in the rhetoric of HRM and more specifically the 'best practice' HRM literature and by extension HRD and especially strategic HRD (which often assumes a mutuality of interests between learner and employer). If the third and fourth of Pillay *et al.*'s conceptions are to be managed and realised organizations and HRD practitioners may need to develop processes to:

- assist workers in recognising and understanding their own conceptions of work and learning;
- implement developmental processes to assist people (perhaps mainly older workers) to understand and embrace the higher conceptions of work and learning.

The research literature suggests that mature students in formal educational settings are generally more self-directed and independent as learners than are younger students. They may also exhibit deeper approaches (i.e. looking for meaning, active critical stance, relating and organizing ideas and using evidence and logic) and less surface approaches (i.e. relying on memorising) (Sadler-Smith, 1996b: 375). It is worth drawing some distinction here between the notions of self-directedness in learning and independent learning. In a previous chapter we discussed Clardy's (2000) work on self-directedness but at that stage we did not distinguish between this concept and that of independent learning. A distinction was made by Morgan (1993) when he wrote:

> there is one view that 'independent learning' means the separation of the teacher and the learner, such that students study in isolation. For other writers independent learning is concerned with students taking responsibility for what they learn and how they learn it, and developing greater autonomy and self direction in learning.
>
> (Morgan, 1993: 123)

In this discussion we draw a distinction between:

- independent learning, which occurs where a learner is separated from the instructor and learns largely on their own;
- self-directed learning, which occurs where the learner takes responsibility for what is learned and how. Self-directed learning can include the learner recognising the range of available potential sources of learning in the workplace, for example that a colleague has the knowledge or skill required, seeking them out and learning from them.

Knowles's (1990: 28–29) used earlier work by Lindeman (1926) to develop a model of andragogical (essentially adult) learning based upon the assumptions that adults are motivated to learn when they experience needs and interests that motivate them to learn. Moreover, their orientation to learning is life-centred and experience is the richest source for adults' learning, allied to which they have a need to be self-directing in their learning. A corollary of this is that there are likely to be individual differences amongst learners which widen with age, and therefore adult education and HRD must take account of these differences (1990: 31). The assumptions of Knowles's theory of andragogy are that:

- Adults need to know why they need to learn something before undertaking it (note that this is commensurate with goal setting theory).
- The adult's self-concept is one of being responsible for their own decisions.
- Adults come into a learning experience with greater volume and variety of life experience than do younger learners.
- Adults become ready to learn those things that they need to know to cope with their 'real-life' situations. [Note this is commensurate with Revans's (1982, 1983) principles of action learning.]
- Adults' orientation to learning is life-centred with the potential of some form of pay-off in work or personal life.
- The most potent motivators for the adult learner are internal pressures such as job satisfaction, self-esteem and quality of life.

The majority of research on age differences concurs with these principles in that it suggests that older, more mature learners are more likely than younger learners to be comfortable with independent and self-directed learning (Woodley and McIntosh, 1979; Holland, 1980; Verner and Davidson, 1982) and have less need for instructor-provided structures.

It may also be useful to distinguish between the effects of age and the possible effects of generation – the former being a measure of maturity (or at least length of time since birth) and the latter a function of the period of time in which an individual was born. There is the potential that different generations have life experiences and contexts which can result in important differences that might impact upon learning. For example, there is often commentary in the popular press on the differences detected between generations (see for example: Cooper, 2004; McCrindle, 2003), with 'Baby-Boomers' (born 1946–1961), 'Generation X' (1961–1976), and 'Generation Y' (1976–1991). Many of these popular writers postulate a set of characteristics for each generation, based on the view that people 'resemble their times' as a result of the experiences they have had.

It is the differing experiences that each generation may have had that might provide some further insight into understanding self-direction more as a function of generational change rather than of age. Research (for example: Bloomer and Hodkinson, 2000; Evans and Furlong, 1997; Bauman, 2001; Dwyer and Wyn, 2001) has shown that the pathways taken by young people as they progress from school to work are much less certain, much less structured, and far more fractured than they were for generations such as the Baby-Boomers. A young person's trajectory is now more likely to be characterized by gaining full-time employment through a number of part-time and temporary jobs, periods of unemployment, and changes of direction as they navigate their way from school to work over a much rockier pathway. Raffe (2003) has argued that it is necessary to provide young people with the signposts and opportunities that enable them to navigate these pathways. Dwyer and Wyn (2001) have observed that younger people are becoming more proactive in making the choices they need to make to develop and secure their futures. Evans (2002) noted that the issue of control over one's life is important and that a sense of agency may be being developed in young people as they negotiate a much less certain set of pathways.

In terms of learner diversities these observations have considerable importance. While the view has been commonly held that self-direction and self-management has been more a feature of more mature learners, it is likely that the uncertainties facing young people, and their need to develop agency over their lives, are the very influences that require them to develop self-direction and self-management at a much earlier age than was previously the case. Indeed, in recent research with vocational learners Smith (2000a) showed that younger apprentices were more self-directed than were their older counterparts. These influences also have a relationship with motivations to learn. While a more mature learner in an already-established career may be motivated to learn in order to develop along an already-established career trajectory, younger people are more likely to be motivated to learn in order to gain purchase into a career trajectory, and to continue to learn in order to maintain agency over a trajectory that will be subject to possibly sudden and discontinuous change. Bauman (2001) made the point that these motivations on the part of younger people are not generally well-understood by older people who have had much smoother trajectories, such that the diversity among them from a lay perspective remains something of a mystery. At the same time Raffe (2003) has argued it is the diversity among young people that becomes much more important in an environment where there is greater diversity in the development of career trajectories.

Abilities

Diversities in the abilities of individuals have commanded an enormous amount of attention from psychologists and educationalists since the nineteenth century. Ability was often seen to fall into two major categories – intelligence and aptitude. Intelligence was viewed as capacity to learn, while aptitude was conceived of as a person's capacity to carry out tasks in quite specific domains, resulting in the concepts of mechanical aptitude, clerical aptitude and so on. In psychology the study of intelligence and aptitude was central to ideas of individual difference. Theories of intelligence developed in the early decades of the twentieth century and were largely influenced by Spearman (1927) who saw it as comprised of a large central component (called the *g* factor), and a number of specific factors associated with particular mental abilities (such as arithmetic ability). Thurstone (1938) departed from Spearman in suggesting that intelligence comprised seven equally important factors (primary mental abilities) each associated with a different domain of mental activity. Over the intervening years since the 1930s there have been other attempts to theorise the nature of intelligence, and to observe it as a dimension of diversity between individuals that can predict and explain capacity to learn, capacity to process information and so forth.

Earlier thinking about intelligence was characterized by a view that it was a reasonably universal concept that could be applied in an unproblematic way across all peoples and manifested in similar ways across cultures. That singular view of intelligence led early workers such as Goddard (1917) to claim through his research that various groups of people were possessed of greater or lesser intelligence than others. Goddard's research was the result of a belief that instruments for measuring intelligence could be applied across all cultural groups with no regard for cultural difference. Through the work of researchers such as Cole, Gay, Glick and Sharp (1971) it has become clear that different cultures have preferred ways of handling information and completing tasks, such that what may be considered 'intelligent' behaviour in one culture may not be perceived as such in another. Hence, not only is intelligence a form of diversity between people, but the very notion of intelligence is a subject of diversity of interpretations as well.

Salas and Cannon-Bowers (2001) in their review of training concluded that *g* does appear to promote self-efficacy, performance and skill acquisition, and that individuals of high cognitive ability (all other things being equal) are likely to learn more and succeed in HRD. However, they also noted that many jobs have requirements that go beyond cognitive ability (and one might include here the ability to use expertise and tacit knowledge and understand and employ emotions effectively). Nonetheless *g* is the most widely invoked factor used to explain differences in performance (Sternberg and Hedlund, 2002). It has also been argued that g becomes even more important as work becomes more complex and unpredictable (Snow and Snell, 1993). However, in spite of its validity as a predictor of performance, g has a number of limitations (see Sternberg and Hedlund, 2002: 144). For example, g leaves between 75 and 80 per cent of the variance in performance unaccounted for (Schmidt and Hunter, 1998). Also, the problems posed in tests which assess g may bear little relationship to problems encountered in occupational and other real-world settings. These limitations have led to the view amongst a number of researchers that there is more to intelligent performance than whatever is measured by an IQ test (Sternberg and Hedlund, 2002).

One of the most influential sets of ideas of the past couple of decades about the nature of intelligence has been Howard Gardner's (1983, 1993) theory of multiple intelligences. Gardner views intelligence as reflecting a unique module of cognitive ability in a specific area; for example: musical intelligence, mathematical intelligence, and so forth which are functional in specific domains (e.g. musical intelligence is likely to have little functionality in a football game). Gardner originally proposed seven intelligences, each of which was also quite modular in that the degree to which an individual possessed each of the seven was largely independent of the degree to which they possessed the others.

The seven intelligences proposed by Gardner were linguistic intelligence, logical–mathematical intelligence, spatial intelligence, musical intelligence, bodily-kinaesthetic intelligence, interpersonal intelligence and intrapersonal intelligence. Although Gardner's theory sounds similar to the primary mental abilities proposed fifty years earlier by Thurstone, Gardner saw the intelligences as separate, while Thurstone viewed them as combinatory in constituting 'intelligence' per se. Gardner's theory has been influential in particular among educationalists since it allows for inclusion of aptitude, and enables differentiation among the abilities of any given individual. Additionally, the theory provides opportunity for an individual low on one of the intelligences to not be typecast as 'unintelligent', since the possession of other intelligences at a higher level can still occur. The model has yet to be fully explored in HRD contexts but provides the potential for a much wider range of abilities to be recognised in the workplace. One manifestation of how this is occurring is with regard to emotional intelligence (a person's ability to perceive and manage emotion, and get along with others) (Goleman, 1995) and which appears to be quite closely allied to the inter- and intra-personal intelligences recognised by Gardner. Emotional intelligence has attained considerable significance in management, HR and HRD practice in organizations.

Sternberg (1985, 1988), in contrast to Gardner, has proposed, in his triarchic theory of human intelligence, that intelligent behaviour is the result of the components of intelligence working effectively together to deal with the internal world (cognitive and meta-cognitive features within the individual); experience (learning from and using experiences); and the external world (using experience to adapt to, shape and select environments). Within this view metacognition is important as an executive function in the controlling and monitoring of mental functions and operations.

In a discussion of diversities among learners some of the more recent theories of intelligence (such as those of Gardner and Sternberg) are of particular importance since they acknowledge not just the diversity *between* individuals, but that there is diversity in intelligence (broadly defined) *within* individuals. Earlier theories that saw intelligence as a single construct led to measures such as IQ which sought to summarise a person's complete mental abilities and potential in two or three digits. Within that inadequate form of descriptor, examples of typecasting individuals and groups of individuals were not difficult to find. The streaming of children into particular areas of schooling based on IQ tests which purported to summarise something as complex as the range of mental abilities possessed by an individual at any point in time was yet another example of major typecasting decisions being made on the basis of a single measure. The more recent theories, such as Gardner's multiple intelligences, enable educators, trainers and HRD specialists to recognise, cater for, develop and use a wider range of mental characteristics without the same forms of typecasting that resulted from much narrower conceptions.

Learning styles and preferences

The idea that people have different ways of internally processing information and of engaging in learning has drawn considerable interest from psychologists, educationalists and HRD practitioners for many decades. As far back as the 1950s psychologists began to take interest in the way that different people, engaging in the same learning task, seemed to go about it in different ways. The term 'learning style' gained considerable currency in the 1970s and has held the attention of researchers and practitioners to the present day. Besides 'learning styles', other aspects of diversity that are pertinent to the different ways in which people learn are 'learning preferences' and 'cognitive styles'. One of the acknowledged problems of the styles research literature is the sometimes considerable confusion between labels and terminologies. Distinct concepts are sometimes referred to using the same names whilst similar constructs are given different names by different researchers. In this discussion we will unpack some of the terminologies and terms and draw some distinctions between them. It should be said that a comprehensive review is not possible in the space available in a chapter and readers should consult other more lengthy reviews for a more detailed discussion (for example, Riding and Rayner, 1998).

In what has since become an influential paper Curry (1983) suggested that individual differences in the ways in which people learn could be separated into three domains, conceptualized as being concentric rather like the layers of an onion. Curry suggested that learning preferences are in the outermost layer and are more influenced by the learning tasks and learning environment. The second of the three layers she suggested was information processing style and the innermost one (and hence least susceptible to environmental influence) was 'cognitive personality style', which she saw as being a relatively stable personality dimension. Others have introduced the notion of learning strategies to the model (a concept we will explore later in the chapter). The following definitions are offered:

- Learning preference: the favouring of one particular mode of teaching or other learning experience over another.
- Learning style: a distinctive and habitual manner of acquiring knowledge, skills or attitudes through particular ways of engaging with the learning process.
- Cognitive style: a distinctive and habitual manner of representing, organizing and processing information in memory.

Learning preferences

The concept of learning preferences appears to have attracted less attention from researchers than have learning style and cognitive style. Smith (2000a) took the view that preferences are a fruitful area of research for HRD practice because of their capacity to be influenced by environmental factors and the ways in which they may be managed (for example, by providing learning methods that suit an individual's preferences or that develop new ones). Smith (2000a) argued that in a practical sense knowing the preferences of learners was important not only in the design and delivery of instruction, but also as a guide to the development and modification of those preferences to better meet the learning demands of institutions and workplaces. The development and modification was likely to be more achievable through managing preferences than through the more stable and less environmentally influenced learning styles or cognitive styles. Canfield (1980) was one researcher who opted to examine the preferences students display in their learning. The Canfield Learning Styles Inventory (CLSI) (1980) provides sixteen learning preference subscale scores in three major categories:

- Conditions of learning: students' preferences for the learning environment, such as instructor-led, team-work, competitive, level of organization.
- Content: relative preferences for working with numeric, qualitative, inanimate and people-related content.
- Mode: preferences for learning through listening, reading, watching or doing.

Note there is some confusion in terminology again here: Canfield named his preferences inventory a 'styles' inventory when in fact it is more akin to a learning preferences inventory. The CLSI has largely been used by researchers and practitioners interested in applied outcomes, such as implementing preferred learning conditions, content and modes into learning programmes to cater more closely for students' learning preferences (for example: Alsagoff, 1985; Heikkinen, Pettigrew and Zakrajsek, 1985; Smith, 2000a, 2000b). Riding and Rayner (1998) acknowledged the practical value of preference inventories for the design of instruction to suit particular learners, or groups of learners. Unfortunately, theoretically well-grounded work using the CLSI is scant in the literature. From a construct validity perspective Gruber and Carriuolo (1991) developed a learner typology based on the CLSI, with the dimensions of conceptual–applied content, and social–independence. Working with Australian vocational education students, Smith (2000b) has developed a similar typology with a dimension of Non-verbal–Verbal learning preferences, and a Self-directed–Dependent learning preference (see below). Smith (2001a) has also argued that it is difficult for designers or deliverers of instruction to know of and take account of the profile of learning preferences that each individual displays. For these reasons he suggested that a higher level of analysis and abstraction may be possible and desirable (on pragmatic grounds), and through large-scale research he developed the simpler-to-use two-dimensional model shown in Figure 5.1.

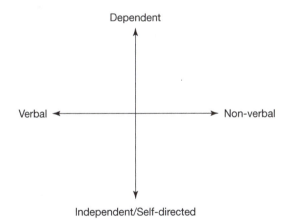

Figure 5.1 Two-dimensional representation of factors describing Vocational Education and Training learners' preferences

In this model, the preferences of a given group of learners can be distributed among the four quadrants described by the two axes. Accordingly, the degree to which a learner may prefer learning that is presented verbally (for example, as printed text, computer-presented text, orally and so forth)

can be balanced against their preference for non-verbally presented learning such as demonstrations, practice, visual display and so on. The model does not suggest that only one of these approaches (for example, verbal or non-verbal) should be employed in any given learning situation or with any given learner; rather it may be used as a guide to deciding on the 'mix' that might be effective. Similarly, the degree to which a learner may wish to engage with learning on a self-directed basis, or with instructor presence and guidance can also be described in the model.

A different approach to instructional preference was taken in research by Sadler-Smith and Riding (1999) in their attempt to explore the relationship between cognitive style (verbaliser–imager and wholist–analytical) and learning preferences. Rather than focusing on the forms of presentation that may be used in delivering instruction, they instead were more interested in identifying the preferred contexts for learning. Their research identified three major domains of learning context preference:

- *Collaborative methods* where learners would work together to achieve learning;
- *Dependent methods* where learners were provided with instructional processes by the teacher and worked through these with instructor guidance;
- *Autonomous methods* where students were provided with learning materials and essentially worked through these on a self-managed basis.

These three identified preferences may serve to unpack Smith's self-directed–dependent dimension further and are, to that extent, consistent with Smith's model. Interestingly enough, in earlier research just with apprentices, Smith (2000c) also noted that the dimension of self-direction–dependence was split into two dimensions, one which described a collaborative learning element, and another that identified the need for instructor-provided structure and guidance.

From the practical viewpoint of assessing and utilising individual differences as they are observed naturally by instructors as they go about their teaching of learners, Smith and Dalton (2005) have shown that preferences are very amenable to observation during teaching. From the results of naturalistic observation during instruction, it appears that teachers and trainers are likely to observe preferences, and to adjust their training design and delivery to meet those preferences. Working with a large number of teachers and trainers in the vocational training sector in Australia, Smith and Dalton were also able to show that a majority of instructors have developed techniques to identify and use preferences to cater to both group and individual diversity. The ability to notice preferences in the learning situation and adjust the learning experience accordingly is an important component of what has been termed 'instructor expertise' (Burke and Sadler-Smith, 2005).

Learning styles

It is probably the second layer of Curry's onion model (termed 'learning style' in our interpretation of Curry's conceptualization) that has attracted most attention in terms of practice-based research. The major contribution to theory and practice in this domain has come from Kolb (1976); whilst in the UK Honey and Mumford (1992) have made a significant impact on management development practice with their adaptation of the Kolb model.

Kolb (1976) (drawing to some extent upon a Jungian approach to psychological type) suggested that individuals learn and solve problems by progressing through a four-stage cycle: *concrete experience* (CE), followed by *reflective observation* (RO); which leads to the formation of *abstract concepts* (AC); which results in the testing of hypotheses through *active experimentation* (AE). Kolb viewed AE and RO as being two ends of a continuum, whilst AC and CE were opposite ends of a second continuum, orthogonal (i.e. at right angles to) the AE–RO dimension. These two continua may be combined to give four quadrants, and an individual's learning style may then be described in terms of the quadrant in which the individual's scores on the Learning Styles Inventory (LSI) fall. Kolb named the four resultant styles as *accommodator* style, *assimilator* style, *diverger* style and *converger* style. Accommodators for example, according to Kolb learn by concrete experience and active experimentation; they rely more upon intuition and trial-and-error methods of problem-solving. Kolb also argued that a person may prefer one style in one situation, and another style in another situation, meaning that the position a person occupies in the two-dimensional plane can vary with the learning task. However, Kolb also argued that in the same learning context the learning style adopted on each occasion is likely to be the same.

Honey and Mumford (1992) in their adaptation of Kolb suggested four learning styles which they named activist, reflector, theorist and pragmatist in accordance with a four-stage learning cycle of having an experience, reflecting on it, drawing conclusions (theories) and applying the lessons learned. In terms of the four styles Honey and Mumford asserted that:

- activists learn by doing, and are keen to move into a learning task or situation and explore it as they engage with it;
- reflectors learn through observation, and by thinking about what they have observed, and constructing meaning through the process of reflection;
- theorists like to understand the underlying concepts and relationships between them (in terms of a theory or model) and they prefer to work with facts and generate meaning through an understanding of relevant theory;
- pragmatists like to see if and how things may be applied to real world situations and they prefer to acquaint themselves with new knowledge, understanding and skill through practical application.

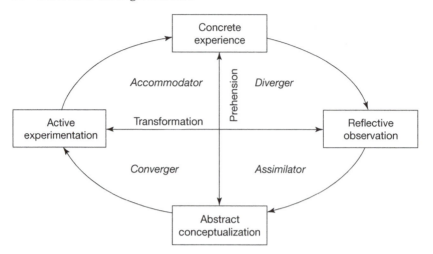

Figure 5.2 Two-dimensional representation of Kolb's (1976) learning styles theory

The Learning Styles Questionnaire (LSQ) developed by Honey and Mumford is designed to identify the relative strengths an individual has for each of the four stages in the cycle. Implicit in Honey and Mumford's model is the assertion that all individuals exhibit elements of each style, but that what defines an individual in a learning situation is the extent to which each of these identified styles forms the basis for thought and action. Both the Kolb measure of style (the LSI) and the LSQ have been the subject of a number of critical examinations with respect to their reliability and validity and some of the issues are still unresolved in both of the areas for the LSI and LSQ (see Coffield, Moseley, Hall and Ecclestone, 2004).

Cognitive styles

As the innermost component of Curry's (1983) model, cognitive style is viewed as a fairly stable set of dimensions which are at the interface of personality and cognition. Two categories of cognitive style based upon a number of specific cognitive functions are relevant in the present context:

- *Mode of representation*: information may be represented in memory as words (a *verbaliser* style) or as images (an *imager* style).
- *Mode of organizing*: information may be organized into wholes (a *wholist* style) or parts (an *analytical* style).

Riding and Cheema (1991) attempted to integrate the many conceptualizations of style, and have developed a two-dimensional model of cognitive style based upon the dimensions referred to above (i.e. the representation and organization of information). One dimension is conceptualized as a

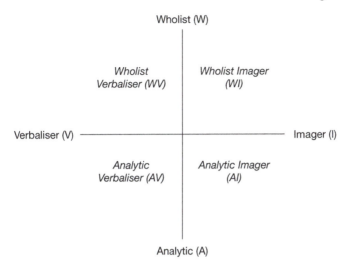

Figure 5.3 Two-dimensional representation of cognitive style (Riding, 1997)

bipolar verbaliser–imager dimension, whilst the other is a bipolar wholist–analytical dimension. A wholist style is characterized by a global or overall view of information, while an analytic style organizes and processes information in its component parts (Sadler-Smith and Riding, 1999). The verbal–imagery dimension refers to the habitual way in which a person represents information in memory: verbalisers represent information primarily in a verbal form and visualisers represent information primarily in visual form. Riding (1997) has also provided evidence that these two underlying dimensions of cognitive style are quite fundamental and may reflect neurological processes and that they are independent of 'learning' style (Glass and Riding, 2000). Similar suggestions of neural correlates have been made earlier by Doktor (1978) and Doktor and Bloom (1977). Figure 5.3 shows the two dimensions of cognitive style developed by Riding and his colleagues.

Sadler-Smith and Riding (1999) investigated the relationship between cognitive style and instructional preference in an attempt to develop predictions to assist the instructional design and delivery of learning programmes to meet the needs of different groups of learners, or individuals. They found that there appeared to be a preference amongst wholists for non-print-based media of instruction, for collaborative learning methods, and for more informal types of assessment. These findings are consistent with Riding's (1991) suggestion that wholists are likely to be sociable and socially dependent. Riding and Sadler-Smith (1997) have also suggested that wholists process information simultaneously, while analytics break it down into parts and process it sequentially. Earlier research by Riding and Sadler-Smith (1992) suggested that imposing a structure upon learning may be beneficial to wholists, since they may otherwise have difficulty breaking information down into its component parts. The wholist–analytic/verbaliser–imager model provides a potentially useful framework for understanding some of the relationship between learning preferences and instructional design matters relating to mode and structure of presentation.

Learning strategies

A further set of diversities that are observable between individual learners comprise the strategies that are used while learning. Curry (1983: 4) described a strategy as 'a translation-like mechanism by which the learner copes with the particular learning environment . . . to translate information from the form supplied into a form meaningful to the individual'. A more general description was provided by Sadler-Smith (1996a: 186) as a conscious plan of action adopted for the effective and efficient acquisition of knowledge or skill. Other researchers have refined the definition of strategy further. For example, in their research into second-language learning O'Malley and Chamot (1990: 44–5) developed a system for the classification of learning strategies into three separate groups:

- Meta-cognitive strategies, defined as higher-order executive skills involving planning, monitoring or evaluating the success of a learning activity.
- Cognitive strategies which are used to operate directly on the information presented, and to organize and process it to enable effective learning.
- Social/affective strategies that represent interactions with others or 'ideational control' over affect.

A similar system for classifying learning activities was developed a year earlier by Short and Weisberg-Benchell (1989) when they classified learning activities into cognitive, affective and meta-cognitive or regulatory activities. Vermunt's (1989, 1992) review of the literature developed a grouping of a wide range of learning activities under the same three identified activity headings. Although there is emerging agreement on the identification of meta-cognitive and cognitive strategies, Brown's (1987: 66) comment that 'it is often difficult to distinguish between what is meta- and what is cognitive' is a potential problem in the reliable classification of strategies. Marland, Patching and Putt (1992a, 1992b) investigated the learning strategies used by distance learning students using the same established framework of meta-cognitive, cognitive, and social/affective, and were able to suggest a 'family' of very specific learning strategies in association with each of the three major classifications.

Researchers such as Marland, Vermunt and their colleagues conducted their research in the context of formal learning and usually within educational settings. Hence the strategies identified tend to be less focused on the situated learning that occurs in the workplace. Billett (1996a: 274–276) drew extensively from the literature on the means of appropriation of knowledge *in situ* in an analysis which resulted in the identification of a number of means of knowledge appropriation that have been observed or proposed by previous researchers. Some of these are strategies used in the appropriation of knowledge from text or other learning resources, while others are appropriation mechanisms derived through engaging with the workplace environment. Smith (2003a) has generated a set of learning strategies based on Marland, Patching and Putt's (1992a, 1992b) work and Billett's (1996a) workplace learning strategies and these are illustrated in Table 5.1.

Table 5.1 Learning strategies and brief definitions

Strategy	Definition
METACOGNITIVE	
Analysis	Reduces, breaks down whole (e.g. problem or task) into parts
Strategy planning	Plans ways for processing or handling textual material during training sessions
Cognitive monitoring[1]	Thinks about, reflects on, evaluates or directs own thinking
Selection	Identifies key material, gist material, or that which is relevant to assessment
Evaluation	Makes judgements about the value of textual materials, activities, in-text questions, own position or point of view
COGNITIVE	
Recalling	Brings back into working memory an idea, opinion or fact previously stored in long-term memory
Confirming	Judges that ideas in text support own beliefs, practices, tactics
Generating	Formulates own questions, examples, ideas, problems; interpolating; going beyond the data
Diagnosis	Identifies strengths and weaknesses in ideas, strategies, points of view
Deliberation	Engages in thinking about a topic, segment
Translation	Expresses segments of text in own words
Categorising	Sorts items, ideas, skills into different classes or groups
Imaging	Creates a mental image of an idea in text to gain a fuller understanding of it
Application	Considers the use of an idea or tactic in a different context
Linking	Associates or brings together two or more ideas, topics, contexts, headings, personal experiences, materials, tasks
Rehearsal	Repeats ideas, facts, etc., two or more times to facilitate recall

continued

Table 5.1 continued

Strategy	Definition
Anticipation	Predicts or states expectations that problem, question, textual feature, etc., will be encountered; looks forward to new material; wonders about the possibility of an event or occurrence in text; relevance of material, content
Comparing	Identifies similarities or differences between two statements, concepts, models, situations, ideas, theories, points of view, etc.
Trialing	Trialling in real workplace of knowledge gained from learning programme
Experimentation	Trying out an idea on equipment or process to test own understanding
Problem-solving	Finding a solution to a problem requiring relevant workplace knowledge
Practice	Engaging in practising the tasks being learned
SOCIAL/AFFECTIVE	
Worker observation	Unstructured observation of a fellow worker carrying out the task as part of everyday work
Demonstration	Structured observation of the process being demonstrated by a fellow worker
Peer discussion	Discussion with fellow worker to assist in knowledge development
Supervisor discussion	Discussion with trainer or supervisor to assist in knowledge development
Scheduled class	Attendance at a formal training programme to assist in knowledge development

[1] Named 'metacognitive' by Marland *et al.* (1992b).

Source: Smith (2003a: 383).

These strategies were used as a framework in Smith's (2003a) research which investigated the ways in which apprentices used learning strategies. While the research showed considerable diversity between individuals, it also showed some characteristics that were common among all apprentices in the study, and also some characteristics that were similar within particular apprentice trade groups. The apprentices were generally able to use the cognitive and social/affective strategies to learn within formal training sessions and in the workplace, but they had poorly developed meta-cognitive strategies. This raised the possibility that learners are likely to require some form of instruction in those meta-cognitive strategies that may be beneficial to them in learning situations (i.e. they may need to be taught ways in which they can think about their thinking and adapt their thinking to suit the task). Learning strategies appear to be amenable to development, for example research by White (1997) and by Smith, Robertson and Wakefield (2002) indicated that learning strategies can be developed not only through experience but also through deliberate interventions.

Focus on practice: the utility of learning styles theories and assessment

In this section we have drawn extensively on a very useful contribution by Delahoussaye (2002) who elicited the views of a number of 'thought leaders' in the area of learning styles in order to explore the practical relevance of learning styles to corporate training. The experts he consulted included Lynn Curry, Peter Honey and David Kolb. The answers given by these and the other experts consulted to a number of questions are summarised below:

1   Can we accurately determine a learner's preferred or dominant style?

    a Many of the so-called tests are better conceived of as tools to be used in order to enable individuals to gain a heightened awareness of their own learning processes.

    b The behavioural tendencies can be measured with more confidence than can the underlying preferences.

2   What is the relationship between learning style and learning effectiveness?

    a There have been problems with the research at the level of method and design but nonetheless the evidence appears to be generally positive with the strongest relationships in the areas of style flexibility.

    b Individuals who have the ability to match their learning processes to the learning environment are at an advantage.

    c Effectiveness can be interpreted in two ways: people can play to their strengths or they can work to become better all-rounders.

    d Any relationship at the individual level can have limited applicability in those situations where learning occurs in a group context, although it can be used to consolidate people into groups. (Delahoussaye, 2002)

3   Should we teach exclusively to an individual's preferred style?

    a It is better to design a curriculum in order that there is some way for learners of every style to engage with the topic.

    b Matching in this way would leave out some of the most important features of effective learning, namely, 'struggle', 'risk taking' and 'learning from mistakes'.

    c Certain topics have to be taught in certain ways. (Delahoussaye, 2002)

4   Are styles stable over time, task, problem and situation?

    a LSI styles appear to be relatively stable over time but do change as a result of career path and life experiences.

   b The underlying preference is more consistent and durable than the behaviours which are changeable depending upon circumstances or will. (Delahoussaye, 2002)

5   Are learners adept at finding their own path through content?

   a Those with inherent flexibility can adapt easily whereas those without are further challenged when the learning does not fit with their style.

   b Learners need to know what to look for – without this it can be very much 'hit-and-miss'. (Delahoussaye, 2002)

6   What are the barriers to making better use of styles? Kolb identified three major barriers:

   a the institutionalisation of the traditional lecture;
   b learners not understating the learning process;
   c teachers who assume that everyone learns in the way that they do. (Delahoussaye, 2002)

7   How can we make best use of learning styles in the corporate environment?

   a Reducing the one-size-fits-all mentality.
   b Understanding one's own decision making processes.
   c Appreciating that different styles may be more prevalent in different parts of an organization.
   d Allowing individuals to use information on their styles to better structure their own learning programmes and processes.
   e Using e-learning to developed customised routes through a learning programme. (Delahoussaye, 2002)

Identifying diversity: questions for situational analysis

In Chapter 1 we explicated some hypothesised relationships between a number of important factors when trying to develop a picture of the various dimensions of diversity in complex and dynamic HRD environments. As may now be apparent, the diversities that exist amongst learners may be further expanded into a large number of complex and interrelated variables which may have an impact on any given learning situation in the workplace. The present chapter has sought to examine some of those variables, their complexity and the underpinning theory and research. The issues that have been explored in this chapter may now be used as the basis for a systematic method for acknowledging and accommodating the diversities that exist amongst learners. HRD should acknowledge that learning-relevant diversities exist between learners and groups of learners and that these diversities need to be thought through and considered in the planning, design and delivery of learning. To this end we suggest a number of questions that may enable enquiry, reflection and analysis as a precursor to any HRD project or activity.

Responding to the target group

1 What are the national cultural backgrounds of the target group?
2 What is the age profile of the target group?
3 What are the educational backgrounds of the learners and what are their likely learning preferences?
4 Do you have any indications of differences in preferred learning styles?
5 Are any of the above based upon supposition and/or stereotype? What evidence are you basing your judgements and decisions on?
6 Which aspects of learner diversity are likely to be critical to success?

Responding to culture

1 Is the group relatively homogeneous or heterogeneous with regard to national culture?
2 What are the likely expectations with regard to learning approaches and methods of individuals of different national cultural groups?
3 What cultures are there among the target group, and how may each culture impact on the HRD initiative?
4 What can be done to cater for any cultural diversity?
5 Is there reason to try and draw some of the cultural differences to the attention of the target group in order to achieve better across-group understanding?

Responding to age

1 Are there likely to be differences within the group in terms of their self-directedness for learning?
2 Are there likely to be differences within the group in terms of their feelings of self-efficacy in relation to learning?
3 How will you respond to these differences?

Responding to learning preferences

1 Which learning media and presentation methods are available to you?
2 What are the learning preferences within the group?
3 Are the methods at your disposal appropriate to the group?
4 Can these individual preferences be catered for? How?

Responding to learning styles

1   What are the learning-style differences within the group?
2   Do you need to cater for these styles differences, or will attention to learning preferences be sufficient?
3   Are the methods that you propose to use appropriate to the individuals' learning styles?
4   Can these individual learning styles be catered for to any extent? How?

Responding to cognitive style

1   What are the cognitive-style preferences within the group?
2   Are you able to or do you need to cater for cognitive styles, or will attention to learning styles or learning preferences be sufficient?
3   Are the methods and techniques that you propose to use appropriate to the individuals' cognitive styles?

Responding to learning strategies

1   How aware are learners of the importance of learning strategies?
2   Do the learners apply particular learning strategies at the moment?
3   How will you provide HRD activities that make use of or enable learners to develop appropriate learning strategies?
4   Which strategies do you believe to be necessary but possibly not developed yet in all target group members?
5   How would you encourage development of those?

6 Diversities in learning methods

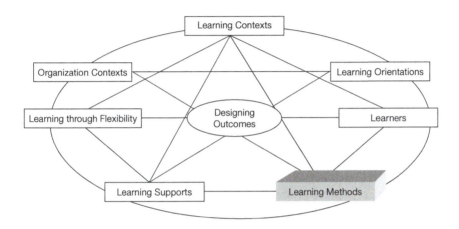

Introduction

The conception of learning in organizations offered in this book is a broad one. It encompasses the notion of training *per se* (for example, training courses), but goes beyond this to embrace learning and working as being closely, and even inextricably, inter-linked in practice. Alongside this we acknowledge huge expansion over recent decades in the range and sophistication of learning methods available to managers and HRD practitioners. This increase in the choices available has been fuelled by a number of factors, including:

- better levels of education of practitioners through professional development and post-graduate schemes (for example the Institute for Teaching and Learning for university lecturers and the Chartered Institute of Personnel and Development in the UK);
- drives to meet diverse learner needs and attempts at differentiation in learning provision;

- increased sophistication of organizational processes within which learning and the creation of knowledge are seen as important for enhancing the performance and competitiveness of businesses;
- higher expectations from learners who may have recently emerged from an increasingly sophisticated school and higher educational system;
- a burgeoning market in the provision of learning media, resources and services;
- developments in information and communication technologies and the emergence of better knowledge relating to the efficacy of different methods (based upon evidence from their practical applications in organizations and from research in universities and other institutions).

These developments may be seen in a context in which human resource development (HRD) is striving to establish itself as a distinctive field of academic enquiry in relation to education, adult education, training and professional development.

Technology is often seen to be a driving force. In recent decades the 'hard', largely electronic, technologies have broadened considerably the options available for training delivery and also the resources and sources of information available to support learning. This has brought increased sophistication which has enabled more complex designs in terms of modes of presentation, structure, adaptability, communication and interaction, assessment, monitoring and recording, and also in terms of general levels of quality of presentation and appearance. These technologies have also increased the flexibility in terms of time and place that is available to learners, as well as the pace at which they may learn.

At the same time 'softer' learning technologies (such as instructional design) and the various non-technology-based methods that are available have not lost any of their power or potential for leveraging learning in organizational and professional contexts where the dividing line between working and learning is quite naturally blurred. Indeed some of the more traditional 'softer' approaches such as coaching and mentoring recently have been the subject of new impetus through developments in areas such as developmental coaching and the management of learning within communities of practice. In some ways we as practitioners are confronted with an embarrassment of riches with almost too many methods to choose from. Where does this diversity leave us in terms of exercising effective choice and making sound decisions about which methods to use under which circumstances? It leaves many potentially insightful questions to be considered from a standpoint that is informed by research and practice. While there is some clear evidence emerging from the rapidly growing literature, there are also many questions left open for conjecture and judgement on the part of designers and instructors which leaves a breadth of possibilities available to them that may enable them to adapt to local conditions in innovative and creative ways based upon a knowledge of what might work best, when, how and with whom.

This chapter will consider the utility of some of the various options that may be available to individuals and organizations in implementing, planning and managing learning. Once again there are no clear right or wrong answers in the decisions that may need to be taken; but there is the process of informed reflection and questioning about aims, processes and outcomes and how these inform judgements and decisions about which methods to deploy. By drawing upon the ever-growing theoretical and empirical knowledge base the challenge for HRD practitioners is to maximise the potential opportunities offered by these methods to enhance the learning of individuals and the organizations of which they are a part in order to address both formal and informal learning needs.

Learning needs may arise naturally in the course of one's work, be diagnosed through performance appraisal, 360-degree feedback or be part of a larger identified need at the job or organizational level. Whatever the impetus for the learning is, there is at the individual level a wide range of methods available; we are not able to consider them all but instead have chosen to focus upon those that appear to us to be relevant in the present context. The methods we have chosen to examine are:

- one-to-one methods;
- one-to-many methods;
- distance learning;
- e-learning;
- games and simulations;
- action-based methods;
- informal workplace learning.

Each of the methods may stand alone; however, it is likely that for any given need a combination of methods is better able to address the relevant need more effectively (for example, coaching may be used to support and follow-up distance learning, e-learning might be a valuable supplementary resource for more traditional methods and so forth). It should also be remembered that at this level broader issues relating to the individual's career and life choices may be raised and should be seen, potentially at least, as part of an ongoing process of lifelong learning and development.

One-to-one learning methods

This section will be concerned with two related one-to-one methods, coaching and mentoring. They are important especially when viewing learning in a socio-cultural context since coaching and mentoring are widely used as one-to-one methods for developing individuals' knowledge and skills *in situ*. Maclennan (1995) suggested that one-to-one approaches such as these may be focused upon particular individual and organizational issues, for example:

- problem-focused to help individuals or teams solve specific problems or to help organizations deal with 'problem people';
- project-focused over the lifetime of a specific project and terminated when the project ceases;
- training follow-up to reinforce the application of new skills in the workplace and aid the transfer of learning;
- induction-focused to overcome any feelings of insecurity and inadequacy when an individual encounters a new work environment;
- qualification-focused to help an individual achieve a particular educational, vocation or professional development goal;
- peer group-focused whereby individuals within the group who are skilled in one area help others who are less strong in that area.

Coaching

In Chapter 3 as part of our consideration of diversities of learning contexts we discussed the concepts of coaching and mentoring and the role that such one-to-one relationships can play in fostering individualised learning. We distinguish between a coach and a mentor thus:

- Coach: someone who provides guidance to others in shaping their performance in specific areas towards achieving greater proficiency in a task, or in broader career and personal development terms. A coach can be inside or outside the organization;
- Mentor: someone who has the competence to pass on knowledge and skills from a perspective of expertise, authority and credibility in broader areas of psychosocial and career development functions. The mentor is usually inside the organization and has often trodden the same path as the protégé. (See Jayne, 2003)

Traditionally coaching was seen as a one-to-one instructional event whereby a skilled employee instructed a less-skilled employee, which is confined to a well-defined task and usually of short-term duration. An analogy is the sports coach: he or she will demonstrate, observe, guide, instruct, monitor and give feedback to a sportsperson with regard to a particular aspect of their performance or technique. Coaching in the workplace is based upon the assumption that people are able to learn effectively by watching others complete a task, and when given the chance to practise with feedback and encouragement will themselves be able to perform to an acceptable level. This approach and its underlying assumptions also underpin much traditional craft apprenticeship training. Coaching can be planned and formalised (for example, in the context of the induction of a new employee) or it can be an ongoing process whereby an employee when faced by a problem that stretches or perplexes them will turn to colleagues for help, instruction, guidance and advice. Indeed, it is sometimes seen in a narrow mechanistic sense of a 'tell–show–practise' sequence. However, it may also be seen in the context of learning as a situated and social phenomenon in which much of the knowledge is held tacitly, owned by the practitioners and is the property of the community of practice in which it is situated (Wenger, 2000: 206) – see Chapter 3 for a more detailed discussion of the socio-cultural context of learning.

Coaching in this narrow performance-focused sense is most suited to tasks where there is no real need to employ extensive, highly structured or lengthy learning programmes. Such an approach, which may seem laissez-faire, need not be a 'hit-and-miss' affair. Its efficacy depends upon a number of factors; for example, the nature of the task and the skills of the coach and the receptivity of the learner and their willingness and ability to ask questions. Coaching can be highly effective if it is planned and executed correctly and it may also help to obviate any difficulties of transfer of learning since the coaching is situated in the context of the job itself. For coaching to be effective it is important to try to ensure:

- the correct sequencing of tasks;
- choosing appropriate coaches who have the technical knowledge, credibility and interpersonal skills;
- back-up materials are provided ('take-aways', job-aids, organization charts, checklists, protocols, flow charts, etc.);
- that the learners themselves are ready and self-motivated enough to learn in what may turn out to be, or at least appear to be, an unstructured and highly experiential approach.

Coaches who possess the expertise and the ability to put this across may be few and far between; it is likely therefore that many potential coaches will benefit from some form of training themselves in how to instruct others (Buckley and Caple, 1992: 186). These are likely to include diagnostic skills, communication skills, feedback skills and assessment skills, and the inter-personal qualities that will create a satisfying and productive coach–learner relationship. The appropriateness of coaching as a method may also depend on the nature of the task: for example high-risk tasks or those using expensive or delicate equipment may mean that the process has to be managed in a more carefully controlled way or in a simulated environment. The support network of colleagues around the individual is important in creating the sense of a community with a shared endeavour and the collective knowledge and skill resource to be drawn upon if and when needed. A further issue surrounds the perception of coaching. It may sometimes be seen as 'training on the cheap'; however, if executed effectively it can be resource-intensive in terms of time and effort, the training of the coaches and the management of the process.

It was stated at the outset of this discussion that traditionally coaching was seen as a one-to-one instructional event in which a skilled employee instructed a less-skilled employee in a well-defined task over the short term.

More recently, however, the concept of coaching has been expanded and given additional impetus as a method with the advent of a more developmental form of this method, often referred to as 'developmental coaching'. Coaching for development, and particularly executive development, appears to be on the increase; for example, in the UK a survey by the Chartered Institute of Personnel and Development (CIPD) found that 80 per cent of the HR practitioners sampled used coaching (Jarvis, 2004). In the USA executive coaching is the fastest growing area of consultancy (Jayne, 2003). The practice of coaching, especially at senior manager and executive level, has grown to such an extent that it is becoming a part of the HRD practitioner's role. In the UK the CIPD has developed a set of professional standards in response to concerns at the lack of accreditation of providers of coaching (*People Management*, September 2004).

A brief discussion of what we term 'developmental coaching' follows on naturally from our consideration of coaching per se. In this case the context and overall aim is different:

- The context may be a specific occupational group (such as senior managers and executives).
- The aim is less specific and more general, going beyond the narrow confines of a specific task.
- The outcomes of coaching may be in relation to personal, career or life goals as well as occupation-specific matters.

Developmental coaching goes beyond the task itself and into the realms of career development and life choices. It is a process whereby a coach and a learner are involved in a longer-term process in which the coach helps (but does not direct) the learner to develop their career and life path in particular ways and to unlock their ability to perform, learn, lead and achieve through developing an awareness of the factors which can impede or facilitate a particular developmental or life trajectory (Maclennan, 1995). The benefits of this kind of coaching can be intrapersonal (for example, self-awareness and confidence) as well as in more externally focused areas such as leadership and management skills, assertiveness, stress management and work/life balance (Wales, 2003: 276).

One of the key HRD decisions is in making the choice of the right coach. Theories of social persuasion suggest that a person who is able to convey experience, expertise and credibility is able to harness authority over others (Sue-Chan and Latham, 2004). Sue-Chan and Latham (2004) asked the question in their research whether one form of coaching is more effective than another. They compared peer, self- and external coaching and found that an external person was superior to peers as a coach in improving the team effectiveness of a group of MBA students. They attributed this to the external coach being more credible for the task than peers. Wales (2003: 282) summarised the benefits of coaching thus:

it is a valuable tool for developing a wide range of learning needs; it may open up personal and sometimes profound insights; it can be used in conjunction with other learning and development initiatives; and it makes managers feel more valued.

On a more practical level the UK's CIPD suggested that a number of guidelines may be followed, such as: setting up a confidentiality agreement from the outset and considering the 'big picture' in terms of overall priorities that take into account work and whole-life issues by the coach asking questions such as 'What is important to you?' (CIPD, 2004). The boundaries between coaching and other more specialised and clinical techniques should be recognised and adhered to since asking certain varieties of questions may surface deeper personal and psychological issues. It is important that coaches recognise where their professional expertise ends and that of their counselling, therapeutic and medical colleagues begins.

Mentoring

The term 'mentor' is derived from the character in Homer's *Odyssey* (Mentor) who guided Odysseus's son Telemachus in the absence of his father. It has come to refer to the process in which an experienced and usually more senior employee provides, in a one-to-one relationship, guidance and advice in order to help less experienced colleagues cope and grow with their job demands within the organization. As noted earlier, coaching and mentoring differ in terms of the nature of the interaction and the skills employed. Jayne (2003: 37) described a mentor as being someone who has 'already walked the path that their protégé is about to tread – they've been there, done that, and have the [business experience] to prove it'.

Whittaker and Cartwright (2000) defined the aim of mentoring as to provide the mentor and the protégé with a cost-effective process of development through constructive reflection that meets their needs and fits into the busy time constraints within an organization. They further held that the relationship is founded upon a trust and respect that enables problems and difficulties to be discussed but that this needs to be structured and within a protected time. The relationship involves a social exchange in which there are mutual benefits. The mentor role may fulfil (Kram, 1985):

- psychosocial functions: for example, role modelling, friendship, counselling, acceptance and affirmation;
- career development functions: including task-related coaching, sponsorship, exposure, visibility, protection and provision of challenging assignments.

There is overlap with some aspects of coaching and the differences sometimes can be subtle. A mentor can facilitate an individual's development in job terms by helping them to overcome problems and make decisions, but also their broader growth through nurturing their development within the organization. Mentors generally have high levels of experience and organizational know-how and are committed to providing upward mobility and career support for their protégés (Kram, 1985). Maclennan (1995) argued that a mentor is more a resource than an expert and is available to fulfil the role with some basic management and interpersonal skills. The coach on the other hand exists in order for someone to achieve more and hence needs to have the necessary expertise in the relevant areas of job content (for performance coaching) or individual growth processes (in the case of developmental coaching). In this regard the interpersonal relationship between mentor and protégé is paramount.

Mentoring can be formalised or it can be informal. The benefits of informal mentoring are fairly well documented; for example, individuals who have been mentored report greater career satisfaction (Fagenson, 1989), career commitment (Colarelli and Bishop, 1990) and career mobility (Scandura, 1992). It appears from research carried out in the USA that the quality of the mentoring relationship is an important factor in determining career and job attitudes. For example, individuals in highly satisfying mentoring relationships showed more positive attitudes than non-mentored individuals; the attitudes of those in dissatisfying or marginally satisfying mentoring relationships were the same as those of non-mentored individuals (Ragins, Cotton and Miller, 2000). This research is important in that it suggests that the mere presence of a mentor is not enough; the outcomes of the process may depend critically upon the quality of the relationship. It is also important to note that bad mentoring may be worse than none at all (Scandura, 1992). The skills of the mentor in cultivating a satisfying relationship may be the key to success, and hence any mentoring programme needs to invest in the preparation of the participants (for example, by carefully selecting and training mentors), the setting out of expectations, as well as in the ongoing process itself.

Pittenger and Heimann (2000) argued that self-efficacy (an individual's feelings about their ability to perform a task) is an important factor in the mentoring process to the extent that the self-efficacy both of the mentor and the protégé may be a key variable in determining their readiness and suitability to enter into the relationship. For example, without high self-efficacy the protégé is less likely to be well suited to taking advantage of the developmental opportunities provided; similarly a mentor with low self-efficacy is unlikely to embrace the demands and challenges of the role (2000: 39). This raises the question of what to do with learners who may be low in self-efficacy. Pittenger and Heimann suggest that an underlying and preliminary goal may be the building of self-efficacy through skills training and career planning. They provided some prescriptive advice for organizations wishing to develop mentoring programmes. For example, there should be consistent organizational goals and shared understanding of these goals – otherwise protégés may be developed in ways that might conflict with the organization's mission and values. They also made the point that mentors themselves should have good interpersonal skills and that there must be opportunities in work schedules and geographical arrangements to enable interaction to take place between mentor and protégé.

One-to-many methods

The term 'many' in this context is intended to refer to a group, hence what constitutes 'many' is variable. One-to-many methods can vary in a number of dimensions of diversity, for example:

- from didactic (designed primarily to *instruct* learners) to participative methods;
- from spatially contiguous (literally face-to-face) to spatially separate (and hence technologically mediated).

In our brief examination of one-to-many methods we will examine a range of factors that may need to be taken into account when designing learning experiences that may involve groups of learners.

Didactic approaches are most often associated with traditional classroom-based methods. Often this can take the form of lecture where an expert such as a trainer, teacher or instructor disseminates information to a group of learners. These interactions often take the form of an exposition of facts, concepts, principles, examples and so forth with opportunities for learners to ask questions, be asked questions and participate in exercises and group work. The degree of didacticism employed can depend upon a number of factors, including:

- The nature of the material to be learned: the dissemination of facts and knowledge is often considered to be achieved efficiently and effectively by this method. However, designers may wish to consider the question of the extent to which such an approach is redundant in the light of the opportunities offered by distance learning, computer-based learning or simply reading from a text book. The prime question to be asked here is 'what is the extent of the value added by having learners and the instructor or teacher in the classroom with their expertise on hand?' There may be unique advantages (for example, the ability to extemporise and elaborate, ask questions, give feedback and enthuse and inspire learners) but it is important that these issues be considered at the outset;
- The style of the teacher: some individual teachers prefer a didactic style, they feel more comfortable with it and may be better skilled in issues of presentation and questioning than they are in facilitative techniques;
- The styles and preferences of the learners: learners themselves will vary in terms of the extent to which they prefer to engage with passive didactic approaches or active participative methods.

When using didactic approaches it is important to structure and sequence the learning appropriately, to be aware of the effects of fatigue and the attention span of the learners and the effects of information overload upon them. Reece and Walker (1994: 117) suggested that it is important to prepare beforehand by identifying the objectives, extracting the key points of content, designing visual materials to supplement the use of voice. Presentation may also be crucial, for example, avoiding a monotonous tone of delivery, emphasising key points, facilitating note-taking (where appropriate), introducing and summarising. The advantages of this method (see Buckley and Caple, 1992; Reece and Walker, 1994) are that:

- The numbers of students addressed is limited only by the capacity of the physical space.
- The teacher has control over the content, sequence and pacing.
- It can convey important points and large volumes of information consistently and efficiently.
- The use of modern visual aids and projection equipment considerably enhances the quality of the learning experience.
- The session can be broadcast and or recorded.

The disadvantages of the method (see: Buckley and Caple, 1992; Reece and Walker, 1994) are that:

- There may be little or no opportunity to question the teacher for elaboration or remediation.
- It is limited to specific types of learning (for example, it may not be used effectively to teach skills).
- The effectiveness is heavily reliant upon the presentation skills of the teacher.
- The human attention span is limited even with the most skilled and charismatic speakers.
- There may be fatigue of the speaker and amongst the audience.
- It is difficult to accommodate individual differences amongst learners in ability, preference and style.

Participative methods of delivery may take any number of forms from group discussions, demonstrations, role play, brainstorming, staged debates and so forth. The difference between these methods and those considered above is that the teacher's role is one of facilitation (meaning to enable learning and make it happen more easily). As HRD practitioners have become more dissatisfied with didactic approaches and as learners' expectations have changed, strategies of small group working have gained momentum, allied to the fact that a much broader range of learning types are amenable to being facilitated in group settings (including the behavioural, cognitive and affective) (Reece and Walker, 1994). Berry (1993) identified the following as amongst the important competencies for facilitating learning in group situations:

- Technical skills: understanding the learning process, group dynamics, subject matter and business context;
- Management skills: planning and preparation, time management and control of the physical environment to make it conducive to learning;
- Interpersonal skills: active listening, clarifying, questioning, summarising, observing, giving feedback;
- Task and human process skills: results orientation, establishment of expectations, pacing and focus, establishing trust, recognising and respecting differences and diversities, accommodating individual differences, managing and resolving conflict.

The actual process of working in a group (irrespective of the content) may also be a valuable outcome from participative methods, especially considering that many work processes are now team-based. Participative methods have the advantages of enabling individuals to express views: there are opportunities for remediation, elaboration and feedback and for learners to bring their experiences to the group to share them. The disadvantages of this approach are that it can be time-consuming and less resource-efficient than large group methods, it can rely heavily upon the facilitative skills of the leader, and a group size of around a dozen is probably large enough to allow optimum interaction.

The didactic and participative approaches outlined above are not, of course, mutually exclusive and some blend of an information-giving approach along with a more participative method may be mutually reinforcing. These traditional approaches in one-to-many learning have relied upon the physical contiguity of learner and facilitator. However, with the advent of high-speed data links, expanded bandwidth and satellite communications, one-to-many interactions may take place at a distance or virtually (i.e. non-contiguously). This type of online interaction will be considered in more detail in our discussion of e-learning below.

Distance learning

There has been much discussion of the terms 'open learning', 'distance learning' and 'flexible learning' in all their various forms (from low technology 'print-based' packages to modern computer-delivered materials and from old-fashioned 'correspondence courses' to ubiquitous e-learning). Keegan (1980) offered the following as distinguishing characteristics of distance learning:

- separation of teacher and learner;
- use of technical media (in its broadest sense from print to computer-based);
- provision for two-way communication.

In a practical context, open learning has been defined in a variety of ways. For example at British Aerospace it is a flexible and efficient alternative to traditional training, allowing employees the option of working at a time, place and pace to suit themselves as well as meeting the needs of the business (Rowe, 1994). Sometimes the terms 'distance' and 'open' are used interchangeably in this context, but they may be seen as separate dimensions of how learning may be delivered. Stewart and Winter (1995) argued that when learning is distant it means that the learner:

- is not continuously and immediately supervised by a teacher or trainer;
- benefits from the support of an institution or organization (for example, in the UK this might be a provider such as the Open University);
- uses a variety of learning media that have been designed in advance and provided by an organization or institution.

On the other hand they argued that open learning aims to offer and provide autonomy, choice and flexibility to the learners in terms of what is learned, how it is learned, when it is learned, where it is learned and how quickly or slowly the learning takes place. Our concern in this section will be with distance learning as a method per se, rather than open learning as a philosophy or general approach.

Distance learning invariably relies on some form of technology to overcome any physical separation which may exist between the learner and the other stakeholders involved in the process (for example, a teacher or tutor, an assessor or examiner). Distance learning relies upon available technology; for example, correspondence education historically has been much vaunted as a way forward in suitable occupational areas such as accounting education because this subject lent itself to being learned 'through the point of a pencil' (Gilman, 1946: 396). The justification offered by Gilman for the use of the most widely available technology of the time, namely pen, paper, print and postage stamp, for written correspondence courses in accounting now sounds like a very familiar mantra that has been repeated many times in the intervening half-century and Gilman's (1946: 400) justifications are not merely of historical relevance:

- 'The student can set his [sic] own pace to harmonize with his own business and personal circumstances'.
- 'Because the cost of its text can be spread out thinly over the student body, the correspondence school can do an elaborate and expensive job of text preparation'.
- 'Provides an excellent balance between accounting study and practice. The student employed in an office does his practical laboratory work by day'.

As better theories of learning became available (for example in Gagne and Briggs's work) the hard technologies and softer technologies (such as instructional design) came together. An example of this is programmed instruction; again in the field of accounting education, Martin (1965: 92); expounded the virtues of programmed learning based upon Skinnerian behaviourist principles:

- the material is broken down into small steps;
- each step is a tiny parcel of information;
- the sequence and presentation are formulated to test whether the information has been successfully learned;
- the student is rewarded if he or she gives the correct answer and clues are given to reduce the probability of a wrong answer.

Again, the benefits are familiar: 'the most careful teacher [in class] invariably misses a step . . . the student is able to review his progress at all stages . . . the instructor can identify which steps the student has not grasped' (1965: 93). Buckley (1967) highlighted similar benefits of programmed instruction: based on learning theory; has explicit objectives; 'bits' of knowledge; active learner role (for example, 'tactile activity'); self-pacing; immediate reinforcement. The programmed learning technique of branching allowed for remediation in response to a specific mistake made by the student, a technique which came into its own with the application of computers to learning and instruction.

Arguably, programmed instruction has not gone away: much of what is considered to be exemplary print-based distance learning material has many of the traditional programmed instruction features built in (for example, clear objectives, small steps, sequencing, interactivity, feedback and remediation). But do programmed texts have any advantage over conventional text books? Fernald and Jordan (1991) looked at this question in the context of an introductory psychology course for students. They found that reading a normal text book and using the programmed text both (thankfully) improved participants' learning; however, the programmed texts were more efficient in that they required less time for the student to learn from them. Programmed instruction also had the additional benefits of encouraging students to be active participants, provision of immediate and continuous evaluation of performance and feedback, and allowing students to learn at different paces (Fernald and Jordan, 1991: 211).

This supported the research findings cited by Goldstein in his review of the field which suggested that programmed instruction groups tend to complete learning more quickly than do groups using traditional methods but that any statistically significant differences in learning in favour of programmed instruction tend to be quite small (effect sizes are often less than 10 per cent) (1993: 241–2). This consideration of impact brings us to a downside of the method: the exceptionally high quality of design and the extensive field pilot testing that is required to iron out any inconsistencies or errors in the content or structure of the materials may mean that the development of company-specific materials requires careful consideration on cost–benefit grounds. Goldstein argues that this is one of the major disadvantages of the approach (1993: 243).

There has been research which has attempted to explore further the relative impact on outcomes of traditional methods, pure distance learning using print material and a more mixed approach using TV programmes, teleconferencing and print materials (distance learning) *in situ*. For example, an Australian study in a higher education context looked at the relative impact of each of these three approaches in undergraduate accounting education. Using a sample of 136 distance learning participants, 329 distance learning partici- pants and 712 on-campus traditional method participants Waldman and de Lange (1996) compared the three groups in terms of assignments and exercises, examination performance and overall performance. As an aside it is worth noting that the study is problematic in that there did not appear to be any controls in the design or the data analysis. That said they found that in terms of overall performance the traditional method participants performed best and the distance learning participants worst (the mean difference being of the order of three and half percentage points between traditional and flexible methods). The drop out rates for distance learning were twice those of the traditional group (nine per cent) and four times greater for open learning (40 per cent). The study whilst interesting is further evidence of the lack of basic research that controls for extraneous variables and hence makes meaningful comparisons *in situ* quite difficult.

Salas, Kosarzycki, Burke, Fiore and Stone (2002) in asking the question 'does distance learning work?' concluded that although return on investment studies had been conducted, every organization must consider its own unique circumstances when deciding on whether or not to invest in distance learning. This can involve the monetary quantification of benefits or the calculation of learning gain ratios. Whilst scientific assessments of impact should and must be pursued, in real-world organizations it is much more likely that evaluations conducted by practitioners and other stakeholders or budget holders will take the form of a subjective judgement of the tangible and intangible benefits in comparison to the monetary and other costs incurred. Salas *et al.* also urged a caution that practitioners should not be caught up in the 'faddish' elements of distance learning and ought to resist embracing high-cost technologies if low-cost approaches are likely to work as well or even better (2002: 149).

Distance learning exists along a spectrum in terms of a number of different dimensions. One way in which it can vary is in terms of the level of instructor support. Take the example of someone intending to visit a foreign country and who wishes to learn a language; the packages that one can pick up in bookshops are perhaps the most extreme form of distance learning: the learner and the author never meet and the physical separation is complete, the cost is low and the learner is completely independent and unsupported. Contrast this with a 'correspondence course' where the physical separation between learner and teacher is still complete: they may be brought closer together through support mechanisms, such as the written word (via print or e-mail) or the spoken word (via telephone conversations).

Distance learning can also vary in terms of the level of collaboration between learners. A collaborativist model of learning would support the view that when learners work together they not only learn themselves but also contribute to the development of other group members (Salas *et al.*, 2002). Learners often report that the most useful aspect of any learning is what they gained (including unexpected things) from other learners. Distance learners are at an immediate disadvantage in this regard given that traditional print-based methods are limited in having had to rely upon postal mail services and occasional tutorials as methods of social interchange and collaboration with other learners. The use of online learning with e-mail and video-conferencing goes some way to addressing some of these issues – see e-learning below.

Whatever the degree of support that is involved, the success of distance learning may depend to a large extent upon how well the materials (print, text, audio and video) are designed given that they are often intended to be used without an instructor immediately to hand, they are relatively inflexible and they are in the public domain (and hence open to scrutiny). The design of a distance learning programme can follow a number of routes: for example, a complete course can be written from scratch, an existing course may need to be converted into a distance learning format (for example, a course may exist but it cannot reach all those who might benefit) or there may be a need to integrate a number of already existing resources into a single coherent package (there may not be any need to 're-invent the wheel'). Rowntree (1990: 39) suggests seven major questions that need to be considered by anyone contemplating designing their own distance learning package:

- Who will be the learners?
- What are the aims and objectives?
- What will be the content?
- How will the content be organized and sequenced?
- What instructional media and methods will be used?
- If the learners are to be assessed how will this take place?
- How will the programme be evaluated?

These questions are typical of a systematic approach to learning design; however, because distance learning materials are, with few exceptions, non-adaptive (they cannot flex and change as learning unfolds) the design of self-instructional materials is a process which requires a great deal of conscientiousness, attention to detail and pilot testing. The theory and practice of instructional design is a field of study in itself and there is an extensive literature on the subject (see for example: Gagne, Briggs and Wager, 1992).

Although distance learning has many advantages, it may not suit the styles or preferences of all learners. Chivers (1999: 269) argued that at its worst it can be an 'inhuman, inflexible, bureaucratic and dreary form of learning provision' and cites this as one reason why very few pure distance learning programmes are used. More often than not it is the human interaction (whether it is with tutors, fellow learners or both) that can be a major factor in maintaining student motivation. This is especially important if one accepts the view that drop-out rates from distance learning programmes may be higher than those of conventional courses (Davis, 1996: 30; Waldman and de Lange, 1996). Technology, and in particular the merging of information and communication technologies, offers great potential for overcoming isolation and promoting person-to-person interaction through networked computer-based learning (see below).

Computer-based learning methods including e-learning

From a historical perspective, as technology moved forward, better 'teaching machines' became available and designs moved from programmed texts to electronic media. For example, magnetic tape for the recording of audio and video was often used to supplement print, and more recently computers and CD storage have been the norm. Indeed, there is a dynamic between the technology and the instructional theory to the extent that developments in technology make more things possible from an instructional design point of view. Moving images, sound and animations of extremely high fidelity are now available, and this makes the choice of what is possible in learning terms much greater. This also creates a new and ongoing research agenda in which the different technologies are tested, validated and evaluated. The specific issue of computer-based learning will be considered in more detail.

Computer-based learning although only one method available for the delivery of distance learning merits separate consideration since it is the technology for which, over many decades, the most potential has been claimed. Rowntree cited the unattributed quip from the 1980s that 'computer-assisted learning is the medium of the future – and it always will be' (1990: 261). The rhetoric and claims appear to have continued unabated over the intervening decade, for example: e-learning will be 'the next killer application for the Internet' which will 'make e-mail look like a rounding error' (Galagan, 2001: 48)! The term 'e-learning' has emerged in recent years and its meaning is ambiguous. We take it to mean the use of information and computing technologies to create a virtual environment for the access to media and resources, facilitation of interaction and collaboration and the provision of support which may enable individual and collective learning to take place. We therefore examine e-learning (as a development of computer-based learning) both in this section of the chapter which is concerned with the individual level, and in the next section of the chapter which is concerned with collective learning methods.

Theoretically at least, a computer should be a powerful medium for learning and instruction. It can present information from a massive memory capacity, in a variety of modes and at a great speed both of information retrieval and processing. Computers may be programmed to guide learners, providing opportunities for practice by responding to learner inputs and dealing with different learning styles in different ways. Computers are also capable of assessing learning, recording progress and providing remediation (Alessi and Trollip, 2001: 7; Rowntree, 1990). Some of the previous disadvantages such as lack of portability, comparatively high cost of PCs and limited disk storage capacity have now all but evaporated. Poor instructional design, for example computer-based learning as boring 'electronic page-turning', is now less of a problem with the advent of hypermedia and increased learner expectations. Its use is undoubtedly growing, but over 40 per cent of respondents to a major survey in the UK reported that they never used intranets or the internet for training, compared with 1 per cent who never used on-job or classroom-based learning (Harrison, 2002: 209). Computer-based learning may be considered to embrace a family of approaches, the application of which should be contingent upon the nature of the learning need. Alessi and Trollip's framework for the design of computer-based learning design identified a number of modes of learning-related applications of computers:

- *Tutorial* (including hypermedia): here the computer takes on a teaching role in presenting information and guiding the learner and providing for learner control, questioning, response judging, feedback and remediation.
- *Hypermedia* (a system for the non-sequential organization, storage and access of information) may serve a tutorial function but is less prescribed in its instructional format (see below for a discussion of web-based learning) and thus allows authors and learners to construct their understandings in a dynamic, flexible, multi-sensory fashion (Alessi and Trollip, 2001).
- *Drill*: this engages learners in practising new knowledge or skill as a means to aiding retention, assimilation of knowledge into long-term memory structures.
- *Games and simulations*: these allow learners to operate freely in exploration mode within a structured environment (see later section).
- *Assessment*: computers can be used in a number of ways, for example in constructing a test (by composing a test from a question bank) and also in administering a test and recording the results (items correct, time taken, wrong answers chosen and so forth).
- *Collation*, *analysis* and *presentation* of test data.

These modes of instruction can be administered across a network or on a stand-alone personal computer; they can be delivered to learners on disk storage or downloaded. In this latter regard Alessi and Trollip also singled out the use of the internet for the purposes of 'web-based' learning as a special case of computer-based learning and argued that it can serve a number of purposes which are in a process of emergence. First, the internet can serve as a delivery medium for learning, enabling a vast number of people to access programmes and information sources. Second, the internet from a learning point of view can serve as a communication medium between teachers and learners and between learners themselves by means of e-mail, 'listservs', bulletin boards, chat rooms and audio- and video-conferencing. They argue that in a learning sense the internet is neutral or 'methodology-free' because it is not a software methodology or an instructional design theory developed explicitly to facilitate learning. Alessi and Trollip consider it more a 'methodology for course delivery or a methodology for developing a learning environment' (2001: 377). This of course does not preclude efforts to develop a theory of instructional design that is based around the internet as a learning method.

Indeed when people talk of e-learning what is often being implied is the integration of different resources and opportunities into an environment which under the right circumstances and with planning may enable effective learning to take place (see our definition above). Alessi and Trollip identified disorientation as one of the potential problems with the internet as a learning environment and urged planners and designers to provide site maps, give printed directions, use bookmarks, provide good orientation cues, use a consistent and memorable navigation system and to not under-estimate the problem of disorientation (2001: 384–5). Potential users should also be wary of the web as a repository of inaccurate information, as a temptation for some learners to plagiarise and as a home for individuals with unsavoury intentions (2001: 398).

As far as the effectiveness of computer-based learning is concerned the literature is large and evolving. We do not propose to give a comprehensive review here, but merely to consider some issues related to its effectiveness. In this way we hope to identify some questions that might be asked by those practitioners who may be considering the use of computer-based methods. We come again to the concepts of self-efficacy and motivation which are recurring themes in our consideration of learning methods. Compeau and Higgins (1995: 189) argued that learners' beliefs about their capability to interact with a given technology are a significant factor in expectations and performance. In a study on the readiness of learners for e-learning in Australia and the United States, Smith, Murphy and Mahoney (2003) showed that ability to self-manage their own learning, and comfort in communicating electronically, were important underlying factors in determining the readiness of any given individual to successfully participate in e-learning. Similarly, learners' motivations, attitudes and predispositions towards technology are likely to play some role in shaping their performance.

The influence of learning style has also been investigated; for example, Ester (1995) found that abstract learners performed better with lectures than computer-based learning, whereas concrete learners performed equally well with lecture and computer-based methods. Other researchers have explored the relationships between other dimensions of learning styles and performance on computer-based learning (for example, Riding and Sadler-Smith, 1992; Riding and Douglas, 1993). The field of style itself embraces a multiplicity of different constructs and measures that often duplicate each other, which can sometimes make the direct practical application of any findings of styles-based research problematic. The findings are sometimes complex (sometimes comprising multiple-way interactions between styles, mode and demographic variables to the extent that they may be virtually uninterpretable) and on balance are largely equivocal in terms of the guidance they provide for designers of computer-based learning. We have identified some of the more salient and applicable general findings in a preceding chapter and will not dwell further on the issue here. In terms of the comparison of computer-based methods with other methods, as was observed in relation to distance learning, where statistically significant findings are observed they tend to be small. For detailed guidelines on the design of computer-based learning we draw attention to the extensive and authoritative text produced by Alessi and Trollip (2001).

In addition to the features of instructional design for computer-based learning and the relative effectiveness of it as a method, the broader implementation, structural and organizational issues are also important. In the UK it was estimated that in 2001, 28 per cent of organizations with an intranet currently used it for the delivery of training, but this was estimated to double within only a few years (Beamish, Armistead, Watkinson and Armfield, 2002), although recent work in the United States (Zemsky and Massy, 2004) warns that these sorts of predictions are hard to make, and have generally been overly optimistic. Whatever the accurate picture is there can be little doubt that the pressures on managers, HR practitioners and learners to make effective use of computers, the internet and intranets for learning are likely to increase simply because the resource now exists in most workplaces and in many homes. There are work design, structural and cultural issues in organizations that need to be considered if the inevitable increase in the use of computers for learning is to make a real impact on performance.

Some of these issues have been explored in the UK by Sloman (2003). His research identified six areas that appear to be important determinants of success (strategic intent, system implementation, blending of methods, learning content, support and motivation, and measurement and monitoring). For example, in his project the introduction of computer-based methods was seen by some organizations as a means to standardise the delivery of learning and of securing efficiency gains. Some organizations appeared to work from the assumption that computer-based methods need to be assimilated alongside traditional methods; others saw it as an 'either/or' question and prefer to 'migrate to e-learning wherever possible' (2003: 33). The migration to computer delivery may be an attractive option against a backcloth of training provision that may appear fragmented; but learning by its very nature meets diverse needs, relies on a multitude of different methods for its effective delivery and needs to be tailored to specific individual circumstances and organizational contexts. Any argument for standardisation whereby all learning is delivered by means of computers is unlikely to meet the needs, preferences and styles of the learners (since the computer as a medium is quite unsuited to many aspects of human learning), may ignore the socio-cultural aspects of learning and miss out in addressing the real learning needs of the organization.

Sloman's research also highlighted the perceived limitations of generic content (an issue that has dogged distance and open learning in general). Some organizations have responded to this in the same way that a number of large organizations in the UK did in the 1980s and 1990s to distance learning by producing their own customised web-based materials. Learner motivation and support infrastructure came out in Sloman's findings as being amongst the factors that have the greatest influence upon the effective implementation of computer-based methods. The concept of 'protected learning time' is vaunted as a solution to the conflict between learning and down-time, but is seen as being problematical to implement when operational pressures may take priority in busy workplaces. Sloman summarised the overall finding of his project thus: the use of computers in learning was seen as important (even 'pivotal' in some cases), with no indications of any withdrawal from its use and emerging evidence of cost benefits. The key success factors of learner motivation, support and line manager commitment (Sloman 2003: 34) are very similar to the factors that need to be put in place for learning in the workplace in general.

These findings are echoed by the study of e-learning in ten major UK corporations (including companies such as BP Amoco, British Airways and Ford) by Beamish *et al.* (2002). Their study found that these major organizations had faith in and commitment to e-learning and predicted increases in its usage as a response to the learning needs of employees in a rapidly changing business environment. However, like the Sloman research Beamish *et al.* found that the end-user factors as much as the technological aspects are key issues in determining the success or otherwise of these initiatives. They highlighted prior use of computers, motivation of learners to engage with the medium, optimising the level of support for learners and maximising employees' external access to resources without compromising security requirements as key issues. They also singled out the management and industrial relations aspects of the introduction of e-learning, and mooted the possibility of the engagement of labour organizations in learning partnerships as a way of initiating positive change.

Interestingly in the Beamish *et al.* study in the UK 'none of the organizations could provide a comprehensive way of measuring the outcomes of e-learning and relating those back to strategic targets' (2002: 114). Bersin (2002) suggested that there are five basic criteria for evaluation: enrolments and usage of the resource; active participation in the programmes; the extent to which programmes are completed; the learning performance of participants;

the reactions of learners to the programme (assumed to be predictive of whether or not they will come back for more). This requires a system of monitoring, assessment and evaluation which needs to be built into programmes and budgets from the outset, rather than, as is sometimes the case, being left as an afterthought. However, a perennial problem in training evaluation emerges: Reddy (2002: 31) pointed out the difficulties of looking for bottom line results from e-learning because, like any aspect of learning, these initiatives do not exist in a vacuum and there may be a separation both temporally (there may be time lag), functionally and spatially between an e-learning initiative and its impact upon organizational performance. Reddy makes a distinction between return on investment (ROI) models for evaluation and cost–benefit analysis (CBA) models thus:

$$ROI = \$ \text{ value of benefits} \div \$ \text{ value of costs} \tag{1}$$

$$CBA: \Sigma(\text{Benefit}_1 + \text{Benefit}_2 + \text{Benefit}_3 + ... \text{Benefit}_n) \geq \text{Costs?} \tag{2}$$

Rather than focus on a hard ROI model (1), Reddy argued for a cost–benefit analysis (CBA) approach (2) which sums the benefits (not necessarily in monetary terms) and compares this to the costs. This approach allows flexibility in the identification of those benefits that may not readily translate into monetary values (for example, increased quality, fewer customer complaints, etc.). At the end of the day when using a CBA approach a judgement has to be called as to whether the sum of the benefits, many of which will be intangible, was worth the hard investment of financial and other resources.

E-learning is broader than stand-alone (i.e. non-networked) computer-based learning; it takes some of the principles of computer-based learning as identified by Alessi and Trollip and allies them to the features and possibilities made available by the internet or web-based learning. Hence, it goes beyond tutorial, drill, simulation and assessment. It also goes beyond computer-mediated communication and online tutorials or supported online learning. The advances in computing and communication technologies that have made the above possible also make feasible the development of communities of learners who are connected and are able to share knowledge and skills and actively construct knowledge only because of the technology that we refer to as e-learning. Hence, it encompasses at least two things over and above computer-based learning (Sloman and Reynolds, 2003: 261):

- *E-learning community*: an individual is part of a recognised group of learners who may have similar needs, may be pursuing the same educational qualification and so forth;
- *Informal e-learning*: the learner employs computing technology to communicate with and learn from individuals within and across organizational, geographical and temporal boundaries.

Groupware systems are available which are dedicated to providing online discussion capability which can be conducted between members of learning groups either synchronously or asynchronously. Asynchronous discussion can be a very powerful learning tool, especially where the learners are separated in time through working different shifts, or where the learning group crosses time zones.

Wenger (2000) argued that just because communities of practice arise naturally it does not mean that organizations cannot do anything to influence their development. In his view to nurture a community of practice requires attention in a number of areas; we argue that the proposals that Wenger offers may also be applied to e-learning communities also. The first of these is knowledge strategy: the organization must have a clear sense of how knowledge and learning are linked to business strategy and the means by which this knowledge is created and shared within this strategic context within and between communities. There may also be a role for e-learning communities in a bottom-up approach whereby the communities themselves and the knowledge they create shape the strategic direction of the organization. E-learning may be a way in which vertical boundaries within the organization may be upwardly permeated. The second factor that Wenger identified was organizational orientation to knowledge and learning. This may mean senior managers and executives supporting e-learning communities by recognising, endorsing and supporting them. In more general terms Wenger argued that merely introducing and articulating the term 'community of practice' can have a positive effect. Perhaps the explicit introduction of the term 'e-learning community' may have positive effects also. Thirdly, Wenger feels that is important that the organization advertently encourages participation and tuning organizational systems, such as performance reviews, so that they 'honor the work of [e-]community building and do not build unnecessary barriers' (2000: 222). E-learning may represent one resource which may assist community members not only in engaging in exchanges locally but also in extending the realm of their participation to the geographical boundaries of the organization and beyond. E-learning may be a cost-effective and efficient way of spreading knowledge and learning across the organization.

One example of e-learning-as-collective-learning and an attempt at creating an e-community of practice is the knowledge-sharing system developed at Shell International Exploration and Production (SIEP). SIEP (part of Royal Dutch Shell) has 30,000 employees but because of the nature of the business they are dispersed across the globe, often in remote and inaccessible locations and sometimes offshore. This creates obvious difficulties for the sharing of information and transferring of new knowledge between employees who may be thousands of kilometres apart and in different time zones but may work in similar fields (such as petroleum well engineering). SEIP developed a knowledge-sharing intranet based on a system called 'Site Scape Forum' which formed a global network of electronic discussion groups. These e-groups provide a forum for asking questions and providing answers. Questions are posted to a 'high traffic' area and, once posted, a question usually generates between three and four responses in the first 24 hours. After 30 days the questions and the answers are archived to create a knowledge base that users are encouraged to search before posing a question as there is a good chance that the problem may already have been posed and solved. Most SIEP employees spend between one and two hours per week on the forum. Examples of the problems solved on the forum include the results of experimental horizontal drilling techniques posted and shared to promote best practice across the division. SIEP's aim was to produce electronic 'communities of practice' in which employees would be motivated to participate by the intrinsic interest that these professionals had in their own discipline and inquisitiveness about related disciplines. In total there are estimated to be about 15,000 users of the forum. The principle of creating electronic communities of practice is an exciting and interesting dimension to e-learning as a collective learning medium (http://www.sitescape.com/next/test_shell. html).

Research conducted with learners in several organizations in Australia (Stacey, Smith and Barty, 2004) has shown that electronic communities of learning can be connected closely to the learner's workplace community of practice such that participation in both of these communities of learning is enhanced through the leveraging of knowledge derived in the one to knowledge being applied and further developed in the other. We should, however, recognise that by making information more widely available e-learning creates wider, more complex and more diversified communities of meaning (Wenger, 1998: 132). E-learning is one means of leveraging the value of socially constructed knowledge and collective meaning to the benefit of individuals and organizations. It raises broader issues in relation to the role of computers in knowledge management and leveraging collective expertise to enhance performance. In their analysis of research gaps in the field of collaborative learning, Smith and Stacey (2003) identified this field as one in need of considerably more exploration. The debates are doubly important since they also ask questions of how training and development and knowledge management relate to each other in order that the acquisition of individual skills (through formal and informal learning experiences) feed into and are fed by the accumulated knowledge of the organization.

Games, role play and simulations

Games, role play and simulations provide an environment in which learners can acquire and practise skills in decision making, communication, interpersonal behaviours, problem solving and so forth in circumstances in which the risk to themselves, workplace tools, other people and equipment is minimised. Simulations can also provide a learning environment that is structured in order that specific knowledge and skills may be developed which might be difficult to isolate, practise or test in a real-world situation. Learners can test and experiment with behaviours that they might not be prepared to or allowed to engage in the workplace and get immediate and unambiguous feedback (Doyle and Brown, 2000: 331). Alessi and Trollip (2001) define a simulation as containing some internal model of a phenomenon or activity (a sometimes simplified representation of reality) that users learn about through interaction with the simulation. The point about simplification is an important one. As Alessi and Trollip note, the aim is to help learners construct their own mental model of a phenomenon and explore, practise and test its features, and this is best achieved when the simulation simplifies reality (2001: 214). That said, simulations may add instructional features such as cues and feedback not found in the real world.

'Micro-worlds' are variations on the simulation theme and are often described as 'flight simulators' for management. They have been implemented in a number of university business schools around the world, for example at the Massachusetts Institute of Technology and the London Business School. A micro-world simuworld (Keys, Fulmer and Stumpf, 1996), business simulator or learning laboratory is any simulation in which people can participate by running experiments, testing different strategies, and building better understanding of the world as depicted in the simulation (Romme, 2003). Such simulators are often computer-based; players may take on a particular role, can ask for information, vary parameters, observe trends, see results and engage in behaviour that is experimental and playful, asking 'What if?' questions in pursuit of a specific goal. We treat them here as a special form of computer-based learning (see Alessi and Trollip's distinction between different modes of computer-based learning (2001)) that create a rehearsal space or practice fields for learning (Keys *et al.*, 1996). Romme also identifies another pedagogical function that such micro-worlds can serve – that of facilitating deep learning for understanding as opposed to surface learning for the mere acquisition of facts and information. In his article Romme went on to describe the evaluation of the application of micro-worlds in a university course on organization and management in the Netherlands. His summary of their effect was that learning processes can be both deepened and accelerated by the use of micro-worlds (2003: 58). Deep learning may also enable managers to sense faint signals or patterns that may otherwise be overlooked without the opportunity and freedom to experiment.

Doyle and Brown (2000) advised those considering the use of simulations to ensure that there is sufficient technical support to ensure the technology works throughout the learning process, to have a game administrator to compile data, progress and decisions and disseminate results, and to pilot-test the game prior to full implementation. Alessi and Trollip offer a staged methodology for simulation development: (a) learn and analyse the phenomenon; (b) decide which factors to include in the simulation; (c) create the model; (d) transfer the model into the software; (e) develop the user interface; (f) develop learning supports in the software (2001: 260). The design of computer-based simulations for learning is a complex task in terms of the expertise needed to create a robust model, in terms of the technical expertise required to transfer the model into the software and the instructional expertise needed in creating a learning environment around the combination of the model and the software. Extensive system testing and piloting is usually required. Invariably it is the case that a team approach is needed to the design and development, with subject matter experts, programmers and instructional designers all bringing their own contribution.

Not all games and simulations have to be technology-based. Woodall and Winstanley (1998) outline four main categories of management games for learning:

- business games in which participants focus on decision-making in areas such as business strategy and so forth (as are often found in university management school courses);
- board games which are a low-tech form of simulation;
- structured experiences which aim to focus attention on transactions between individuals in the group. Content is less important than process and examples include building a paper tower (1998: 176) and team-based games such as 'lost at sea';
- role plays which aim to bridge the cognitive, affective and behavioural skills by allowing participants to take on roles and associated feelings and act them out.

Role plays are often used in management development and people-related HRD for the purposes of interpersonal skill development. The usual format is that the role players act out the characters assigned to them in a scenario. The technique is based on the assumption that active experience, human modelling (either real or video-presented) and practice are better than passive methods for the learning of conflict management, negotiation, active listening, giving and receiving feedback and so forth (Gist and McDonald-Mann, 2000). Such approaches can help participants experience, in a safe simulated environment, their emotions and potential reactions that may surface in a real-life scenario where interpersonal issues are involved (such as disciplinary, appraisal and selection interviewing) (Woodall and Winstanley, 1998: 173–5)

The 'beer game' is a well-known example of a management game; it was developed at MIT in the 1960s as a model of a production distribution system for a brand of beer with three main characters in the game: retailer, wholesaler and marketing director. The details of the game are discussed in Senge (1990), but as with many simulations the aim is for the laboratory replica of a real-world setting to enable the learning 'disabilities and their causes' to be isolated more easily than is possible in the real-world (1990: 27). Senge described the deepest insight from the game as the understandings developed by the players of their own thinking processes and the way individuals often fail to learn from their experiences because the important consequences of their actions occur elsewhere in the system. Although we have included the use of simulations such as the beer game in this section on individual learning, the learning process involved is a collective one which helps groups to surface and share mental models and hence facilitates organizational learning. Games such as this may be one means by which individuals can develop insights into their own cognitive processes.

Action-based approaches

Action-based approaches are based upon the principles of the surfacing, sharing and collective reflection upon our own and others' understandings and actions and the impact of the reflective process upon our subsequent actions. Reflection can also be an individual process. However, in the context of the action-based methods such as action science and action learning, it is generally seen as collective reflection-upon-action. Two similar action-based approaches will be examined: the action science model of Chris Argyris and Donald Schön (1996) in the USA, and the action learning approach of Reg Revans (1982, 1983) in the UK. Both models are concerned with how to understand and narrow the gap between managers' thoughts and their actions.

The conception of learning that underpins the action-based approaches is somewhat different from that found in instructional design and in education and training. For example, in Argyris and Schön's work it goes beyond problem solving and experiential learning and into the realm of questioning how the problem is defined, why it is defined in a particular way. On a practical level it concerns itself with the ways in which managers may screen out certain information in an attempt to control their environment through what may often turn out to be defensive routines (Woodall and Winstanley, 1998: 155). In Revans's work the argument is put forward that managers should be more concerned with the asking of insightful questions rather than searching for pre-programmed knowledge or pre-programmed solutions to a problem.

The basis of action science is that learning occurs when errors are detected and corrected. Argyris distinguishes two types of learning: single-loop learning occurs when errors are detected and corrected without altering the underlying governing values or assumptions that govern action (the actions change but the assumptions do not). Double-loop learning on the other hand occurs when errors are detected and corrected by changing the governing values or assumptions and then the actions (Argyris, 2002). The analogy that Argyris offers is that of a room thermostat which exhibits single-loop learning if it merely turns on the heat when the room is cold, and turns off the heat when the room is hot. Double-loop learning in this analogy might be when the thermostat asks why it is programmed to measure and respond to temperature.

The formal method of action science is a body of theory and research for exploring the reasoning that underlies our actions. This involves inward

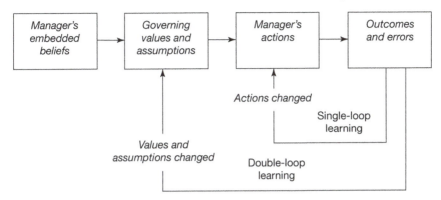

Figure 6.1 The processes of learning within an action science framework (adapted from Argyris and Schon, 1996)

reflection and analysis about the way in which problems are defined and our: (i) espoused theories, these are the personal assumptions that a manager will subscribe to and claim that they use; and (ii) theories-in-use, which are the assumptions and beliefs that are used to guide action but which managers are very often not aware of but can be inferred from behaviour. Managers may trap themselves in defensive routines that insulate their mental models from critical examination with the result that a skilled incompetence is developed and used to shield managers from the 'pain and threat posed by learning situations', but in doing so they also protect themselves from getting the results that they want to achieve (Senge, 1990: 182). Many managers espouse double-loop learning but are unable to produce it and moreover are blind to their incompetence and, even worse, are unaware that they are blind in this regard (Argyris, 2002: 206). The practice of action science in the hands of a skilled facilitator draws out the subtle and potentially erroneous assumptions and patterns of reasoning that underlie behaviours. The individual learning which occurs in this way may serve as the basis for organizational learning and transformation. Argyris also makes a distinction between Model I theory-in-use and Model II theory-in-use. In Model I the governing variables are to be in control, to be rational and to maximise winning; the action strategies are: advocate a position that enables you to be in control, appear to be rational and win; the consequences of this are: miscommunication, self-fulfilling prophecies, self-sealing processes and escalating error. Individuals behave with a skilled incompetence that produces unilateral control (Argyris, 2002: 213). Contrast this with Model II theory-in-use: the governing variables are to have valid information, make free and informed choices and be committed to the choice; the action strategies are: advocate a position but combine it with enquiry and public testing; the consequences are: reduced self-fulfilling, self-sealing and error-escalating processes and improved problem solving and learning (Argyris, 2002: 214). A Model II learning system (Argyris and Schön, 1996) is one in which organizational defensive routines are cut through and instead organizational learning processes are created that may lead to double-loop learning.

A different approach to a similar issue was developed by Reg Revans in the UK in the 1960s. He called his method 'action learning' and based it on the argument that in a turbulent, fast-moving and uncertain business environment the rate of learning must exceed the rate of change if an organization is to stay ahead and remain competitive and effective. He expressed some of the principles of action learning as two 'equations':

$$L \geq C, \tag{1}$$

$$L = p + Q, \tag{2}$$

where L = rate of learning, C = rate of change, p = pre-programmed learning, Q = the ability to ask insightful questions. Revans argued that managers need a small amount of p in comparison to the large amount of Q they needed. Action learning relies on facilitating enquiry that enables managers to ask insightful questions (content) and also to develop the ability or skill to ask insightful questions (process). The ability to ask insightful questions may be blocked by idealising solutions that worked in the past, being charmed by the charisma of other managers, acting impulsively rather than reflectively (Revans, 1982, 1983). The process of action learning is organized on the basis of groups of learners known as 'action learning sets'. A set usually comprises between six and ten participants and is facilitated in its content and process issues by a skilled set adviser. The content of the learning is a live project (usually a complex organizational problem that cannot be answered using p) that each individual participant is engaged with.

Informal and incidental workplace learning

Whilst all of the above methods are applicable in those situations where it is planned that learning should take place, learning is a naturalistic process that can happen in involuntary, unexpected, surprising and disconcerting ways. Learning is as much an informal and unplanned process as it is a planned process, and indeed many planned learning events turn out to have unplanned consequences. The focus of this section will be on how some of these unplanned happenings may be managed more effectively by the various stakeholders (for example, those with the responsibility for managing learning and the learners themselves). Some might argue that 'planning' and 'learning' is an oxymoron (see, for example, Weick and Westley, 1999). Our view is that like many involuntary processes unplanned learning can be left to be 'un-managed' but this leaves much to chance, and we prefer to offer some suggestions (in addition to those already discussed) about how unplanned learning might be maximised for the benefit of individuals and the institutions or organizations of which they are a part. In this regard Mumford (1995) argued that there are a number of ways that managers can learn from experiences:

- The first of these is intuitively, where the learning is not conscious and it is difficult to articulate but nevertheless managers feel that they are learning something (but what it is they are not quite able to say).
- The second way is through an incidental approach of learning by chance or accident when things don't go to plan or something surprising or unusual happens and which causes a jolt and makes managers take notice, absorb and reflect. In the retrospective approach managers consciously reflect on an event and draw conclusions from it. The process of review in a more or less structured form is a key to the effectiveness of the retrospective approach.
- The final approach Mumford identified is one he terms 'the prospective approach': here a manager will approach an informal learning opportunity with the direct intention of learning from it. This often involves a conscious planning process in which the opportunities are anticipated and planned for ahead of time.

Dobbs (2000) described a number of organizations where managers had taken deliberate steps to promote informal learning. For example, in a manufacturing company the way work was designed militated against learning; employees rotated between jobs every few hours but never saw a job through from start to finish and hence were unable to see how the process as a whole functioned and how they contributed to this. In order to facilitate informal learning the company moved its customer service department down to the shopfloor and introduced 10-minute overlaps between shifts so that employees had the chance to mingle with people from other shifts and other departments. When these conversations veer towards work, as they inevitably do, 'simple moments of learning' take place (Dobbs, 2000). This contrasts with the perceptions of some managers that such congregations are unproductive and need to be guarded against as a waste of valuable work time.

The physical layout of the workspace can be as important as job design: Dobbs cited the example of Xerox Business Services condensing office space to make room for an open gathering area where a lingering coffee break could take place and where the chat turns to work because that is the thing employees have in common to talk about. Cross (2003) also made some suggestions for how the informal and natural learning processes might be facilitated: for example, provide time and space for informal sharing, encourage cross-functional gatherings, use coaches, informal mentors and experts, teach employees how to learn, and set up a budget to support informal learning. Indeed it should not be seen as 'cheap' or a 'quick-fix' since it may take some time and resource to plan for and implement and support with the necessary physical and work re-design necessary.

Focus on practice: narrowing the gap between HRD rhetoric and reality

In this section we have drawn extensively on previous work of our own (Sadler-Smith, Down and Lean, 2000; Smith, 2002), where we examined the realities and the rhetoric surrounding discussions on 'modern' training methods. The research by Sadler-Smith *et al.* set out to explore if a gap existed between the rhetoric that has surrounded 'modern' learning methods (such as distance learning) and actual practice in organizations. They surveyed 235 firms in the UK across a range of sizes and sectors and asked questions related to the perceived frequency of use and perceived usefulness of eight training and development methods (off-site courses, on-site courses, at-job learning, video, distance learning, computer-based learning, work shadowing, job rotation). As expected there was a correlation between frequency and effectiveness, and no firms were frequent users of ineffective methods (encouragingly). The methods formed eight subjectively determined clusters ranked as follows in terms of frequency and effectiveness: (a) at-job methods; (b) taught courses (on site and off site); (c) computer- and work-based (job rotation, work shadowing and computer-based learning); (d) distance learning and video.

The general picture that emerged from their data was that at-job methods were widely used and considered to be effective while distance learning was less widely used and considered to be less effective irrespective of firm size. The implication that they drew from this is that at-job learning needs to be fully incorporated into HRD pedagogy and subjected to the same level of attention as technology-based methods. One means to this end is by developing a coherent and integrated model of work-based learning that draws upon the action learning, experiential learning and reflective enquiry-based methods (amongst others). This is especially important given the widely held view that learning is socially constructed in the work environment through engagement with real problems in real time. Given the nature of human learning the use of virtual realities is unlikely to supplant this.

Smith (2002) described evidence from Australia that supported some of the views presented by Sadler-Smith *et al.* For example, out of 542 vocational learners surveyed over four-fifths chose face-to-face methods of delivery as the overall preferred method of learning. Other research in Australia supports the assertion that self-directed learning is not generally favoured. These findings, however, should not be taken as an indication that distance learning may not be used within a framework of flexible delivery. Such techniques do need to be integrated into a wider mosaic (what has come to be known as a 'blend') of learning delivery methods and in conjunction with at-job methods such as practice, demonstration, coaching and mentoring. Where distance learning methods are used without support they are likely to be unsuccessful and firms need to develop the policies, structures and systems to support learning in the workplace (Smith, 2002: 110–11).

Identifying diversity in learning methods: questions for situational analysis

Many of the learning needs in modern organizations go beyond simple training solutions involving the acquisition of bodies of knowledge and particular sets of skills. Traditional training can be ineffective and inefficient because it may not be delivered at the right time, it may not be relevant to employees' needs and the conditions may not be in place for it to be applied in the workplace. Against this backcloth we have argued that conventional training cannot cater for the diversity that exists in terms of needs, contexts, learners and desired outcomes. Hence the methods that practitioners must bring to bear upon those needs also should be similarly diverse. To this end we have avoided simply considering different approaches and media (lecture, tutorial, audio, print, video and so forth, although these do figure in our discussions) and instead we have chosen to focus on a spectrum of learning methods which may add value to organizations for planned and unplanned learning, for formal and informal learning and for learning that is concerned as much with process as it is with content.

In an overall or general sense there are no right answers or best methods, and the appropriate answer and 'best' method for a particular problem or context comes through an informed questioning regarding the aims, objectives, content and process of learning. What the practitioner may arrive at is a solution to a need, or set of interrelated needs, that involves the skilled combining of a range of methods. This approach is increasingly being referred to as a blending of the right 'ingredients' to make the most appropriate 'mix' for the identified learning need. It is to the issue of this process of blending that we turn our attention in the next chapter. Below we offer some questions about each of the learning methods we have discussed. The questions are designed to enable you to examine each method with regard to its suitability of use in an organizational setting.

What is the target group?

Are the learners to be involved in the HRD you are planning likely to profit most from a one-to-many method, a one-to-one method, or a combination of both? What makes you think that? Which approach best suits their work context? Is there an expectation that learners will share their learning with others in their workplace? How will you know that the shared learning is occurring in a systematic and useful way?

What is the purpose of the learning?

Does the learning relate to specific tasks that need to be demonstrated and practised? Is the learning very task-focused or is there a career-development intention as well? Are there colleagues available with the expert knowledge to fulfil a coaching or mentoring role? Are the relationships between people well enough established to support a coaching or mentoring approach? Is the time available for learners and mentors/coaches to engage in that form of learning?

What resources are available?

Are space and teaching resources available to support a one-to-many approach? Are there sufficient learners available at the same time to ensure efficiency in a one-to-many approach? Should the one-to-many approach be commonly located in a training room or distributed across locations and technologically mediated? Are there hardware, software and other learning resources available to support an e-learning approach? Are the learners sufficiently prepared to be able to engage with e-learning in a meaningful and profitable way? Are their instructors available to support an e-learning approach? Can games and simulations be used to support the learning? How could action learning be useful? Are participants and their managers receptive to an action learning approach?

Performance coaching

Questions that may be useful to ask when considering performance coaching as a method include:

- Is the task narrow, definable and comparatively simple?
- Are experienced, skilled and motivated coaches available who have the necessary interpersonal communication skills and personal qualities?
- Does the culture of the work group encourage and support the sharing of knowledge and skills?
- Is the organization willing to devote appropriate resources (for example, down time will most probably be incurred) to the process?
- How receptive is the learner to this form of instruction?
- How will the learner and the coach relate to each other, and does the coach have a stake in the learner's performance in the longer term?
- Are there any 'take-aways' available or that could be produced to support learning after the direct coaching has ended?
- How will you know if the performance coaching has been successful?

Developmental coaching

Questions that may be useful to ask when considering developmental coaching as a method include:

- Is the overall purpose as coaching clearly understood by all parties? Have the boundaries between *coaching* and counselling been anticipated and recognised?

- Is there a contingency plan and the commitment to deal with those matters that may go beyond the remit of the coaching and the competence of the coach and into other professional domains (for example, counselling)?
- Have the individuals got a clear career development plan? (This does not necessarily preclude the use of developmental coaching but it means the starting point will be further back.)
- Are the objectives for the coaching definable in reasonably precise terms?
- Who are to be the coaches? Will it be more appropriate to use internal or external coaches? What are their qualifications and experience?
- Does the coach have the necessary interpersonal skills and expertise to be credible in the eyes of the learner?
- Are the resources available (for example, finance, space, time and so forth)? Can the organization commit to the time needed away from the job for the coaching process?
- Is the organization prepared to face the issues that may arise?
- How will you know if the developmental coaching has been successful?

Mentoring

Questions that may be useful to ask when considering mentoring as a method include:

- Are there individuals of suitable levels of experience, expertise, commitment, motivation and self-efficacy available to fill the mentor role?
- Will the mentoring process be formal or informal?
- What will be the focus of the mentoring system?
- How will it fit with other more formal procedures such as performance appraisal?
- How will the quality of the mentor–protégé relationship be monitored (if this is necessary)?
- Are there systems and processes in place to terminate the mentoring arrangement if it appears to be being unsuccessful or counterproductive?
- Are there likely to be any personal barriers (e.g. bad past experiences, negative attitudes), organizational barriers (e.g. culture, resource constraints, threat to management control) or process barriers (e.g. conflict and frustration) to mentoring (Maclennan, 1995)?
- How will you know if the mentoring has been successful?

One-to-many methods

Questions that may be useful to ask when considering one-to-many methods include:

- What is the nature of the learning objective(s)? Can they be achieved in a large-group setting or does it require a more participative approach?

- What is the nature of the group and can they be reached by other means such as distance learning, e-learning and so forth?
- Are the facilities and resources available to enable large-group learning? What are the costs? Are there operational (for example, down-time) implications?
- Does the learning require participative approaches? Can it be achieved in any other way?
- Who are the teachers? Do they possess the necessary skills to present to large groups or facilitate smaller-group learning? What are their preferences?
- What are the preferences of the learners likely to be? Can they be accommodated?
- How will the learning transfer from the non-work setting to the workplace? Will the support be there? Have managers bought into the learning?
- How will you know if the one-to-many method has been successful?

Distance learning

Questions that may be useful to ask when considering distance learning include:

- What are the objectives and can they met by other means?
- What type of instructional design will meet the objectives?
- Why is distance learning being used? Will it be educationally effective and economically cost-effective?
- Do materials already exist or will they have to be designed from scratch?
- How will the necessary resources be acquired?
- Do the organizational infrastructure and culture support the use of distance learning? What will be the reactions of other HRD practitioners?
- Who are the learners? Do they have the learning skills, the motivation, and the self-efficacy to undertake a distance learning programme?
- What level of support will be required by the learners and how will this be provided?
- Do those responsible for the support of learners have the necessary skills, knowledge and resources?
- How will the effectiveness and smooth operation of the programme be monitored?
- How can the learning be transferred and applied in the workplace?
- How will you know if the distance learning programme has been effective?

Computer-based methods and e-learning

Questions that may be useful to ask when considering e-learning in its networked and non-networked forms include:

- Do the learning objectives require the use of computer-based learning? Could the objectives be achieved just as effectively by other means?
- Do computer-based learning materials exist that will meet the learning need? Is there some requirement to develop bespoke materials?
- Is the mode appropriate to the objectives; is the package more than just electronic page-turning? What value do computers add to the learning?
- Who are the learners? What is their experience of computers, what is their motivation to learn from computers? Will they need any support or IT skills training as a preliminary?
- What equipment will be used to deliver the learning? Will it be desk machines or dedicated PCs for e-learning? Will there be an IT support infrastructure to deal with any problems?
- How will the learners access the materials? Will it be in work time, their own time or in protected time for learning?
- Who will support the learners? How will their progress be monitored? Will the learners be assessed? Will the assessment be by means of computer? For what purposes will the learners be assessed; to what use will the scores be put?
- How will the learning be monitored and evaluated? To what purposes will the evaluation data be put?
- How will you know if the computer-based learning has been successful?

Simulations, role plays and games

Questions that may be useful to ask when considering simulations and games include:

- What is the nature of the skills that need to be developed? Are they cognitive, affective, psychomotor or behavioural?
- Do they require practice, experience, experimentation and play?
- Are suitable games already available? What will the learners' reactions be; will all learners react in the same way or will it conflict with the styles and preferences of some? Can the facilitators handle the motivation and group dynamics? How might these issues be addressed?
- Do they require a high-technology solution? For example do the learning objectives require individuals to master complex cognitive and psychomotor skills in a safe environment?
- Can the relevant organizational system or process be modelled? Is the software available that will enable the model to be created? Does the organization have the hardware to deliver the model to end-users?

- Is the ability to experiment and play an important part of the learning strategy? How important is fidelity in the simulation?
- Are the resources, infrastructure, end-user skills available to enable this to happen? What expert and tutorial support will be available to learners?
- How will you know if the games or simulations have been successful?

Action-based methods

Questions that may be useful to ask when considering action-based methods include:

- How resistant are participants to learning?
- Are participants ready for double-loop learning?
- Do participants expect pre-programmed knowledge in preference to the skills of questioning and enquiry?
- How willing are participants to learn new skills of enquiry and to question and confront their assumptions?
- Are senior managers and the organization willing to face up to and listen to negative messages?
- Are skills and resources available to facilitate and support the processes involved?

Informal and incidental workplace learning

Questions that may be useful to ask when considering how to maximise the benefits from informal and unplanned learning include:

- How is learning perceived in your organization? Does 'learning' equate to 'training'?
- Who 'owns' learning? Who are the stakeholders?
- Do HR practitioners, learners and managers see working as learning and learning as working?
- What processes are in place which might enable interchanges to take place that could enhance individual and collective learning?
- To what extent could these processes be managed in your organization?
- Do the culture, work design and physical layout of the organization create opportunities for learning?
- To what extent is technology being harnessed to capture knowledge?
- How will you know if unplanned learning is taking place? How will you know if it is adding value?

7 Diversities in learning supports

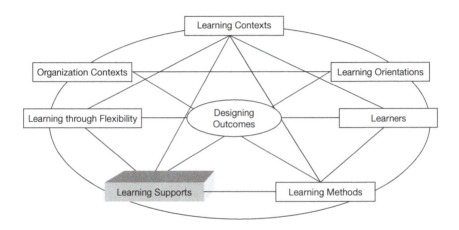

Introduction

Supporting learners is widely recognised in the education, training and HRD literature as an important means of maximising the effectiveness of learning (Blanchard and Thacker, 2004; Collis, 1996; Laurillard, 2002). The assumption even that a large minority of adult learners are likely to be wholly self-directed and autonomous is a fallacious one. Garrison (1995: 138), in the context of resource-based learning, argued strongly for the need for learner support when he cautioned against a 'naïve constructivism', where educators and trainers have a 'blind faith in the ability of students to construct meaningful knowledge on their own' in circumstances where the resources are provided to learners, but no further assistance is given to them in the use of those resources. The work of Vygotsky (first published many decades after his death, see for example Vygotsky 1978) is often used to invoke the concept of a 'zone of proximal development' which embodies the notion that for learning to be fully optimised there needs to be timely and appropriate intervention and instruction, dialogue, interaction with and support from another person. In the zone of interaction between a novice and an expert, the learner can participate in performance at a higher level of complexity than he or she could achieve alone (Borthick, Jones and Wakai, 2003). The activity in the zone is focused not on the transfer of skills to the learner but on collaboration between an expert and the learner that enables the development of understanding of the complexity of the system or activity (Borthick *et al.*, 2003: 111). Such an approach is likely to involve instruction, study, collaboration, practice, feedback, questioning and coaching through assistance from the expert via modelling, providing cognitive scaffolding, encouragement and a fostering of self-awareness and self-efficacy. 'Scaffolding' is a term used to refer to devices or strategies to support learners (Rosenshine and Meister, 1992). The function of a scaffold is to initially provide the support to enable a learner to achieve a goal not achievable without the support, and because excessive support can hinder learning the scaffold should be withdrawn (faded) until it is no longer needed (van Merriënboer, Kirschner and Kester, 2003).

The concept of constructivism is important here in its observation that learning is not achieved through learners merely passively receiving knowledge, but that knowledge and the meaning of that knowledge is actively socially and culturally constructed in collaboration with others. McLoughlin (2002: 150) provided a set of guidelines for designing constructivist learning that included: enhancing learners' understanding of the knowledge construction process; creating learning tasks that are relevant and authentic to the individual; encouragement of ownership and a say in the learning process; situating the learning in social experiences and the social context of practice and encouraging multiple ways of representing knowledge. McLoughlin pointed to the importance of 'scaffolding' in a constructivist approach to learning. Scaffolding aims to enable a learner to engage the use of skills or knowledge already developed, and to extend that learning through guided practice provided by a mentor or trainer who assists the learner to further develop (Billett, 2001). 'Fading' refers to the practice of removing the scaffolding as the learner becomes more proficient. Much of workplace learning support focuses around the effective provision and management of scaffolding and its subsequent fading.

However, there is more to learner support than the interventions that occur during the actual process of learning. As we have discussed elsewhere in this book there are other relevant variables, such as the culture of the workplace, the capacity and willingness of the workplace and its personnel (including other workers, managers and supervisors) to support learning, the structures put in place to support learning, the value placed on learning by both the learner and others in the workplace environment, and the availability of a range of learning, physical and human resources that can be deployed to support the learning process. Taking that broader concept of learning support, Smith (2001b) has proposed a workplace learning model that included a consideration of the organizational and contextual factors that impact on learning, and the individual learner elements that similarly impact.

Model for developing effective support to workplace learning

Drawing on Kember's (1995) model for supporting student progress in educational institution environments Smith (2001b) identified two major components of effective workplace support; the first of these was the development of learners themselves, and the second was the development of the workplace context to support learning. Smith's research reflected and drew upon other research (for example, Brooker and Butler, 1997; Cornford and Gunn, 1998; Fuller, 1996; Unwin and Wellington, 1995). This research suggested that the systems and structures in place in workplaces to support learning are often not developed strongly enough to provide adequate cultural and managerial support for learning, for valuing learning as it is achieved, or for encouraging learning. Robertson's (1996) research with small enterprises showed that role clarity for personnel with training and HRD responsibilities is important if HRD initiatives are to succeed and to change. As Berge (2001) has pointed out, moving learning within an organization away from the more traditional face-to-face instructor-led training-room contexts into a more learner-centred form of HRD may sometimes challenge the existing skills, role perception and confidence of HRD specialists and managers more generally. This is likely to be especially true in those situations where the role perception is that of a didactic provider. Smith's research indicated that the problem here was not so much an unwillingness to move towards a learner-centred paradigm that provides effective support to learners, but that it was more a problem of not knowing how to do it. Smith's (2001b) model is shown in Figures 7.1, 7.2 and 7.3.

There are three principal elements:

- The various foci within the Learner Development Space indicate the areas in which it is necessary to develop and support learners.
- The various foci within the Workplace Support Space areas required to develop a supportive organizational environment for learning.
- The Strategy Space represents the combination of learner development and workplace support strategies that are brought to bear to achieve objectives that are important at any given time, either long or short term.

The Strategy Space, therefore, provides opportunity for a considerable diversity of strategies to be combined to suit diverse circumstances and requirements. The foci within the Learner Development Space and the Workplace Support Space provide a useful framework for identifying the issues relevant to this chapter, and also to suggest some of the strategies that may be useful to deploy within the Strategy Space.

Learner Development Space	Strategy Space	Workplace Support Space

Focuses on:
• development towards self-directed learning
• develop skills and concepts through a range of learning strategies and materials
• development towards structuring own learning in a community of practice
	Identifies specific strategies for development of learner and workplace preparedness for effective workplace learning	Focuses on:
		• development of clear training policies
		• development of training structures
		• development of trainer skills to support:
		  • self-directed learning
		  • acquisition of skills and concepts
		  • participation in a community of practice

Figure 7.1 Spatial model for development of workplace learning

Learner development space

The model is expanded in Figure 7.2 and emphasises the need to pay specific attention to learners' capabilities for:

- using their own experience to develop cognitive schemata and new learning;
- setting their own learning goals and taking responsibility for their own learning;
- developing intrinsic motivation;
- evaluating and monitoring their own learning;
- adopting a problem-solving approach to learning involving the use of authentic workplace tasks;
- selecting their learning materials and learning strategies from a wide range of options.

A deep approach to learning embodies conditions in which, according to Candy (1991), learners: engage tasks appropriately; use abstract frameworks for conceptualizing the task and for illuminating the content to be learned; are independent and reflective, meta-cognitive in planning ahead and in monitoring their own progress; achieve well-structured and integrated outcomes; and actually enjoy the learning process. Some of the conditions conducive to this type of learning are suggested by Biggs (1994: 23) as being:

- a positive motivational context, hopefully intrinsic but at least one involving a felt need to know and a warm emotional climate;
- a high degree of learner activity, both task-related and self-related;
- interaction with others, both at the peer level with other students and hierarchically, within scaffolding provided by an expert tutor;
- a well-structured knowledge base that provides depth (for conceptual development) and breadth for conceptual enrichment.

Wright (1987) has drawn attention to the importance of experience as a basis for the development of new knowledge. Dreyfus's (1982) model of the five stages of development of expertise from novice through to expert, introduced in Chapter 3, suggested that at the novice stage, behaviour is limited, inflexible and rule-governed. At the expert stage actions are performed in a seemingly intuitive way from a deep understanding, rules are not immediately apparent and performance is fluid and flexible, invoking the use of abstract understandings (Nisbet, Fong, Lehman and Cheng, 1987). Cognitive psychologists (e.g. Case, 1985; Kirby, 1988) have referred to the significance of automatising lower-order task components in order to free working memory for the higher-order ones. This cognitive reorganization of knowledge to enable accurate and accessible indexing has also been suggested by Billett (1993, 1994) and by Ericsson and Charness (1994).

While the model proposed in Figure 7.1 and expanded in Figure 7.2 suggests the importance of the development of self-directed learning, it is also important to note Fuller's (1996) contention that learners need to be able to work and learn alone, as well as within the context of a work team, or a more informal community of practice. Several writers (for example, Brown, Collins and Duguid, 1989; Collins, 1991; Rogoff, 1984) have proposed that learning takes place through meaningful, authentic environments and tasks. Other writers have stressed the importance of these experiences within a community of practice (Billett, 1993; Lave and Wenger, 1991). Brookfield (1985) has also made the observation that successful self-directed learners are adept at the construction of knowledge through social mediation. Accordingly, in the development of stronger preferences and capabilities in self-directed learning, it is important to retain the willingness among learners to engage in learning in a social context as well. The need for self-directed learning in a workplace environment has been argued in Chapters 4 and 5, as has been the notion that self-directed learning includes the setting of one's own learning goals, and taking responsibility for one's own learning. In the model presented in Figure 7.2 the development of the learner's ability to set learning goals and take responsibility for learning within a community of practice is regarded as an important element of learners' preparedness for effective learning in the workplace.

In Chapter 4 we discussed in detail some of the theories of motivation that may impact on learning. In particular, development of intrinsic motivation has been identified by Bransford and Vye (1989), Caine and Caine (1991), Kember (1995) and Rojewski and Schell (1994) as necessary for the effective engagement with self-directed learning. Furthermore, these writers have viewed intrinsic motivation as an important component in the acquisition of situated knowledge, or in the use of experience to construct new learning. While much of traditional HRD processes provides extrinsic motivation to learners through the provision of a structured programme to meet identified needs, and structured external feedback, the model depicted in Figure 7.2 suggests that personal interest in knowledge acquisition (for example, curiosity)

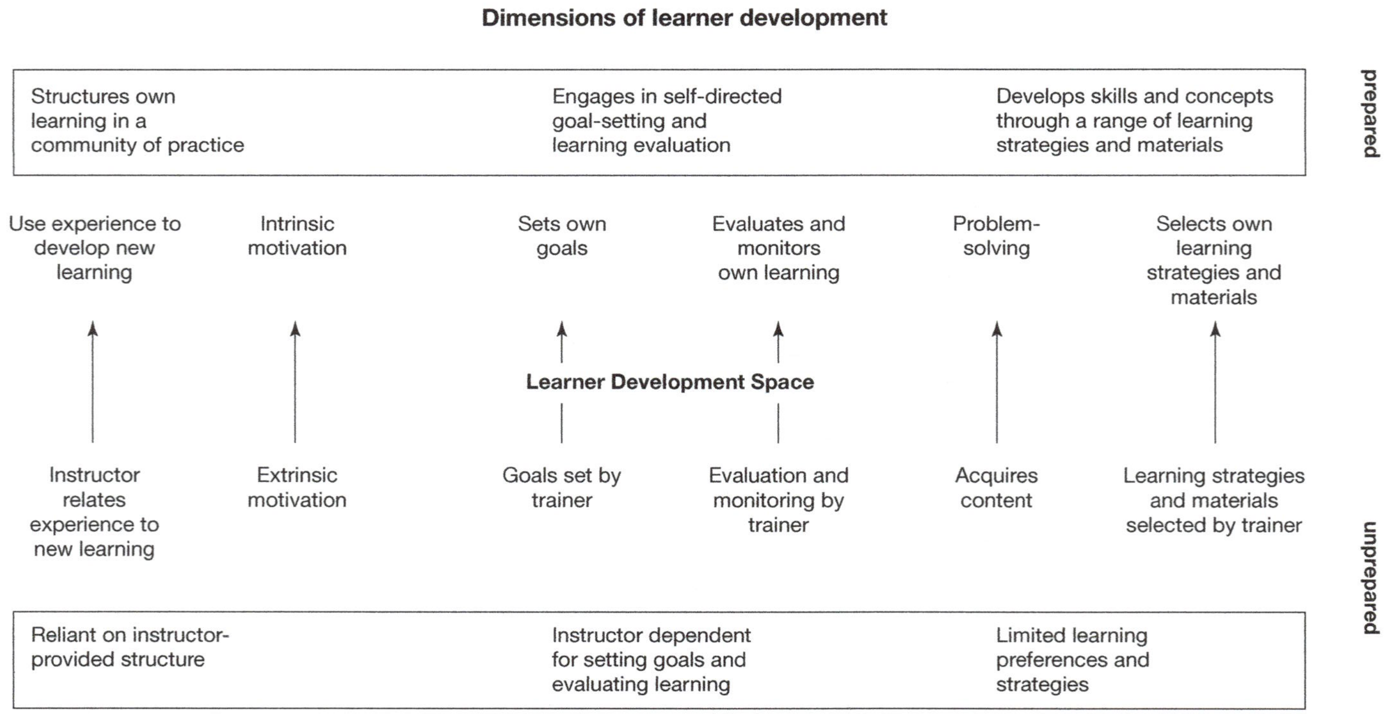

Dimensions of learner development

prepared				unprepared

Structures own learning in a community of practice	Engages in self-directed goal-setting and learning evaluation		Develops skills and concepts through a range of learning strategies and materials	
Use experience to develop new learning	Sets own goals	Evaluates and monitors own learning	Problem-solving	Selects own learning strategies and materials
Intrinsic motivation				

Learner Development Space

Instructor relates experience to new learning	Goals set by trainer	Evaluation and monitoring by trainer	Acquires content	Learning strategies and materials selected by trainer
Extrinsic motivation				

Reliant on instructor-provided structure	Instructor dependent for setting goals and evaluating learning			Limited learning preferences and strategies

Figure 7.2 Dimensions of the Learner Development Space

is an important characteristic to develop in learners, and that the situated learning context provides opportunities for that to occur (e.g. Brown, Collins and Duguid, 1989; Collins, 1991; Resnick, 1987; Rogoff, 1984).

The evaluation and monitoring of one's own learning in preparing for a learning environment that demands greater self-direction has been commented on by Biggs and Moore (1993), Boote (1998), Kember (1995), Manning and Payne (1996) and White (1997). Consistent with constructivism, the essence of the evaluation and monitoring captured by each of these writers is that the learner is an active participant in their own learning at meta-cognitive, motivational and behavioural levels. Biggs and Moore (1993) saw this as taking a responsibility at a meta-cognitive level for planning, deciding, monitoring, evaluating and terminating learning – notions clearly linked to the need to set learning goals and take responsibility for learning. Manning and Payne (1996) also argued that the evaluation and monitoring of one's own learning is an active process requiring skills to be developed in the learner. As a result, the model proposed in Figure 7.2 suggests that these skills require development in many workplace learners, and represent an important component of preparedness for effective HRD.

The value of a problem-solving approach to the development of situated knowledge through engagement with authentic tasks has been noted by writers such as Brown, Collins and Duguid (1989), Collins (1991), Cunningham (1998), Rogoff (1984) and Young (1993). Kember (1995) has identified a problem-solving approach as an important component of independent adult learning, and has contrasted problem solving with an approach of acquiring the content of the learning. The proposed model suggests that an effective learner engages in a problem-solving approach to workplace learning involving the use of authentic tasks. There is evidence from the literature that whilst workplace learners may relate well to problem-solving approaches, there may be a need to assist them to develop problem-solving as part of a set of strategies relating to the identification of their own learning goals, and the monitoring of the success of problem solving in achieving these goals (Billett, 2001; Smith, 2003a).

The proposed model of learner development has identified the need to develop a willingness to work comfortably with a wide range of learning resources and to engage a range of learning strategies. In Chapter 5 we discussed the differences that occur between individuals in terms of their preferences, and abilities, for learning from different forms of experiences and resources. Several researchers have pointed to the need for workplace learners to engage with a wide range of modes and structures of presentation of information (e.g. Riding and Sadler-Smith, 1997; Sadler-Smith and Riding, 1999; Smith, 2000a, 2000b). Others have made the point, at a more general level, that the complexity of modern workplace tasks and the rapidity with which they change demand the ability to access information from a wide range of sources (e.g. Blanchard and Thacker, 2004; Berryman, 1993; Calder and McCollum, 1998).

There is also evidence from research on learning preferences and strategies, discussed in Chapter 5, that learners can be developed to engage with a wider range of presentation formats and instructional approaches (e.g. Curry, 1983; Sadler-Smith and Riding, 1999; Sternberg and Grigorenko, 1997; Vermunt, 1996). Furthermore, writers such as Cleverly (1994) and Gregorc (1979) have argued that development of non-preferred learning strategies is important in order to enable learners to engage with a wider variety of learning situations. Vermunt (1996) has shown that learners tend not to develop those strategies that are provided for them by their instructors, and that the development of different strategies depends, at least in part, on the instructor developing instructional methods that require the learner to develop different, that is non-habitual, strategies. Effective engagement with learning in the workplace demands that learners can develop skills and concepts from a range of sources and learning experiences, as we discuss in some detail in Chapter 7. The same observation, although not in a workplace context, has been made by Candy, Crebert and O'Leary (1994). The need among learners to select learning materials and strategies from a wide range of sources has, therefore, been included in the proposed model as an important component of preparedness for skills and knowledge development in contemporary HRD. The model shown in Figure 7.2 suggests that a learner prepared for effective HRD is effective in:

- self-directed learning;
- participation in a community of practice;
- developing the skills and concepts required at the workplace.

Strategies to develop these characteristics will later be located within the 'Strategy Space' of the model, which describes the collective strategies for a workplace to achieve effective learning.

Development of workplace support

The model proposed at Figure 7.1 indicated that, for organizations to become prepared for effective workplace learning, specific attention needs to be given to the following:

- clear workplace training policies and identifiable training structures;
- the development of trainer skills to support the processes for learner development, skill development and for the facilitation of learning through communities of practice.

The model shown in Figure 7.1 has collected these specific focuses under the three dimensions of policy, structures and trainer development. Figure 7.3 expands on the Workplace Support Space to show the dimensions of a supportive workplace environment and how it may be developed.

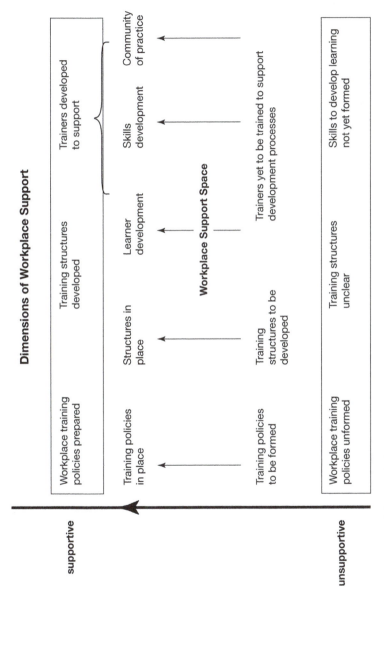

Dimensions of Workplace Support

supportive			
Workplace training policies prepared	Training structures developed	Trainers developed to support	
Training policies in place	Structures in place	Learner development	Skills development	Community of practice
Training policies to be formed	Training structures to be developed	Trainers yet to be trained to support development processes	
Workplace training policies unformed	Training structures unclear	Skills to develop learning not yet formed	
unsupportive			

Workplace Support Space

Figure 7.3 Dimensions of the Workplace Support Space

A wide range of shortcomings in the support that workplaces provide to learners is clear from research by Brooker and Butler (1997), Calder and McCollum (1998), Fuller (1996), Harris, Willis, Simons and Underwood (1998), Smith (2001b) and Unwin and Wellington (1995). It is clear from these studies that workplace learners require considerable support if they are to be effective in their skills and conceptual development, but that support is not always well developed or, in some cases, even provided at all. Apart from learners support components in HRD policies, also required is the recognition of the tension between the worker as a learner and the learner as a worker, such that HRD is understood to be valued (Harris and Volet, 1996; Unwin and Wellington, 1995), and time out from production is available for learning (Calder and McCollum, 1998; Harris *et al.*,1998; Whittaker, 1995).

Lack of training policy at the enterprise, or workplace, level has been identified by each of the cited studies. The research by Calder and McCollum (1998) suggested that in the UK training policies or training plans were not that common, and it is likely that they are even less common in smaller firms. Brooker and Butler's (1997) work in Australian enterprises indicated a lack of training policies, and Harris *et al.* (1998) have made similar observations. Moreover workplace learners are not always embraced in a community of practice nor, in Lave and Wenger's (1991) terms, are they viewed as legitimate peripheral participants. The proposed model suggests the identification and articulation of clear training policies as an area of focus for development of preparedness of workplaces.

Training structures have also been shown by Brooker and Butler (1997), Calder and McCollum (1998) and Harris *et al.* (1998) to be an area of need in the development of better training provision and support for learners. Calder, McColllum, Morgan and Thorpe (1995) have suggested that senior managers and line managers need a greater level of understanding of, and involvement in, training matters than was evident in their study of enterprises in the United Kingdom (see also the discussion in Chapter 2). As mentioned previously, training plans were not always evident in the enterprises surveyed by each of these researchers, and Harris *et al.* (1998) remarked on the perception among apprentices, for example, that their training 'just happened' (p. 124).

More broadly, writers such as Billett (1994, 1996b), Rojewski and Schell (1994) and Smith (1997) emphasised the importance of the role of mentors to assist learners in the development of skills, conceptual knowledge, and the social ethos and values of the workplace. Feedback to learners on both task and learning performance has been shown in work by Barry (1996), Brooker and Butler (1997), Burns, Williams and Barnett (1997), Gott (1989) and White (1997), to be important in the development of skills and learner confidence both in the workplace and in self-directed learning contexts. Training structures include processes for performance monitoring and feedback. The need for developed training structures has been included in the model as an important component of preparedness. This is echoed in two parallel streams of work to our own. Rouillier and Goldstein (1997) identified a series of features (referred to as 'situational cues') that facilitate transfer, including making sure:

- learners have the opportunity to use their newly acquired skills;
- learners and experienced managers share their knowledge and skills;
- equipment in the learning situation is similar to that in the job situation;
- an experienced co-worker is assigned to a new recruit to give feedback and coaching on their application of the skills;
- managers ease the pressure for at least a short time on new recruits to enable them to get up to speed.

Holton and his colleagues have developed a Learning Transfer System model (Ruona, Leimbach, Holton and Bates, 2002) in which learning is effected by motivation, ability and perceptions of L&D (learning and development) and individual performance, as well as being related to learning, is effected by motivation to transfer, the transfer climate and the transfer design (i.e. the features of the learning design that promote transfer). Organizational performance (related to individual performance) is effected by links to organizational goals, expected utility (given that L&D that has low expected utility will be less able to demonstrate results) and return on investment (ROI) and external events (i.e. those factors which are extraneous to training but which may affect the organizational results, for example equipment failures).

The development of workplace learning skills is an important element in the proposed model of workplace support. There is a need for learners to develop skills necessary for structuring their own self-directed learning within the community of practice, and also a need to develop skills to enable them to utilise a wide range of learning resources and opportunities. The research indicating the importance of these skills in a workplace learning environment has been discussed in Chapter 3 and establishes the need for workplaces to incorporate learner development processes within a broad framework of learner support.

Clearly, no model of support to workplace learning can ignore the need for the learners to develop the propositional, procedural, dispositional and strategic knowledge necessary to competently carry out the tasks required of them. Accordingly, processes to develop these forms of knowledge are seen as important components of workplace supportiveness. While an apparently obvious inclusion, here is the research evidence that the HRD processes for the development of these various forms of knowledge may not be well developed in enterprises (Brooker and Butler, 1997; Calder and McCollum, 1998; Harris *et al.*, 1998; Unwin and Wellington, 1995). The research cited here indicates that these processes are somewhat haphazard, unplanned, and sometimes reliant on workers' 'having a go' (Harris *et al.*, 1998: 119) or watching and trying to 'pick it up' (Harris *et al.*,1998: 119). Adequate support for knowledge development in enterprises requires:

- provision of organized demonstrations, practice, trialling (Billett, 1993; Collins *et al.*, 1991; Harris *et al.*, 1998);
- selection of authentic tasks (Billett, 1993; Young, 1993);
- provision of feedback on task performance (Brooker and Butler, 1997; Gott, 1989; Smith, 1997);
- exposure to a diversity of learning and implementation experiences (Brooker and Butler, 1997; Hayton, 1993).

There is also the need, as noted above, for the organization of demonstrations, the 'time out' from production to enable practice (protected time for learning), and for the progressive development of expertise through scaffolding and withdrawal (Farmer, Buckmaster and LeGrand, 1992; Rojewski and Schell, 1994). These processes need to be implemented by the enterprise in order to support and develop learning. They are an important component of the model.

Finally, in the model in Figures 7.1 and 7.3 we propose that the development of support processes that help learners to engage in a community of practice are an important component of the preparedness to support workplace learning. Developing a community of practice depends on communication between practitioners and mutual acceptance (Lave and Wenger, 1991). It also depends on learning about the organization, its values, and one's place in it (Billett, 1993; Mezirow, 1991). Mezirow (1991) and Welton (1991) have each taken the constructivist view that learning is an action shaped by the interests of the learner, but also shaped by the interests of the workplace and its trainers (see also Harris *et al.*, 1998). Several writers have argued that communication between the learner and another more expert worker is necessary to acquire skill (Billett and Rose, 1996; Cunningham, 1998; Pea, 1993), and that communication is an integral part of conceptual development in the workplace (Billett, 1994, 1996b; Brookfield, 1986; McKavanagh, 1996). A community of practice also requires commitment to observation and guided practice (Billett, 1994, 1996b; Collins, Hawkins and Carver, 1991). That community is enhanced through the siting of learners close enough to a more expert worker such that observation and discussion can occur in a casual and continuous way (Harris *et al.*, 1998; Unwin and Wellington, 1995). The model proposed in Figures 7.1 and 7.3 argues that the establishment of processes to yield and sustain a community of practice is important in the development of support for workplace learning.

The third stage of the model, shown in Figure 7.3, suggests that a workplace supportive of workplace learning exhibits:

- clear and articulated training policies and clear and accountable training structures;

- training personnel adept at the processes required to develop and support knowledge construction by learners (which is likely to go beyond a passive provider role).

Strategies to develop these characteristics are then also placed in the 'Strategy Space' of the model, describing the collective strategies for a workplace to prepare for effective learning.

The Strategy Space

The emphasis here is on the strategies identified that may be deployed to promote the development of effective workplace learning, both for learners and for workplaces. The Strategy Space component of the model proposed in Figure 7.1 combines the development of self-directed learning among the learners, their participation in a community of practice and the development of relevant skills and concepts along with the strategies required to develop the features of effective workplace learning. The strategies that are discussed in the following sections are shown in Tables 7.1 to 7.8. They can be selected from and combined into the Strategy Space to provide an appropriate mix of strategies for deployment at any given time to achieve the relevant developmental objectives. These strategies combine in the Strategy Space to provide a diverse set of strategies to develop learners and workplace support for learning. Some overlap among these strategies as they appear in the tables will be apparent; this is inevitable since some strategies can be applied to more than one developmental objective.

Strategies for development of learners

DEVELOPMENT OF SELF-DIRECTED LEARNING

The literature drawn upon to identify the areas of specific attention required in the development of learners indicates that the achievement of self-directed learning involves developing skills in:

- goal setting and determining what is to be learned;
- how it is to be learned;
- evaluating and monitoring learning;
- developing intrinsic motivation;
- problem solving, questioning and reflection;
- having at one's disposal a repertoire of learning preferences and strategies to enable real choices to be made in how learning is to be engaged with.

In the context of learning in the workplace, these features of self-directed learning can be developed within an authentic, real-world environment where there is access to authentic tasks and expert guidance (Brown, Collins and Duguid, 1989; Young, 1993). Additionally, these features can be developed through careful integration of off-the-job and on-the-job learning (Fuller, 1996; Harris *et al.*, 1998). Strategies for the development of these identified features of self-directed learning are highly integrated, and it is intended in this discussion to provide a set of integrated support strategies that can be used in the workplace.

The integration of goal setting, evaluation and monitoring of learning, and issues of intrinsic motivation is alluded to by Morgan, Ponticell and Gordon (1998: 138): 'self-motivation results from setting and making commitments to goals and defining standards by which one evaluates his or her goal-setting behavior'. The setting of goals requires careful consideration on the part of the learner and the trainer or mentor. Goals need to be achievable and set in relation to meaningful tasks of importance to both the learner and the workplace. This same integration of goals, goal commitment and meaningful tasks is reflected also in Locke and Latham's (1990a, 1990b) High Performance Cycle Model, which indicates a significant relationship between goal setting and performance in organizational contexts. Reeve, Gallacher and Mayes (1998: 19) have stressed the importance of setting goals from which structured experiences and learning opportunities can be derived. They make the point that a lack of self-directedness can make goal setting and structuring difficult for learners. Goal setting requires consultation between the learner and the trainer/mentor to develop the goals, to identify how learning outcomes are to be evaluated, and to design a structure through which the goals are to be pursued. The importance of feedback to learners has been established by Brooker and Butler (1997) and Harris *et al.* (1998). Feedback needs to be provided on a continuing basis as learning goals are pursued. The process of setting goals, monitoring the learning process to achieve them, and receiving feedback provides a basis for the evaluation and monitoring of learning.

Central to the setting of learning goals is a clear training plan developed by the organization or its HR or training function, the establishment of HRD personnel with clear role definitions, clear expectations of the learner on the part of the organization and its managers and a structured approach to guidance and communication with the learner. Also necessary are the opportunities, 'spaces' or protected time in the production schedule such that both learners and trainers can attend to setting and achieving the learning goals. Collins (1991) has argued the necessity for the learner to move back and forth between the accomplishment of new learning and the setting of new learning goals.

Gibbs, Morgan and Taylor's (1984: 170) conceptualization of intrinsic and extrinsic motivation among student approaches to study provides a useful insight here into the development of intrinsic motivation. They argue that intrinsic motivation in a vocational orientation to study is derived through an understanding of the relevance of learning to future career.

Table 7.1 Strategies designed to develop self-directedness among workplace
learners

---

1 Assistance in grounding new learning goals in a context of experience, existing
   knowledge, and an appreciation of the place of learning in 'becoming' skilled
   and knowledgeable;
2 Assistance to learners to understand their learning within the broader context
   of the workplace;
3 Assistance to learners in development and negotiation of learning goals;
4 Assistance to learners in developing and negotiating a learning plan and
   learning contract, starting with limited contracts prior to developing towards
   more comprehensive contracts;
5 Assistance in the identification of authentic tasks and learning resources
   through which the learning contract is to be pursued;
6 Assistance in the identification and accessing of other experts who can provide
   demonstration, discussion and guided practice;
7 Working with learners to develop a structured approach to completing the
   learning contract negotiated between the learner and trainer;
8 Working with learners to develop monitoring of learning as it proceeds, and
   the self-evaluation of learning outcomes;
9 Provision of regular discussion with learners on their learning contract;
10 Recognition and review of achievements as learning proceeds, and assistance
   to modify learning contracts on the basis of that feedback;
11 Encouragement of cognitive and meta-cognitive skills such as anticipation and
   question-asking; strategy planning and analysis; wider use of learning
   resources; monitoring of learning processes; articulation of knowledge;
12 Provision of opportunity within the production schedule for withdrawal to
   make use of learning resources.

Achievement in this regard is enabled where learning goals can be readily
understood by the learner as contributing to 'becoming', and are developed
in a holistic context. In Candy, Crebert and O'Leary's (1994) terms, this is
part of the ability to see the inter-connectedness of the knowledge and skills
being acquired.

Specific strategies to be pursued in workplaces to achieve the development
of self-directed learning, and a reduction in the reliance on the instructor are
shown in Table 7.1.

DEVELOPMENT OF SKILLS AND CONCEPTUAL KNOWLEDGE

Strategies for skills and concept development will necessarily involve
scaffolding and modelling, and the fading of the scaffolding (Farmer,
Buckmaster and LeGrand, 1992; Rojewski and Schell, 1994). Also needed is
the opportunity for the learner to appreciate the place that the new skills and
knowledge hold in their extant knowledge structures, the workplace context
and in the development of personal expertise (Ausubel, 1968; Caine and
Caine, 1991; Harris *et al.*,1998). Opportunities to discuss the learning with
other learners (Biggs, 1994; Candy, Crebert and O'Leary, 1994), and to

reflect on and to articulate the knowledge gained from learning (Berryman, 1991; Caine and Caine, 1991; Collins, 1991) will also provide opportunity to enhance the meaningfulness of the learning. Coaching, dialogue and observation may assist with the identification of heuristics used by the more expert worker in carrying out the task.

Fuller (1996) has argued for a stronger relationship between off-the-job and on-the-job training. Whether off-the-job training is provided by the organization itself or by an external training provider, the importance of the link between the two has been also identified by Harris *et al.* (1998). However, Harris *et al.* (1998) have identified a number of different forms of integration between on- and off-the-job training. First, one view of integration they identified was that to do with timing, where the material to be learned in both environments was contiguous. A second concept of integration was the degree of relevance between the two, while a third was the degree of utility that learning in the one environment had for learning in the other. While it is arguable that all three of these forms of integration are important, integration of timing may not be reliably achievable given that production and other workplace imperatives and learning sequences may not coincide. Research also suggests that the transfer of learning from the off-job situation to the on-job situation is enhanced through the principle of identical elements (i.e. the degree of similarity of the training and workplace situations) and the acquisition of general principles that transfer between situations rather than the acquisition of specifics. Hence there is a clear need for the development of strategies that link the meaning of learning derived off-the-job with that constructed on-the-job, and the linking of that learning to experience and prior knowledge.

Prior knowledge may come from outside the workplace altogether; it may come from theoretical learning off-the-job to be deployed on-the-job; or it may derive from experience on-the-job and be used to inform the off-the-job learning. The judicious selection of tasks (Young, 1993) for the learner to focus on in setting learning goals, and the development of movement between what has been learned and experienced (Collins, 1991) is an important component of learning design. The integration between the two, however, requires careful management between the learner, the trainer and the off-the-job training provider where there is one (Fuller, 1996). In a report of training design in the wool-processing industry Smith (1997) proposed a supportive 'triad' arrangement between the learner, the industry trainer and the training provider to ensure that the off-the-job and on-the-job training informed each other through authentic experience as much as is possible. This suggested triadic model results in a rather different and much more participatory role for instructors from training providers than conventional teaching in a decontextualized environment. A similar triadic arrangement between learners, learning advisers and management-school academics was implemented by Sadler-Smith, Gardiner, Badger, Chaston and Stubberfield (2000) in their action-based research with small firms.

The development of skills and conceptual knowledge through structured experience and the integration of relevant theory form a mechanism through which lower-order skills can be automatised (Biggs, 1994) and the development of higher-order skills can be achieved (Case, 1985; Kirby, 1988). The automatisation of skill is an important element of enabling the development of expertise through Dreyfus's (1982) stages, and the organization of knowledge to enable accurate and ready access for the deployment of knowledge and skill (Billett, 1993, 1994; Ericsson and Charness, 1994; Glaser, 1984; Greeno, 1989). Integral to the use of experience to inform new knowledge is the need to plan for a diversity of workplace experience and problem solving (Brooker and Butler, 1997; Hayton, 1993). Lave and Wenger (1991) have explored further the idea that, as skills develop, learners move from peripheral engagement in activities towards tasks that are of more central importance to the workplace. Kornbluh and Greene (1989) have similarly developed their notion of the 'spiral of increasing responsibility' (pp. 260–3), whereby the learner is provided with more responsible and more challenging authentic tasks as experience and skills develop. They have further argued that it is partly through the process of spiralling responsibility that the learner will develop the sense of 'becoming', that Harris *et al.* (1998) identified as an important intrinsic motivator. Biggs (1994) has argued that these twin objectives, of providing a breadth of knowledge through a diversity of experience, and a depth of knowledge through increasing the level of responsibility, will enable conceptual enrichment and conceptual development respectively. Diversity of experience can also be deployed towards the acquisition of the skills required to access and use a wider range of learning resources.

Research by Smith (2003a) with vocational learners in the workplace has shown, for example, that little or no use was made of learning materials other than those supplied by the training provider, and a dislike for appropriating knowledge through reading and textual sources. However, the appropriation of knowledge through reading can play an important part in the development of expertise, where there is a need to use technical manuals, technical journals, instructions, and textual information accessed on-screen in online learning environments. Curry (1983) and Sternberg and Grigorenko (1997) have both argued that new strategies can be developed, while Riding and Sadler-Smith (1992, 1997) have proposed a number of techniques for developing learners' repertoire of learning strategies which may enable them to use a wider range of learning materials. Candy, Crebert and O'Leary (1994) have also identified a repertoire of learning skills as integral to their definition of a lifelong learner. The suggestions of Riding and Sadler-Smith (1992, 1997) are based on the notion that new learning skills can be developed through existing ones, such that knowledge appropriated through a preferred mode may be enhanced through exposure to a non-preferred mode.

In practical terms, these various proposals would mean there may be value in trainers providing learners with alternative forms of learning material to enhance knowledge in areas where there already exists a basis of under-standing. In strategy terms, this might indicate that there is some value in providing early exposure to new knowledge through the modes of learning preferred by the learner, but to follow that learning with the provision of further information in a different form. Articulation of what has been appropriated from that non-preferred mode may aid in development of confidence (Barry, 1996) with the mode and recognition of its value in developing skill and conceptual knowledge.

Time-out to participate in structured guided practice and observation (Rojewski and Schell, 1994) forms an important part of workplace knowl-edge development, and requires design in the learning environment that includes appropriate scaffolding and the provision for the eventual with-drawal of the scaffolding (Brown, Collins and Duguid, 1989; Farmer, Buckmaster and LeGrand, 1992). The authenticity of the learning task is important (Young, 1993), but this should be selected on the basis of the learning needs of the individual and the enterprise. External education and training providers can be of assistance here in choosing the tasks, since there is advantage in the task also informing the off-the-job learning and calls for close collaboration between off-job providers of learning and clients.

There is evidence (Healy *et al.*, 1992) that long-term retention of skill and knowledge is enhanced where the situation of recall is similar to that of acquisition. To enable generalization of the learning beyond that acquisition–recall context, Brown, Collins and Duguid (1989: 40) argued for the need for multiple practice in diverse contexts, and the opportunity for deliberation on and articulation of the learning and its generalizability. The articulation of new learning has been identified by Brown, Collins and Duguid (1989) and Collins (1991) as important in consolidating the learning in a relevant schema. However, the opportunities for the articulation of knowledge were shown to be deficient in the workplaces studied by Brooker and Butler (1997) and Harris *et al.* (1998). Within the opportunities provided for diversity of experience and problem solving, there also needs to be oppor-tunity for some reflection and deliberation on those experiences, and the placement of them in a context of skill and knowledge development (Berryman, 1991; Caine and Caine, 1991). Provision of such opportunities needs to be built into the HRD process. 'Deliberation' can include the devel-opment of cognitive strategies to enable comparing of concepts and skills, and to categorise them into a developing schema. The specific strategies to be pursued by workplaces in the development of skills and conceptual knowledge among learners are summarised in Table 7.2.

DEVELOPMENT WITHIN A COMMUNITY OF PRACTICE

The importance of the community of practice is a cornerstone of theories of situated learning and cognitive apprenticeship. A community of practice

Table 7.2 Strategies for the development of workplace skills and conceptual knowledge

---

1 Assistance in the development and negotiation of learning contracts that clearly specify the skills and concepts to be learned;
2 Provision of regular meetings to discuss and receive feedback on progression towards completion of learning contracts;
3 Provision of assistance to recognise current skills and knowledge as a basis for the acquisition of new learning;
4 Assistance in the identification of authentic tasks for learning;
5 Providing opportunity for demonstration, structured practice, guided practice, and observation;
6 Provision of opportunity for deliberation, reflection, and articulation of knowledge;
7 Provision of learning scaffolding and its planned withdrawal;
8 Exposure to a diversity of experiences and problem-solving situations;
9 Development through an increasing 'spiral of responsibility';
10 Assistance in the integration of on- and off-the-job learning experiences;
11 Encouragement and facilitation to use a broad range of learning strategies, and a wide use of learning resources;
12 Provision of access to other workplaces, or to an education and training provider, to enable learning of a diversity of skills and concepts not available for learning within the workplace.

---

provides the context for learners to understand the values and ethos of the system of activity and enables the appropriation of knowledge through authentic and situated tasks. The community of practice provides an opportunity for the development of transferable knowledge through socio-culturally rich and authentic learning experiences guided by expert mentors (Billett, 1994, 1996b) and acknowledges that learning is a social activity (Rogoff and Lave, 1984). The use of social learning is arguably part of the arsenal of self-directed learning skills that a workplace learner may need to deploy. Choosing between situations where learning is pursued independently and where it is to be pursued through social mediation is in itself a skill that needs to be developed.

Additionally, there may be some need to support learners in ways such that they use their opportunities for social learning. The community of practice demands that there be effective communication established between the learner and instructor, such that learners may need assistance with establishing the confidence for communication, and the understanding that two-way communication and dialogue will be well-received and reciprocated by the instructor (Pea, 1993; Billett and Rose, 1996; Cunningham, 1998). Communication is a vehicle for meaning negotiation, and for developing understanding and skill. Learner-initiated communication may require direction to ensure that its content is relevant to learning and assists in identifying meaning and testing knowledge (Berryman, 1991, Caine and Caine, 1991, Collins, 1991). Billett (1996b), Brookfield (1986) and McKavanagh (1996) have also emphasised the importance of peer communication to assist in negotiating meaning and developing conceptual knowledge. Opportunities to enable learners to engage in focused communication needs to be provided through, for example, meetings and structured discussions between them.

The development of a community of practice has been shown by Harris *et al.* (1998) and others to be largely unplanned and unstructured in the workplace. In Lave and Wenger's (1991) terms it appears that the move from peripheral activity to legitimate involvement is not necessarily planned and thereby may prove difficult for many workplace learners. Learners require assistance with securing themselves a place in the legitimate practices of the learning community in the workplace. Candy, Crebert and O'Leary (1994), similarly to Brookfield (1985), have suggested that a characteristic of a self-directed learner is being able to identify and to ask the relevant questions. To do so presupposes a level of deliberation and the confidence to ask the relevant and appropriate question. Also necessary in this context is the ability to listen to and use feedback from others.

In Smith's (2003a) research with apprentices, there was evidence of frequent use of social strategies, such as demonstrations, scheduled classes, peer discussion and supervisor/trainer discussion, but they were not able to make similar use of worker observation and observation of the broader workplace. Rectification of such difficulties would appear to lie more with the workplace than with the learner. Worker observation is often thwarted by the frequent siting of learners away from the expert workers whom they could observe and restrictions placed on their capacity to move about the workplace to observe. A similar feature of workplaces was observed by Harris *et al.* (1998), and apprentices in Unwin and Wellington's (1995) study complained of the fact they were largely ignored by the organizations. Under these circumstances, learners may need to develop the skills necessary to identify what it is they wish to observe, and then request that they be able to make those observations. A better response in developing the engagement with the community of practice may be for the workplace to ensure that learners are included as legitimate contributors, and sited in places that enable observation and casual interaction with a more expert worker. Strategies to develop learning within a community of practice are summarised in Table 7.3.

Strategies for the development of workplace support

The Workplace Support Space of the proposed model identifies five areas for specific development of workplaces to enable effective learning:

- training policies to be developed, articulated and publicised;
- identifiable and accountable training structures to be engendered and publicised;
- process for the recognition of self-directed learning to be developed;

Table 7.3 Strategies to develop learning within a community of practice

1 Developing an understanding among learners of their work and training within the context of the workplace, and others within the workplace;
2 Development among learners of a clear understanding of the workplace ethos, values and policies;
3 Development among learners of their dual role as learners and as workers;
4 Encouragement and facilitation to learners to form relationships with trainers, supervisors, managers, HRD personnel, peers and other experts to enable discussion of developing skills and knowledge;
5 Assistance with identification of learning objectives to be pursued through interaction with others, through discussion, demonstration, articulation etc.;
6 Assistance with skills of structured observation and question-asking;
7 Provision of a 'spiral of responsibility' to increase responsibility and work complexity as learning progresses, and to move from legitimate peripheral participation towards full participation;
8 Provision of regular opportunities within the production schedule for discussion of learning, of skills and of work.

- processes for the development of required skills and knowledge to be developed;
- processes to develop a community of practice to be developed.

Within the Strategy Space, these areas are identified in three sets of strategies and processes, namely the development of training policies, training structures and HRD personnel to support development of self-directed learning, skills and concept development, and participation in a community of practice.

DEVELOPMENT OF LEARNING SUPPORT POLICIES

The development and articulation of clear enterprise HRD policies is an important component in the support by workplaces for effective learning. Unwin and Wellington (1995) observed the importance of enterprises being explicit about the value and expectations of HRD. Harris and Volet (1996) have commented on the need for support and genuine commitment to be shown by enterprises, and Smith (2000b) has also commented on the need for the development and articulation of clear training policies and procedures. In the literature, several sources of tension in the workplace that may act as barriers to successful HRD have been identified. Harris *et al.* (1998) have argued that there may be different conceptualizations of learning among the different stakeholders. For example, employers typically had a behaviourist orientation to training, being mainly interested in the behavioural, or skill, outcomes of training, whereas trainers were more 'humanist' (Harris *et al.*,1998: 186) in their orientation, adopting an orientation towards learning facilitation based on trust and respect. Trainers in the study also saw value in a cognitive orientation that took account of the processes and contexts for learning. These different orientations are most likely attributable to the outcomes of learning that are of most interest to each of the stakeholders, with employers being most interested in the skill and knowledge that enhance business outcomes such as productivity and quality. Other stakeholders are more likely to have an interest in the outcomes of learning associated with a broader conceptual understanding of the knowledge that lies behind the behaviourally represented skills. Hager, Athanasou and Gonzci (1994: 5) have discussed these orientations in terms of an atomistic or a holistic approach, where the former regards the discrete and specific tasks as forming the competencies, while the latter views competency as 'attributes of workers that underpin competent performance of an occupation'.

The development of HRD policies that address the different, and sometimes conflicting, needs and interests of the different stakeholder groups is important. An effective HRD policy needs to address the learning outcomes required for the development of skills and knowledge required for business enhancement, but also needs to recognise the value of conceptual knowledge that will enable transfer of skills to new tasks and to new technologies and may even be instrumental in facilitating new and innovative working practices. Also required in HRD policies are statements of what is expected of learners and of trainers and mentors, and how the achievement of these expectations may be assessed.

It is important that learners develop a sense of belonging to the community of practice; this necessitates the inclusion of learners in communications and dialogue (Unwin and Wellington, 1995), their siting in positions where they are naturally included in observation, demonstration and discussion with more expert workers (Harris *et al.*, 1998), and the explicit recognition of their legitimate participation in the workplace (Harris and Volet, 1996; Lave and Wenger, 1991). Several writers (Fuller, 1996; Harris and Volet, 1996; Harris *et al.*,1998; Lave and Wenger, 1991; Unwin and Wellington, 1995) have pointed to the need for learners to develop a sense of being valued and belonging. Taylor (1996) remarked on the need for environments conducive to learning; however, there may be a tension in the role of individuals as both learners and workers. This tension between learner-as-worker and worker-as-learner requires some stance on the part of the organization that will legitimise the learning role within the production schedule and against the backcloth of the business and performance imperative. Hence there is a need for recognition that learning on-the-job is a negotiated experience, and that work and learning shape each other (Harris *et al.*, 1998). This negotiation process requires a certain amount of legitimised 'time out' for learners to engage in meetings with trainers and mentors to set learning goals, to review progress, and to plan learning. The time necessary to make effective and efficient use of learning materials and other resources also needs to be viewed as legitimate and protected rather than being viewed as taking unproductive 'time-out' (Calder and McCollum, 1998). There is also a need to legitimise the asking of questions (without being dismissed as wasting time) and activities such as guided practice, demonstrations, trialling and experimentation.

The need for diversity of experiences, and the development of the 'spiral of responsibility' have been commented upon by several writers (Brooker and Butler, 1997; Hayton, 1993; Kornbluh and Greene, 1989) and require recognition in HRD policies. Evans (2001) and Sadler-Smith, Gardiner, Badger, Chaston and Stubberfield (2000) have drawn attention to the fact that the scope of work an organization undertakes is a limiting factor in the diversity of experience that can be provided to learners. They have commented, similarly to Fuller (1996), that organizations may need to establish a clear relationship with an education and training provider to enable the acquisition of knowledge and experience that is unable to be provided by the knowledge and skill resources within the organization itself. The relationship with the education and training provider and the expectations o   f the training provider (e.g. 'who does what') needs attention, along with the processes to be followed in establishing the learning partnership with the provider. Support from an external training provider may also be necessary where HRD staff's training skills are deficient, or when the knowledge set of the workforce is inappropriate or outdated. HRD policies need to include the identification of any external training providers, the expectations of those providers and of the organization's personnel, and the processes and protocol to be used in the partnership with the provider. There is some comment in the literature (Calder and McCollum, 1998) on the value of learning 'resource-banks' (such as an e-learning room) and a designated learning withdrawal area within enterprises to enable learners to access a variety of materials, and to use those resources away from the production site. HRD policies need to include consideration of what resources will be acquired and made available to learners, and what the conditions of use are to be, along with expectations on the use of any withdrawal space provided. Finally, Brooker and Butler (1997) have identified some deficiencies in the record-keeping typical of the firms they observed, and have pointed to the need for adequate records (see also Calder *et al.*, 1995) to be kept of learning plans, learning activities and achievements. HRD policies, it is suggested, should include requirements for the keeping of adequate records. Table 7.4 shows a number of strategies that may be used in developing HRD policies designed to support effective learning in the workplace. HRD policies and plans contextualise learning in the organization, and indicate its commitment, and for these reasons they need to be clearly articulated to the workforce (Unwin and Wellington, 1995).

DEVELOPMENT OF LEARNING SUPPORT STRUCTURES

Within the development of the necessary HRD structures and the identification of roles, attention also needs to be given to the development of

Table 7.4 Suggested diverse strategies in developing training policies designed to support effective learning in the workplace

---

1 A statement of the purposes for learning within the enterprise, and the value that is placed on it;

2 A statement of the form of knowledge that the enterprise wishes learners to construct, including whether skilled performance only is to be pursued, or whether skilled performance is expected to be accompanied by conceptual understanding;

3 Details of the HRD structures in the enterprise, and the roles of each of the personnel involved with training, and the role of any external education and training provider;

4 A statement of the nature of assessment, and by whom those assessments are to be made;

5 A statement of recognition that values workers as learners and learners as workers, and with legitimate need to ask questions, seek guidance and demonstration, and to be provided with opportunities to experiment, trial and practice;

6 A statement that learning is a legitimate part of the enterprise activity such that learners are expected to participate in the workplace community;

7 Recognition that diversity of experience is necessary and will be provided through different work experiences in the enterprise, or provided externally by education and training providers;

8 Recognition that time needs to be made available within the production and other business schedules for meetings, discussion, practice etc.; and that time is also required for the use of learning materials and opportunities, or attendance at classes;

9 A statement of what learners can expect in the provision of learning resources, and to where they may withdraw to use these resources;

10 Recognition that self-directed learning requires the regular negotiation of learning goals between the learner and the trainer/mentor, and the need to jointly review these goals and discuss progress;

11 An expectation that learners will work within the community of practice as a member of a team, but will also progressively develop the skills to take responsibility for their own work and learning;

12 A statement that training plans, activities and achievements will be adequately recorded.

---

workplace instructors, trainers, coaches and mentors. These roles need to include the development of learning plans, the negotiation and monitoring of learning goals and achievement, the design of learning experiences and access to guided practice. Also necessary is the provision of appropriate learning resources, opportunities for trialling and experimentation, the liaison and planning with external education and training providers where necessary, and the commitment to and championing of HRD by management. Clearly identifiable responsibilities for HRD, and accountability for learning outcomes are important. The integration of on- and off-the-job experiences also requires careful management to ensure that off-the-job learning is relevant and timely (Fuller, 1996). Responsibility for performance monitoring and evaluation, assessment type, implementation and recording of these functions also require management by HRD personnel.

The significance of access to more expert workers for questioning, demonstration and guided practice has been noted by several writers (Brooker and Butler, 1997; Fuller, 1996; Unwin and Wellington, 1995), and part of management and HRD responsibility is to try to ensure that such access is available. There is evidence (Harris *et al.*, 1998) that learners can be met with some hostility if too many questions are asked, or if time is demanded from other workers for demonstration. Robertson (1996) has shown that trainees in the workplace are expected to accept what they are told or shown without criticism, and yet at the same time they were expected to have a level of understanding that would enable them to contribute ideas for new processes. Part of the role of a workplace trainer, coach or mentor is to communicate an individual's learning needs to other workers, and facilitate access to the knowledge held by these more expert employees. Furthermore, to provide the diversity of experience suggested by Brooker and Butler (1997), Evans (2001) and Sadler-Smith, Down and Lean (2000) requires the identification of authentic experiences (Young, 1993), planned rotation (Hayton, 1993), and access to external education and training providers where the experience cannot be provided within the organization. Responsibility for the access to a suitable diversity of learning experiences requires management through the learning plan.

The accountability of HRD personnel and trainers to management lies in an expectation that learning will be conducted in an efficient manner that enables appropriate skill and knowledge outputs which can be achieved within the goals and production schedules of the organization, and which also ensures that learners are engaged in consistent and ongoing learning activities. Additionally, some organizations may wish to charge HRD personnel with a responsibility to develop self-directed learning among learners such that goal setting and scaffolding activities can be progressively reduced. Table 7.5 summarises a diversity of strategies to develop effective HRD structures to support learning in the workplace.

DEVELOPING HRD AND TRAINING PERSONNEL:

The importance of professional development of HRD personnel, trainers and mentors has been observed by several writers (Blanchard and Thacker, 2004; Raelin, 2000; Calder and McCollum, 1998; Harris, Simons and Bone, 2000), suggesting that deficiencies in learning support at the enterprise level are likely to be at least partially related to a need for training among these staff. Research by Peoples, Robinson and Calvert (1997: 59) concluded that in Australia 'virtually all staff in training organizations' require some form of training, and that within large enterprises there was evidence in their research that trainers may be 'locked into traditional modes of delivery' (1997: 59). Among small businesses surveyed, the major problem lay with convincing them of the value of any form of training. Peoples, Robinson and

Table 7.5 Strategies to develop effective HRD structures to support learning in the workplace

---

1 Identification of HRD personnel and others who take responsibility for individual learners;
2 Development of roles for personnel that include responsibility for each learner in:

   • learning plan development;
   • learning design and implementation;
   • goal negotiation with learners and monitoring of learning;
   • assessment of learning outcomes;
   • enabling access to learning materials, physical resources and more expert personnel;
   • enabling access to people and experiences as required;

3 Implementing learning within the policies of the enterprise;
4 Representing learning needs of individuals to management and other staff;
5 Developed documentation for learning plans, recording of learning activity and achievement;
6 Identifiable partnership arrangements with external education and training providers, and management of that relationship and the training provided;
7 Commitment to the professional development of trainers and other personnel involved in the design and of learning sequences, in the delivery of training, and the development of self-directed learning.

Calvert's research showed that at both management and trainer level there was a shared view of a need for developing a 'flexible orientation' (1997: 60–1) towards training, for understanding the need to identify and use a variety of learning resources, and to utilise workplace-based learning as a major strategy. For practitioners there was an identified need to understand and use a wider variety of learning strategies.

As noted earlier, several decades ago research in the UK examined the roles assumed by training practitioners in organizations. For example, Pettigrew, Jones and Reason (1982) surveyed trainers in the chemical industry and identified five trainer roles:

1 The passive provider sits back and waits for clients to come forward and then provides training aimed at maintenance and improvement of performance.
2 The provider is concerned with the maintenance and improvement of performance but without reference to any major change.
3 The practitioner whose role is in transition is no longer content to provide training courses but desires to have a more proactive and influential role.
4 The change agent's main concern is organizational development and complex issues of cultural change.
5 The training manager is concerned with the smooth running of the

training function.

Again, other research in the UK back in the 1980s by Bennett and Leduchowicz (1983) suggested that trainers occupy four roles which vary according to two dimensions, a traditionalist versus an interventionist orientation, and maintenance versus a change orientation:

- Caretaker (traditional/maintenance): Provides training to maintain smooth running of organization. Adopts traditional educational practices. Responds to requests for training (i.e. passive and reactive).
- Educator (traditional/change): Sees need for training to change systems and procedures. Adopts traditional educational approaches. Anticipates the need for change.
- Evangelist (maintenance/interventionist): Concerned with training to maintain present systems and procedures. Adopts learner-centred (not 'educational') approaches. Facilitator of learning rather than subject expert.
- Innovator (change/interventionist): Sees need for training to change systems and procedures. Attempts to understand real needs and causes; persuasive, problem-solver and catalyst for change

Bennett and Leduchowicz noted some polarisation of roles along the diagonal caretaker-to-innovator. This broadly corresponds to a continuum that may be detected in the Pettigrew *et al.* framework (from passive provider to change agent).

In the USA, the American Society for Training and Development (ASTD) has produced a competency model based upon foundational competencies (for example, interpersonal and management skills), areas of expertise (for example, designing learning and delivering training) and workplace roles (for example, learning strategist, business partner, etc.) (Rothwell and Wellins, 2004). There have been similar efforts at defining professional competencies in the UK by various government and professional bodies (such as the Employment National Training Organization and the Chartered Institute of Personnel and Development).

Mitchell (1999) described the outcomes of the Australian National Training Authority's LearnScope projects, which focused on registered training organizations within Australia. The research has shown that the success factors for developing training and development skills among practitioners were the identification of a need for such skills, the enterprise attitude and support for professional development, flexible approaches to learning, and the level of resource that could be provided to project-based professional development of relevant skills and knowledge.

In conclusion, it is suggested that for HRD managers and front-line HRD personnel to be effective in the terms depicted in the model shown in Figure 7.3, there is need for them to be able to support the processes of developing self-directed learning, the acquisition of skills and concepts, and

Table 7.6 Strategies for trainers/mentors to assist learner development

1	Providing assistance to learners in developing and setting learning goals;
2	Providing assistance to learners in developing a learning plan and learning contract;
3	Understanding of, and preparedness to negotiate learning contracts and outcomes with learners;
4	Provision of assistance to learners in self-assessment of existing knowledge and skills;
5	Assisting in the identification and use of other resources, both human and material;
6	Provision to learners of positive feedback on self-directed learning skill development;
7	Developing an expectation among learners that it is legitimate to ask questions, and assisting in the identification and framing of questions;
8	Providing encouragement for reflection through discussion with both the trainer/mentor and with fellow workers;
9	Assistance in self-evaluation of learning progress and outcomes;
10	Provision of regular monitoring of the learning contract with learners, and negotiation of changes;
11	Understanding the need to develop an equality with the learner in the learning partnership;
12	Making use of the learning contract as the basis for communication between the learner and trainer/mentor on matters to do with learner learning;
13	An understanding of learning preferences and learning strategies.

Table 7.7 Knowledge, skills and responsibilities to be developed among trainers and mentors to support the development of skills and conceptual knowledge

1	Ability to negotiate learning contracts that integrate learner off-the-job learning through the use of learning resources and other forms of instruction, with the tasks to be learned on-the-job. These learning contracts clearly specify the skills and concepts to be learned;
2	Ability to systematically identify authentic tasks available on-the-job to support learning;
3	Understanding of the processes required to provide for a diversity of problem-solving and learning experiences on-the-job;
4	Ability to identify learning tasks that cannot be undertaken at the workplace due to enterprise scope of work, and a process for negotiating for these learning tasks to be undertaken through an education and training provider, or through another enterprise;
5	Understanding of the processes for designing and supporting scaffolding and fading;
6	Capacity to provide demonstration and practice opportunities, and to facilitate trialling and experimentation;
7	Understanding of the need to provide time out from production schedules to enable discussion, articulation and purposeful reflection;
8	Skills required to provide feedback as learning progresses, and at the conclusion of a learning contract;

Table 7.7 continued

9	Commitment to provide an organized repository of learning resources, and methods to encourage use of those resources;
10	Ability to develop a supportive learning environment where there is encouragement of question-asking and the engagement of other experts in willingly assisting learning;
11	Commitment to a system of recording and recognising skill acquisition and development.

Table 7.8 Strategies of use to trainers and mentors to support the development of participation in a community of practice

1	An understanding of workplace training policies that emphasise the value of training, the value of learners and learning, and the need for shared experience;
2	An understanding of the respective roles of trainers and learners, as well as the contributions other workplace personnel can make through the willing sharing of their knowledge and experience;
3	A recognition and valuing of dual roles of workers as learners, and learners as workers;
4	An understanding of the need to 'champion' the needs of learners in the workplace;
5	Commitment to the provision of a spiral of responsibility that enables learners to move from peripheral to central participation as skills and knowledge increase;
6	A commitment to providing opportunities within the production schedule for discussion and articulation of learning, skills and knowledge.

the participation in a community of practice. Tables 7.6, 7.7 and 7.8 provide a set of strategies aimed at the development of HRD staff to support learners' development of self-direction, acquisition of workplace skills and knowledge, and the managed participation in communities of practice:

- The specific strategies for trainers and mentors to enable them to implement strategies to develop learner skills are shown in Table 7.6;
- Table 7.7 proposes the knowledge, skills and responsibilities that may need to be developed among trainers and mentors to support the development of skills and conceptual knowledge in the workplace;
- Finally, in Table 7.8, we suggest some strategies for trainers and mentors to support the managed development of participation in a community of practice.

Focus on practice: developing learner support at a high-tech wool-processing plant

In this section we draw on the experiences of a high technology wool scouring plant that formed part of the research conducted by Smith, Robertson and Wakefield (2002). The HRD issue to be addressed in that plant was the diagnostic and maintenance knowledge and skills that needed to be developed among workers whose experience had been in more traditional low-technology wool-processing companies. Management, working initially with training personnel at the company, developed a set of learning outcomes that they believed were necessary for successful plant operation and maintenance. To support worker achievement of those learning outcomes they also developed and articulated a set of training policies to include training time to be provided, remuneration schedules that were tied to the achievement of learning outcomes, and a publicly articulated strong support for training that recognised the value being placed on the learning and its outcomes. Trainers were further developed to work with individual operators to assess prior knowledge, new knowledge to be gained, a schedule for the learning, and to identify and acquire relevant learning resources that could be used by diverse learners within a twenty-four-hour shift pattern. Those resources included printed material as well as the setting up of a learning room that had within it computer-based learning materials that could be accessed at any time. The schedule for learning included milestones to be reached as well as identifying the resources that each learner would need and have available. That learning schedule formed a 'contract' between the learner and their trainer.

The company also developed a relationship with a training provider to enable external support to be available to trainers and learners in developing learning contracts, but also to assist with resource identification and the effective use of those resources.

In terms of the model we have suggested in this chapter, the company had developed opportunities for learners to develop their level of self-directedness as they pursued the learning contracts and learning outcomes. The company had also developed several forms of workplace support for learners. The strategy space was represented by the set of strategies put together by the company, and outlined in this section.

Although the initial development of these support features was developed by management and HRD staff, operators were included in some substantial ways. First, operators, together with their trainer, had considerable latitude in the ways that they pursued the learning outcomes, so that they suited their own circumstances and individual characteristics. These inputs were reflected in the learning contracts by adjustment through discussion as the learning progressed. Additionally, operators were encouraged, through regular discussion meetings, to talk about their learning progress, and to share the experiences.

Responding to diversity: questions for situational analysis

The model portrayed in this chapter suggests a number of areas in which the development of workplace support for learners may be secured. A consideration of the following set of questions may provide a systematic analysis of the wide diversity of learner development and workplace support issues that may need to be considered.

Identifying development areas

- Using Figure 7.2, identify which of the dimensions in the Learner Development Space you believe may need to be pursued in your organization. Note that these may vary between different individuals or groups within the organization, so you may need to be fairly specific again about the target individual or group that you have in mind;
- Now move on to Figure 7.3 and identify the dimensions of workplace support that you believe will need to be pursued to develop learners in the ways you have identified through Figure 7.2;
- Now select from the relevant tables the strategies that may be useful to you in achieving the development along the chosen dimensions.

There will be other strategies that you might generate which may work well within your own organizational context besides those we have suggested. The strategies you ultimately choose may be collected together into the Strategy Space of the model (see Figure 7.1).

Selecting the strategies

Now use the relevant tables that relate to the development areas you have chosen, and choose those that you believe can be feasibly deployed in your organization to assist in working towards development along the dimensions that you require. As discussed earlier in this chapter, our previous research indicates that some of these strategies are perceived by organizations as being fairly universally feasible for effective use, while others need modification to be feasible within any given situation. Some of the strategies were shown by our research to be not at all feasible in some organizations.

It is important to bear in mind that diversity of individual circumstances and organizational contexts means there will be a diverse range of strategies that is likely to be effective; furthermore there will be variations in the ways in which the strategies are actually implemented. In the next chapter we will give further consideration to the various options that might exist for the design of workplace learning such that you can begin to operationalize the strategies chosen in this chapter.

8   Responding to diversity through flexibility

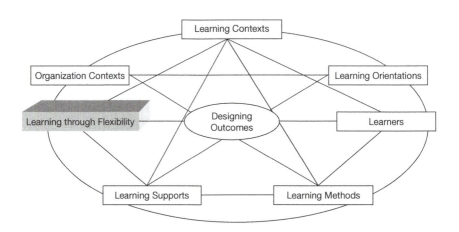

Introduction

In the previous chapter we provided a detailed analysis of the options which may be available to support HRD learning programmes and other more informal learning activities, along with an analysis of the delivery options available in planning and executing HRD programmes. We have also discussed in earlier chapters other important HRD issues associated with learner characteristics, and with organizational contexts for learning. In this chapter we aim to develop some planning and decision-making tools that will assist HRD practitioners in the identification of the diversities that they may be confronted with in terms of learners, outcomes and contexts. The first model we develop is designed to assist in the identification of the range of design responses that may be available in planning, designing and delivering HRD. The second approach is also designed to identify appropriate resources and knowledge development processes, but also addresses issues of learner control and the development of self-directedness. We then present a third model which attempts to encapsulate the issue of the levels of responsiveness that an instructor or facilitator may provide to individual learners as the learning proceeds and which accommodates many of relevant aspects of diversity.

Flexible or blended learning

The first concept to be addressed is that of flexible delivery, and what has more recently been referred to as 'blended learning'. The concept behind both of these terms is that learning can be provided in a number of different ways, using a range of different resources and teaching methods. Although the term 'flexible learning' can be traced back to the United States in the 1970s (Yinger and Eckland, 1975), at that early stage it was used to describe a shift from teacher-led instruction of children to the development of pupil-led problem solving. Ellington (1997) has traced the concept of flexible learning in Britain back to the 1980s when Roebuck (1987) used the term to describe an approach which is characterized by flexible approaches to educational provision and the design of ways of meeting learners' needs through open learning and self-study. This conceptualization of flexible delivery when applied to adult learning developed into common use during the 1980s and beyond and is still in currency at the time of writing. In Australia, the Flexible Delivery Working Party (1992) proposed the following definition of flexible delivery:

> Flexible delivery is an approach to vocational education and training which allows for the adoption of a range of learning strategies in a variety of learning environments to cater for differences in learning styles, learning interests and needs, and variations in learning opportunities.
> (Flexible Delivery Working Party, 1992: 2)

Arguably one difficulty with this definition of flexible delivery is that it fails to identify any unique features that are not present in the competent teaching of any group in any situation. Indeed, it implies that all teaching that is not 'flexible delivery' is rigid in method, content and expectation and that, without flexible delivery, teachers would behave in a rigid way taking no account of learner needs or circumstances. Burns, Williams and Barnett (1997: 16) have interpreted the definition to mean that flexible delivery is characterized by the following key features:

- flexibility in terms of entry, course components, modes of learning and points of exit;
- learner control and choice regarding the content, sequence, time, place and method of learning;
- appropriate learner support systems;
- the application of learning technologies where appropriate;
- access to information on courses and services;

- access to appropriate learning resources;
- flexible assessment processes.

Burns, Williams, and Barnett (1997) acknowledged that this set of characteristics is based on the widest possible view of flexible delivery systems and, through implication, they do not suggest that all flexible delivery must encapsulate all of these characteristics.

Although the term 'flexible delivery' is still in widespread use, there has been more recently the introduction of the term 'blended learning'. There are a number of reasons for the coining of this term. The term 'flexible delivery' has been conflated with concepts of more independent forms of learning that we would normally associate with distance education. Accompanying the drift in meaning there has also been a close link drawn between flexible delivery and online learning. The term 'blended learning' is increasingly in use to quite clearly convey the idea that the learning experience will comprise a number of different teaching methods and a number of different resource formats, which may include components of face-to-face learning with an instructor, learning which may occur with a mentor in the workplace, and learning that may be resource-based using learning materials that may be print, video or online. Misko (1994), writing in the context of flexible learning, identified a range of different forms of learning experience that may be incorporated into a flexible delivery programme, clearly recognising the 'blended' nature of flexible learning. In the previous chapter we discussed a small selection of the various options available for learning and which can be put together to form the mosaic, or blend, that will eventually form the learning programme.

Flexible delivery had its origins in distance education, where the learner is typically separated from the instructor because of distance, time inconveniences such as may occur with shift workers, or because of an inability to attend face-to-face sessions. The wider application of distance education teaching methods to supplement face-to-face methods, or to substitute for them in learning institutions or workplaces, was a response to the availability of newer technologies that enable learners to access learning materials through technologically mediated communication devices (such as computers connected to the Internet), and the ability for learners to communicate readily with their instructor or with fellow learners through e-mail or other electronic systems. Distance education methods traditionally relied on the use of learning materials and resources for independent study. As we have noted in an earlier chapter, the factors that were necessary for success in distance education contexts are by no means unproblematic, for example it cannot be assumed that all learners have the skills to enable them to succeed in these resource-based learning contexts (Smith, 2000a; Boote, 1998; Warner, Christie and Choy, 1998).

In their research with training managers in UK firms, Sadler-Smith, Down and Lean (2000) showed that training methods based on distance education techniques were not favoured since they were not in general seen to be effective with learners. A strong preference for on-the-job learning was prevalent amongst participants in the research. In a rejoinder to the Sadler-Smith, Down and Lean research, Smith (2002) identified the tension between the requirements distance-education methods place upon learners and the characteristics that typify learners in workplaces, and the expectations and policies of workplaces themselves. However, Smith argued that these tensions were not a reason to ignore distance education or other resource-based learning systems but to consider them more strategically as part of a blended learning approach that includes learning that is embedded in the situated learning context of the workplace, and that makes use of the advantages for learning that can be afforded within the learner's community of practice. Smith (2002) also made the point that the use of resource-based methods for HRD can provide considerable advantages to learners who need to fit their learning into the demands of a production schedule (Evans, 2001). He suggested that

> There is considerable commercial value in encouraging employees to become effective self-directed learners such that they can develop and pursue their learning goals and outcomes that contribute to competitiveness without the need for all learning to occur only when there is direct training by an instructor.
>
> (Smith, 2002: 111)

Planning the blend

It is one thing to establish the value of a blended learning approach, but yet another altogether to identify what that blend might be. We intend to approach the planning and decision-making activities associated with choosing the blend through a strategic planning model adapted from the corporate sector. We have chosen the planning model developed by Viljoen and Dann (2000) as a starting point; we have adapted their approach to the context of planning of blended HRD learning programmes.

Most strategic planning literature is focused on the plans that organizations make in order to identify where they wish to go, what goals and objectives they wish to achieve, and how they are going to get there. In developing strategic plans organizations need to be cognisant of the resources at their disposal and the environments (both internal and external) that will impact on them now and in the future in the achievement of their identified goals. Viljoen and Dann (2000: xii) defined strategic planning and management in the following way:

> The process of identifying, choosing and implementing activities that will enhance the long-term performance of an organization by setting direction, and by creating long-term compatibility between the internal

skills and resources of the organization, and the changing environment within which it operates.

Important in Viljoen and Dann's description are the notions of identifying, choosing and implementing, and the notion of long-term compatibility between internal capabilities and external demands and influences. These are the key ideas in strategic planning and management. Viljoen and Dann suggested a framework that includes the four domains of self-analysis, strategy analysis, strategy choice and strategy implementation. In our adaptation of the model we have recast these four domains as follows:

LEARNER ANALYSIS

This includes, among other things, thinking through the short- and longer-term learning outcomes that are being sought either by the learners or by the organization through its HRD. Also in this analysis there is need to consider the characteristics of the learners themselves in terms of the knowledge and skills they already have and that are relevant to the acquisition of the new knowledge; their abilities and their sophistication as learners; the contexts within which they work; and their styles of learning. When planning learning that is to be undertaken by a group of learners, a crucial question here is diversity of the learner group. Can you expect some similarities between the learners and, if so, what are those similarities? Or are you likely to be working with a group that has considerable diversity across the individuals? What are those diversities likely to be?

ENVIRONMENTAL ANALYSIS

At this stage we can separate the environmental analysis into those components that are under the control of the HRD personnel who are planning the learning and those components that pertain to the environment within which the learner operates and over which less control may be exercised. The analysis of the environment that is under the control of HRD personnel or trainers includes the personnel available and their content and process knowledge and skills. The questions are: What physical resources such as space for training, instructional technology and learning resource materials are available in-house, or can be made available through external sources? Are the physical resources accessible to the learner group? What amount of time can realistically be invested in the learning? What is the budget for the learning programme?

The workplace-environment component includes an analysis of the contexts within which learners operate in their workplace, the supports that they may have in the workplace that will enhance their learning opportunities, and the barriers that they may face in learning and its application to the job. Is the culture of their workplace one that will support their learning, inhibit it, or even be hostile towards it? What resources (human, plant, instructional) are available in that workplace already to support the learning? What amount of time is the workplace prepared to allow for the learning to take place? A third set of environmental analyses relate to the stakeholders, as we discussed in Chapter 4. Who are the stakeholders in this HRD, and what are their expectations?

STRATEGY CHOICE

In this stage the task is to review each of the instructional options, as discussed in Chapter 7, that may be available to deploy towards the learning programme and to identify which of these is feasible for use in terms of cost and availability (including those available in the workplace), fitness for purpose, and context of intended delivery. Having identified those which are feasible, the issues of desirability or preference for use are then assessed as a function of the characteristics of the learners' and the instructors' or facilitators' preferences, including the consideration of the desirability of using a number of different resources and methods that may address the extant differences amongst the learners within the group and the contexts within which they work and learn.

STRATEGY IMPLEMENTATION

At this stage the task is to develop more detailed plans and ideas to implement the chosen strategies, the resources that will be needed, and the ways to manage the process. Finally, in this phase goals and strategies may need to be adjusted as circumstances change and in the light of the results of ongoing monitoring and assessment. The model is shown in diagrammatic form in Figure 8.1.

The processes of interrogating each component of the strategic planning process shown in Figure 8.1 are complex since there a large number of questions that need to be asked. In Tables 8.1 to 8.4 we offer a number of the questions that may be helpful in this planning process. The precise questions are likely to vary between organizations, their contexts and the learning outcomes being pursued.

Developing individual learners through flexibility

Our discussions thus far have concentrated largely on groups of learners, although many of the issues, questions and recommendations may be applied readily to HRD that involves individual learners. We commented earlier in this chapter that the skills of self-directed learning cannot be simply assumed to exist among learners (Smith, 2000b 2000c; Boote, 1998; Warner, Christie and Choy, 1998), and moreover it has also been shown that training managers may have a degree of scepticism towards independent learning

Learner Analysis		• Identify learner characteristics • Identify learner contexts for learning
Strategy Analysis		• Analysis of the learner workplace environment and opportunities • Analysis of HRD training environment and opportunities • Analysis of stakeholder needs and expectations
Strategy Choice		• Generate strategic options: What methods and resources are available? • Evaluate strategic options: What methods and resources are feasible? • Choose a preferred strategy: Which of these methods and resources are preferred?
Strategy Implementation	Implement the Strategy	• Develop short-term goals linked to actions and milestones • Develop program and sequences in detail • Secure resources and personnel necessary • Make organizational arrangements
	Evaluation and Monitoring of Strategy	• Develop processes for ongoing monitoring of programme effectiveness, smoothness of running, and progress towards outcomes for all stakeholders

Figure 8.1 The process of strategic planning

methods (see Sadler-Smith, Down and Lean, 2000). Drawing on the work of Smith (2002) and Evans (2001) we also observed earlier that the development of the skills for independent and self-directed learning has considerable value in a business environment where there is a constant need for people to identify their learning needs and to pursue the new skills and knowledge. The work of Poell *et al.* (2000) was also reviewed in an earlier chapter, where it was indicated that some forms of learning and labour networks, most notably the liberal and the horizontal networks, not only required forms of self-direction but also were environments where the development of those skills was to be valued and encouraged.

In this section we focus on the strategies and processes that may be used both for skills and knowledge acquisition but also which may contribute towards the development of the capability to be self-directed on the part of

Table 8.1 Indicative questions to interrogate the Learner Analysis phase

Learner analysis questions

- Who are the people who will participate in this programme?
- How many of them are they?
- What is the gender mix?
- What sort of work does each of them do?
- What relevant knowledge and skills does each already have?
- Are they all competent and experienced learners – or is there a mix among them?
- Do they all know each other? Some of them know each other? None of them know each other?
- Do some of them work together already?
- Are they typically people who like to interact and learn in social contexts?
- Are they visual or textual learners, or is it a mix?
- Are they hands-on learners or do they like more theoretical approaches – or is it a mix?
- Are they self-directed and independent learners – or is it a mix?
- What is the cultural mix of people in the group?
- What is the geographical distribution of the learner group?
- What is the distribution of time availability across the group?
- What sorts of learning resource formats are learners likely to find engaging?
- What can I expect to be fairly similar characteristics across the learners?
- What can I expect to be important differences across the group?

Table 8.2 Indicative questions to interrogate the Environmental Analysis phase

Environmental analysis questions

HRD environment
- Who will conduct the programme?
- Should the trainer have a facilitative or an instructional style?
- What skills does the instructor/facilitator require?
- Should we have mentors deployed with individual learners?
- What physical resources can we access?
- What learning resources can we access?
- What instructional technology can we access?
- How much time do we have to plan and organize the programme?
- How much time do we have to conduct the programme?
- What is the budget we can allocate towards this programme?

Workplace environment
- Are the learners' workplaces likely to be supportive of the learner?
- What characterizes the workplaces that can be used to enhance the learning?
- What characterizes the workplaces that may inhibit the learning?
- Are there possible mentors or expert others in the workplace?
- Can those people be deployed to support the learner?
- What learning resources are already available in the workplace, and in what forms?
- What equipment is in the workplace that the learner can use to practise?

Table 8.2 continued

- What opportunities are there for the demonstration of processes and skills?
- Is there an active community of practice already in the workplace?
- What amount of time can the workplace provide to enable the learner to engage in learning and to support the learning?
- Does the learning need to be part of the work schedule, or is it separate from the work schedule?

Stakeholder environment

- Who are the stakeholders in this learning programme?
- What does each set of stakeholders expect in terms of process and outcomes?
- Are there tensions in these different sets of expectations that need resolution?

Table 8.3 Indicative questions to interrogate the Strategy Choice phase

---

Strategy choice phase

Feasibility/Availability identification

- What independent learning resources and methods are feasible/available?
- What learning technologies are feasible/available to support resource-based learning?
- What classroom/workshop learning processes are feasible/available?
- What learning technologies and resources are feasible/available to support classroom/workshop-based learning?
- What learner discussion and other collaborative learning methods are feasible/available?
- What are the workplace community of practice opportunities for learning?
- What mentoring or coaching opportunities are feasible/available?
- What distance education resources and methods are feasible/available?
- What job rotation opportunities are feasible/available?
- What teambuilding opportunities are feasible/available?
- What role playing/games and simulation opportunities are feasible/available?
- What action science opportunities are feasible/available?
- What action learning opportunities are feasible/available?
- What e-learning opportunities are feasible/available?

Preferences identification

In this sequence of questions each of the above questions is asked again but this time, to establish the list of preferences, each option is included or excluded on a basis of consideration of the:

- Learning outcomes to be achieved
- Available learning contexts and workplace contexts and characteristics
- Group and individual learner characteristics
- Stakeholder expectations
- Time available for planning and for learning
- The relationship between learning and the work schedule

Table 8.4 Indicative activities in the Strategy Implementation phase

---

Strategy Implementation

- Check that the preferences we have established above achieve the objectives of the learning programme, and serve the needs of each stakeholder.
- Develop the detail of the programme schedule and organization.
- Develop the short-term objectives and milestones that are required to monitor the progress of the programme and the progress of the learners.
- Ensure all identified human, physical and learning resources are in place when required.
- Check that budgetary allocations are adequate.
- Consult with workplaces to ensure they are fully aware of their responsibilities and that their expectations are understood by trainers/facilitators and by learners.
- Consult with learners to ensure they are fully aware of their responsibilities and that their expectations are understood by trainers/facilitators and by workplaces.

---

the individual learner. As noted above, the skills of effective learning are becoming increasingly important along with the need for the development of knowledge and its continual updating. Although vertically organized training management systems will continue to have a place in some forms of HRD, there is argument for the liberalisation of a vertical organization if employees are to develop as effective and self-directed learners. We have argued that the effectiveness of flexible HRD is enhanced where workers have self-directed learning skills that enable them to identify learning needs, to pursue them, and to monitor their own progress towards those goals. Research by Smith, Wakefield and Robertson (2001) has indicated that while these more liberal mechanisms may operate effectively at higher levels they are not seen to be as feasible at lower levels. A barrier to the provision of more liberal networks at lower levels appeared to be the time that might be consumed by personnel whose primary purpose was seen as production. A further barrier was the level of the skills needed by supervisors to effectively implement and monitor such arrangements. It did not appear that the learners themselves were not capable of effective learning within liberal networks, and there was evidence that these already existed informally. In proposing a set of recommendations on the feasibility of the development of learners' skills it is necessary to take particular account of the time constraints, the competition between learning and production, and the skills of supervisors who may have responsibility for implementation and monitoring.

To provide a framework for the determination of agreed learning goals, the activities to support that learning, and the monitoring of progress towards them, Smith, Wakefield and Roberston offered a pro forma that can be completed by learners themselves, modified and agreed in consultation with a supervisor or trainer, and easily monitored by each. The data collected by Smith, Wakefield and Robertson (2001) resulted in the development of specific recommendations for practice, based on what was shown to be generally feasible across the diversity of organizations that formed the focus of their research. Smith, Wakefield and Robertson's specific recommendations were to the development of a pro forma that required employees to provide answers to the following questions:

- What is my work over the next (say) six months?
- What do I need to learn to be able to do that work?
- What activities will I use to learn?
- Who do I need help from?
- What do I need to have demonstrated to me?
- What do I need to practise?
- What learning resources do I need to help me?
- How will I know that I am learning?

Smith, Wakefield and Robertson (2001) recommended that these issues be reviewed by the supervisor or HRD specialist and discussed with the learner, and modified where necessary. Identification of any barriers to the achievement of the plan would take place at that time. Additionally, supervisors or HRD personnel would then put in place the required structures and relationships for the accessing of resources. It also provides capacity for the employee to furnish a brief statement of achievement against each learning objective on a periodic basis, and advise of any barriers in the way of achievement, and any adjustments to the plan that are required. Also recommended was the identification by each learner of the network of individuals within which they may learn, including co-workers, expert others, supervisors or trainers. Smith *et al.* also recommended that external training providers may be used to set up and maintain such a system. A process for implementing this set of recommendations is shown in Figure 8.2.

The process outlined in Figure 8.2 may contribute to the following outcomes:

- Learners take responsibility for their own learning.
- A more liberal learning network is developed.
- The learning is situated in the workplace and makes systematic use of the existing community of practice.
- Supervisors and HRD personnel are not in a position of needing to identify the learning needs of each individual.
- Supervisor time is conserved as much as is possible.

The suggested process can also sit comfortably alongside other more vertically driven training processes. For example, where reward is directly related to the achievement of identified competencies, or in other situations where learning outcomes are necessarily prescribed by management for such

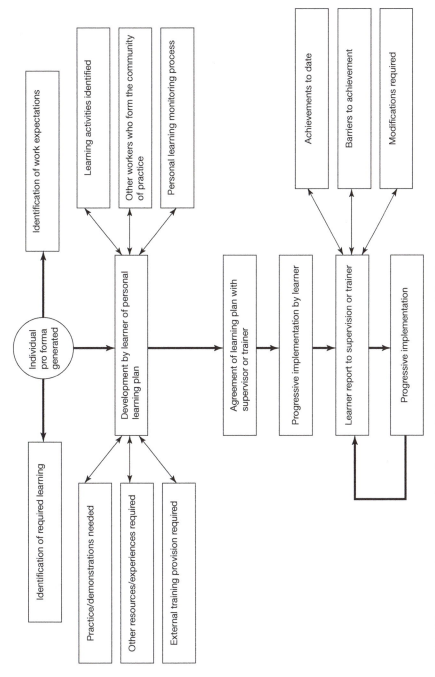

Figure 8.2 Diagrammatic representation of enterprise-based learner-centred development system

reasons as safety, due diligence and so on, the self-identification of all learning needs and their pursuance may be neither desirable nor feasible. As suggested by Poell *et al.* (2000), there is no necessity for any given individual to operate only within one form of learning network, nor within only one set of learning expectations. The process we suggest here can be easily implemented in a context where other learning needs and their achievement are determined through other, probably more tightly controlled methods. The process described above has the advantage of contributing to the development of learners' ownership, implementation and monitoring of their learning and engaging in self-direction.

Monitoring and ongoing adjustment

We have thus far focused on the issues of planning and designing HRD that caters for diversities among learners and the contexts within which they learn. Although in the model we have introduced the capacity for adjustment to the planned processes as a result of the feedback received while the learning progresses, we have not dealt in any depth with the changes that can be made on the basis of any such observations. As learning proceeds trainers and facilitators are in a position to make observations of learners and identifying characteristics that may have been opaque to them at the time of planning the HRD. The strategic-planning model we outlined in Figure 8.1 and the attendant tables calls for identification of broad learner characteristics and diversities but, of course, is unlikely to be able to focus on those characteristics and the diversities since these are observations that cannot be made until the learning is under way.

A large national project undertaken throughout Australia by Smith and Dalton (2005) with vocational trainers and teachers showed that the aware-ness of learning styles and preferences was common among them, although the participants in the research did not have any theoretical understanding of those issues. What was clear, though, was that at a practical level voca-tional trainers and teachers recognised that styles and preferences were an expression of the individual differences that exist between learners and that taking account of and responding to those differences formed part of an effective set of training and HRD strategies. Few participants in that research distinguished between styles and preferences in any formal way and tended to use these terms interchangeably, with the understanding that they described the way that an individual 'likes' to go about learning. There was some distinguishing between learning strategies and styles, with an under-standing that strategies represented the activities and processes students used to learn. Although style was commonly conceptualized as the way an individual likes to go about learning, there was a range of understandings. Some participants saw style differences between individuals as representing the different ways people make meanings from information while others saw it as a different mix of preferences associated with sensory modalities such as visual, auditory and kinaesthetic. Although a number of participant trainers spoke of particular theories and models of styles that they were familiar with, the majority of people identified the styles of learners they taught at a fairly pragmatic macro-level in terms of the sensory modalities mentioned above, together with student preferences for:

- self-paced learning, self-direction and independent learning;
- reading;
- hands-on experience;
- learning with structure and guidance;
- learning through social interaction with others.

It was evident here that trainers analysed learner styles at a level they could observe in the classroom or the training room, and that they could actually use in their training design and delivery. The pragmatic approach was evident among most participants in the research and meant that they could work with styles at a usable level of analysis. The model shown in Figure 8.3 indicates that an instructor or facilitator may begin with some ideas about the likely group style of learning, based on some preconceptions derived from their experience with similar groups in the past.

As the group learning proceeds, the instructor/facilitator may make observations about individual learners in the group, based on their apparent preferences for different learning contexts (shown in the top box on the right of Figure 8.3); and the preferences of individual group members for the different content presentation methods. Through those observations a picture of individual student preferences may be developed, together with a sense of the diversity among these that exists within the group. The Smith and Dalton (2005) research indicated that these perceptions of the individual characteristics of learners were processed cognitively by the instructor/facilitator to develop a composite picture of the general style of the group, together with the individual variations within that general style. The general style picture served to challenge the original set of preconceptions and expectations such that those become tested and modified as the interactions with the group and its component individuals proceeded. On the basis of the emerging picture of the group style and preference, the instructor/facilitator may modify the strategies used for group teaching and learning (bottom box on the right of Figure 8.3), as well as modifying those used for each individual in the group (bottom box on the left). There was also evidence in the research that trainers would 'test' individual and group preferences by trying things out that they expected to work well on the basis of their observations and then evaluate whether or not that initiative had worked. The feedback arrow in the model indicates that these processes were ongoing and iterative. Accordingly, through a mix of ongoing observation the trainer continuously developed and improved her or his understanding of the group and individual's style and preferences, and developed and adjusted their methods.

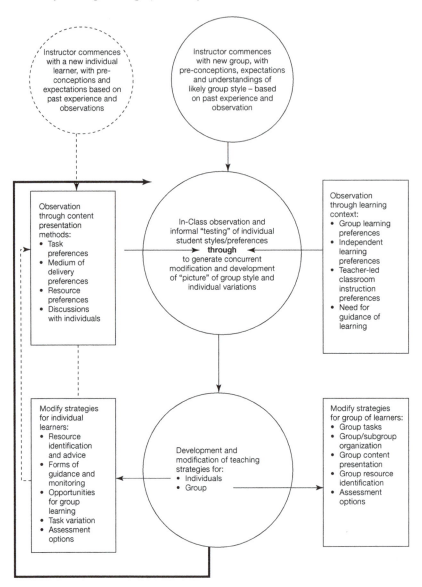

Figure 8.3 Model for a responsive and interactive pedagogy based on learner style/preferences

The model in Figure 8.3 is likely to work best with smaller groups of no more than around ten to fifteen learners. The model can also be interpreted at an individual level, and the dashed lines in Figure 8.3 indicate how the process may work with individual learners. Where the learning is delivered through an independent learning approach, perhaps in a distance-education format, the instructor/facilitator has less opportunity for naturalistic observation and, therefore, less opportunity to make adjustments on the basis of those observations. However, it may be possible to include in the HRD delivery design some ways in which interaction occurs at a level sufficient for limited insight into learner styles and preferences, as was evidenced in the Smith and Dalton (2005) research where they observed that some conclusions about learners were reached by trainers on a basis of what they understood to be occurring outside the scope of their direct observation.

Focus on practice: responding flexibly to learner needs

The following section is based on research conducted by Smith and Dalton (2005). Part of that research focused on training within a mining environment, where learners worked in remote locations and were developing knowledge and skills in supervision of mining operations. The company had developed a number of methods for achieving learning, including the development of printed material, some computer-based learning materials, and workshops that were held in group settings. The learner analysis showed that learners were from different backgrounds and with different learning experiences and preferred methods of learning. The learning context had some complexities, since learners were involved in different parts of a large plant, and in shift work; as much as was possible the learning needed to take place in independent learning format. Some learners were ready for that while others were less so. The company was able to support occasional group components where all participants assembled in the same place at the same time.

The strategy put in place to achieve required learning outcomes needed to recognise those limitations and opportunities, and deliver quality learning outcomes that enabled full competence to be developed in as short a time as possible. Due to safety requirements that were imposed legislatively as well as through company policy and desired performance levels, the training needed to be thorough and to be assessed.

The strategy developed was a flexible one, based on an initial workshop of two days for the twelve participants. The company hired an experienced trainer with a strong interest in the Honey and Mumford (1992) learning styles theory. Using a technique similar to the interactive model we have provided in Figure 8.3, the trainer devoted considerable time during the group workshop to identifying each individual's learning style. Once the trainer felt she had developed an understanding of each style, she worked with each individual to develop the written learning plan (see Figure 8.2) most likely to suit that learner, to include activities, resources and milestones to be reached. Resources were identified from those available already within the company resource bank and made available to each learner as required. Additionally, managers of each learner were involved in developing an understanding of each learning plan so that support could be provided, and time made available for the learning to proceed.

The trainer then continued to work with each individual as the learning proceeded, to evaluate progress towards learning achievement as the learning continued. Adjustments were made to the contract in a way similar to the model we have shown in Figure 8.2 through regular interaction between the trainer and the learner.

Once both the trainer and the learner were satisfied that the learning outcomes had been achieved to the required level, assessment was conducted by a third party.

The process used in developing this approach to the learning mirrors substantially the strategic planning process we have shown in Figure 8.1, and was strongly based on a flexible and responsive model that took account of trainer observations of preferred style.

Responding to diversity: questions for situational analysis

In this chapter we have presented a series of frameworks that may be used to plan HRD that enables a more tailored response to diversities amongst learners and their environments.

Planning the blend

The models shown in Figure 8.1 and Tables 8.1 to 8.4 may enable a flexible response to the learning needs of a group or an individual and the 'blend' they may use in the learning to be planned. Once the target group of learners has been identified, the questions posed in Tables 8.1 to 8.4 may assist in the learner and environmental analysis and the selection from the various strategy choices which should then enable an implementation plan to be put together.

Developing individual learners through flexibility

Figure 8.2 illustrates a sequence which addresses the various activities associated with developing individuals' knowledge and skills and also serves to develop the learner towards greater self-direction. The sequence has a number of associated questions:

- Who is the appropriate person to develop the plan with the learner?
- What is to be achieved through the plan?
- Who should work with the learner to facilitate and guide achievement, as well as monitor progress?
- What is the reward for successful pursuit and achievement of the plan?
- What are the planning, discussion and control actions and the schedule that needs to be put in place around this plan?

- Who is responsible for identifying necessary resources and acquiring them for learner use?
- Who should put in place the relationships with others that will facilitate achievement of the plan?
- Can barriers be successfully identified and strategies developed to overcome them? Who should do that?

Ongoing monitoring of learning

Figure 8.3 shows how trainers and other HRD personnel can observe individual learners in action, or groups of learners, and adjust learning delivery in a flexible way to suit the learning process. The major issues relate to the sensitivity of trainers and HRD personnel to the characteristics of learners as they go about their learning and upon which adjustments to the learning may be made. The major questions here are:

- Can the people in my organization make the sorts of observations and adjustments that may be necessary?
- What training and HRD skills do I need to put in place with them to ensure that they can make informed judgements?

9 The reflective HRD practitioner

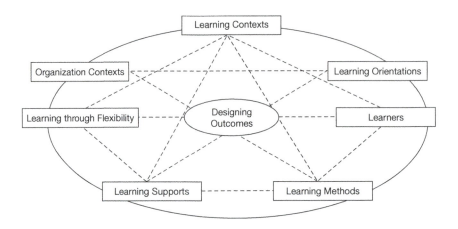

Introduction

A fundamental argument of this book is that an organization's human resource base is a strategically important source of competitive advantage; a corollary of this is that managers and HRD practitioners have a key role to play in the development of the knowledge and skills which are a crucial aspect of this. The argument draws upon a resource-based view (RBV) of the firm (see Colbert, 2004: 341). The RBV has been one of the theoretical drivers of strategic human resource management (SHRM) (see Barney, 1991), and by extension strategic human resource development (SHRD) (see for example: Garavan, Costine and Heraty, 1995) over the past decade and more. The RBV states that a firm's competitive advantage is based upon the acquisition, development and effective combination and deployment of its resources (physical, human and organizational) in ways that add value and which are difficult to imitate (Barney, 1991).

The effective acquisition, deployment and development (the latter is our prime interest) of a firm's human resource base and the associated intellectual and social capital depend upon consideration of a wide range of interacting factors. Traditionally the principles that underpin HRD policy, planning and practice have tended to take a technical, rational and systematic (not necessarily systems) approach to the analysis, design, implementation and evaluation of HRD projects in organizations (see, for example, Goldstein, 1993). Whilst this approach has undoubted strengths it also has inherent limitations (reductionism and over-simplification being two of these).

We have argued that a complementary but less reductive approach is needed which:

1   First, provides tools which may help managers to identify, explore and reflect upon the ways in which their firm's human resource base may be utilised and developed in more effective ways. In this book we have sought to provide a set of tools to assist this process.
2   Second, enables practitioners to more easily recognise and suggest ways of accommodating the complexities of the organizational and business environments in which managers and learners operate. Again, throughout this book we have provided tools which may aid reflection.

Recognising the need for a less reductive approach, but one that can more readily embrace the diversities and complexities that form the contexts for organizational learning, requires an acknowledgement of at least three significant issues:

1   The concept of complexity in professional HRD practice. This must be set against a background of environmental dynamism, uncertainty and ambiguity and be based upon the assumption that an organization is a system that is composed of a large number of agents which interact in linear and nonlinear ways (see Stacey, Griffin and Shaw, 2000).
2   The importance of the situated nature of learning and the significance and implications for HRD theory and practice of the acceptance of and adherence to the principles that underpin this assertion, that is, the assumption that work-related learning incorporates the process of participation-in-action in a community of shared understandings and accountabilities.
3   The role played by reflection-in-action and reflection-on-practice (Schön, 1983) and the ways in which reflection can influence current and future HRD practice.

A theme which runs through each of the above is that of the range of issues and their diversities that the HRD practitioner is faced with and which render the arena of HRD practice complicated and complex. The various dimensions of a number of these diversities have been the main concern of each of the chapters that make up the body of the book. In this, the final chapter, we will turn our consideration to the three issues of complexity, the situated nature of learning, and reflection. These should be seen against a backcloth in which the book's overarching aim has been to provide a framework for enquiry which acknowledges the complexities of learning for practice and in practice.

Complexity and HRD practice

A central concept in complexity theory is that a complex system is more than a 'mere' complicated system. With time and effort a complicated system may be reducible to its component parts whereas a complex system may be quite simple but irreducible – the essence of the whole is impossible to quantify (Lee, 2003). This is not to say that relationships and underlying principles cannot be inferred in a complex system (Lee, 2003), but a reduced representation of the world trades complexity for simplicity. Allen (2001) has identified the assumptions that underpin a tendency to simplify (which we elaborate and interpret here in the context of HRD):

1   Defining the relevant system boundary in order that the 'less relevant' is excluded. In HRD this may occur by defining inputs (e.g. needs) and outputs (e.g. effects) of the system and by specifying discrete levels of analysis (e.g. individual, job, group, organization) (see Sadler-Smith, 2006).
2   The reduction of full heterogeneity to a typology of elements. In HRD this may occur when diversities at the individual level are glossed over, for example, by making the assumption that 'one size fits all'.
3   (Related to the above.) Assumes individuals of an 'average type', and hence ignores important sources of and expressions of individual difference.
4   Processes are assumed to run at an average rate (for example, when employing generic HRD solutions or implementing organization change programmes).

Whilst we are not elaborating here a complexity-theory-based interpretation of HRD (that would be a much bigger task – see Lee, 2003), we are suggesting that HRD principles and practice have sometimes attempted to reduce the inherent complexity of the system with a consequent loss of richness in the picture that confronts the practitioner. As a result, there may be premature reduction in the possible responses that may be made within a given context. Whilst this is understandable, the application of the four assumptions listed above in HRD practice often results in a reduced representation of the complexity of the system. The simplification techniques used in practice manifest themselves in various guises, for example the systematic approach (a 'plan–do–check' cycle), functional analysis and the production of generic competence statements, task analyses, the derivation of behavioural objectives and pre-planned outcomes and so forth. Rather than attempting to create a reduced representation of reality in what is a complex and causally ambiguous situation, an alternative way forward may be to provide a means by which questions relating to the complex whole may be framed. Hence in this book we have taken the approach of providing the practitioner with a framework and a set of tools that may help to develop and focus queries or conjectures which may then serve as a basis for an enquiry-based interpretation of the HRD system of interest.

In the preceding discussion we have alluded to causal ambiguity. In this context it may be defined as the uncertainty surrounding the causal relationships between actions and results. When competitive advantage is derived from causally ambiguous competencies the potential exists for averting imitation by competitors (Reed and DeFillippi, 1990: 91). Colbert (2004) has pointed out one of the problems of RBV and SHRM research is the very causal ambiguity that is claimed as one of the distinctive features of an RBV paradigm. One reason that it may be potentially problematic is that it may be ambiguous to the managers themselves and hence uninterpretable. In HRD for example, causal ambiguity has bedevilled much of the evaluation of training research at the results level (the fourth and highest level in Kirkpatrick's (1998) original four-level evaluation framework). This may sometimes render investment in training decisions to be based more upon expert judgements than meticulously calculated bottom-line pay-offs. This is not to say that such analyses are impossible but they may be difficult to achieve in practice, see for example the practitioner work of Phillips (1996) and the econometric analyses of Bassi, Ludwig, McMurrer and van Buren (2002) and Molina and Ortega (2003). Colbert also noted that this causal ambiguity may only be a problem in so far as the researcher, theoretician or practitioner attempts to untangle the causal ambiguity in order to render simple that which is complex. An acceptance of the unpredictable and emergent properties of the system allows more effort to be focused upon the processes by which the elements of the system 'mingle and interact' (2004: 342). Colbert elaborated upon these issues in the context of the universalistic, contingency and configurational perspectives of SHRM and it is from his discussions that we attempt to draw some lessons for HRD.

UNIVERSALISTIC APPROACH

A specific problem that Colbert identified in the universalistic approach to SHRM (i.e. that some practices are always better than others) is that it is unconcerned with interaction effects (for example, some HRD practices might work better under certain sets of circumstances than under others). This view is problematic in that such practices are likely to become widely adopted and institutionalised and might not therefore provide a unique or difficult-to-imitate source of competitive advantage. So for example, if induction training is one of the HRD practices that reveal universal benefits, then clearly it will be sensible for all firms and departments to provide induction training for new employees, but this largely ignores a whole host of issues pertinent to the design and delivery of such training. An induction programme that works well in one setting may work less well in others and vice versa. Therefore, over and above the universal value of certain forms of HRD there are detailed issues at the local level that must be taken into account in the fine-tuning of HRD practice. 'Sameness' and institutionalisation cannot, by definition, cater well for diversities. One argument of this book is that the acknowledgement of complexity and the accommodation of diversity are critical to the success of HRD. This represents one way of circumventing the sameness of a universalistic approach and thereby may provide a unique and difficult-to-imitate set of HRD practices. Throughout this book, and most particularly in Chapters 7 and 8, we have described in some detail tools that will enable context-specific HRD responses to be generated. It is their uniqueness that may make it difficult for imitation by competitor organizations. Copying may be futile because context-specific HRD is a specifically developed response to particular sets of local issues and it is from this that value may be derived. Any attempts at benchmarking HRD practice should take this into account.

Colbert (2004) noted that in the contingency view the effectiveness of HR practices (including HRD) depends upon how well they fit with other aspects of the organization. The main concern of the contingency approach is the vertical fit with business strategy (an external variable) and 'internal system interaction effects are not a central concern' (2004: 344). This presents a potential problem for HRD in the sense that HRD is clearly concerned with external factors (for example, the skills needed to compete successfully in a particular market or the appropriateness of certain forms of HRD in particular national cultures), but the successful implementation of HRD depends also upon a cognisance of a whole host of internal factors such as the organizational culture (some forms of HRD will fit whilst others will not), the unique needs of the individual and the way in which he or she prefers to learn and so on and so forth. These can be recognised, acknowledged and, where it is possible and appropriate to do so, may be accommodated in the design of HRD through effective use of the tools we have provided.

CONFIGURATIONAL APPROACH

The configurational perspective in SHRM goes some way to acknowledging the limitations of the contingency perspective in that it recognises the role played by 'multiple dimensions of organizations' and focuses upon the patterns that together may go to make up an internally consistent whole (Colbert, 2004: 344–345). From a research perspective one of the disadvantages of the configurational approach is that within a positivist paradigm it is difficult to construct and test models of more than a small number of variables (Colbert, 2004). The practical advantage of the configurational perspective is twofold (Nelson and Winter, 1982):

1   It enables practitioners to blend together a range of what are perceived to be significant factors in the local organizational system.
2   The 'recipe' thus derived is one which is likely to be difficult for competitors to imitate by copying or 'reverse engineering'.

The ingredients available to the firm in these circumstances, and from which a 'recipe' might be constructed, depend upon, amongst other things, some of the contextual, organizational and individual-level diversities outlined in the preceding chapters.

A further paradox highlighted by Reed and DeFillippi (1990) is that causal ambiguity may be derived from knowledge and skills which are themselves tacit and may be acquired through processes of implicit learning (for example as a result of exposure to expertise or a human model *in situ*, perhaps as a member of a community of practice). With this in mind it is important that organizations recognise the significance of implicit learning, tacit knowledge and the development of expertise, and where possible take steps to encourage the development of tacit knowledge and skill. The proactive management of communities of practice through 'design' (see the discussion of Wenger's work below) is one way in which managers and HRD practitioners may take steps to enable both explicit and implicit learning.

Colbert's (2004) analysis takes the heuristics (i.e. principles used in taking decisions when all possibilities cannot be fully explored) for nurturing complex living systems and translates these into HR principles, policies and processes. Although his focus is on the broader domain of HRM, some of his suggestions arguably are pertinent to HRD, for example:

*   'Distribute being' by eradicating arbitrary boarders and building broad-based identity. This might be achieved through cross-functional working (secondments and postings), induction training, team building and leadership development.
*   'Control from bottom up' by feeding information to all levels. This might be achieved by creating an understanding of the whole business, coaching at all levels and formal and informal communication and learning processes and the use of technology (such as intranets) to support the distribution of information and informal learning, and the gathering of information by workers who are at the organization's boundaries (see Pedler, Burgoyne and Boydell, 1997).
*   'Cultivate increasing returns' by creating positive reinforcement in the system and being deliberate and precise with language and symbols. This might be achieved by using consistent models and language in

development programmes and a high level of customisation of HRD programmes rather than using generic off-the-shelf packages or over-relying on outsourced programmes.

- 'Grow by chunking' though local innovation and building learning capacity: this might be achieved through allowing inconsistencies across departments (as a source of creative tension) and fostering and supporting communities of practice and other learning forums.
- 'Honour your errors' by encouraging reflective practices and having reward systems that recognise the 'greatest learning experiences'.
- 'Pursue multiple goals' by incorporating the perspectives of different groups of stakeholders and being tolerant of multiple aims and the definition of value from diverse stakeholders' perspectives (Colbert, 2004: 354).

Allen (2001) advocated that rather than trying to create a 'true' representation of the reality of the complex system, the analyst provides 'causal conjectures' that can be compared with and tested against reality. When a fit is found with our perception of reality he argued that we may feel temporarily satisfied; when there is not a fit we can set out to explore why. The production of such causal conjectures requires an interpretative framework for sense-making and knowledge-building (Allen, 2001: 26). The interpretative framework furnishes questions to which attempts are made to provide answers; the questions are those of interest to the practitioners and other stakeholders; they are a means to interpret reality but will in all probability change over time. At any given juncture there are multiple possible behaviours (Allen, 2001: 29), the range and diversity of which may be identifiable through a process of questioning and enquiry. The questions that we have provided at the end of each of the chapters are an interpretative framework whereby HRD practitioners and managers may jointly construct what appear to be relevant questions and use these as the basis for enquiry, interpretation and action in situations that may be complex, dynamic and uncertain and which in the light of experience may require reinterpretation and reframing in practice.

The situated nature of HRD practice

When interpreting HRD from an RBV perspective, the situated nature of knowledge and skill emerges as being of crucial importance. Work-related learning is situated in a context, affected by and affecting the context (hence a 'situated' view of learning), the context being the community of practice (CoP) defined as:

> a set of relations among persons, activity and the world, over time and in relation with other tangential and overlapping communities of

practice. A community of practice is an intrinsic condition for the existence of knowledge, not least because it provides the interpretive support necessary for making sense of its heritage.

(Lave and Wenger, 1991: 98)

Newcomers become included in a community of practice through a naturalistic process of legitimate peripheral participation (LPP). Peripherality, which is a precursor to full inclusion, gives two things: first, access and exposure to real-world practice from the edge; second, a sense of how the community operates. Legitimacy operates in the sense that those individuals chosen to participate may be treated as potential members of the community. The structure of a community of practice is complex, unique and variable between contexts and over time and hence is organization-specific and difficult to imitate. However, as we have demonstrated in preceding chapters, a community of practice can be strategically deployed to assist in the development of a unique HRD response.

A strategically valuable HRD system is organization-specific, and the capabilities that underpin it are likely to be distributed amongst the members of the organization. Any attempt by competitors to 'poach' key players may be futile in the sense that once taken out of context the socially embedded knowledge and skills of individuals may be of limited value in the new context (Becker and Gerhart, 1996; Colbert, 2004). For the displaced individual this may entail building new sets of localised knowledge through engagement with other practitioners. The difficulty of transplanting knowledge and skills constitutes what Peteraf and others have referred to as 'imperfect mobility'. Socially embodied, contextualised firm-specific knowledge and skills are amongst the most imperfectly mobile of resources (Peteraf, 1993). What is more mobile is the capability to learn (i.e. the skills to exploit learning opportunities effectively). The ability to engage with learning and learning to learn is a valuable individual and organizational competence which transcends localised knowledge and skills. Given that learning belongs to the realm of experience and practice, Wenger argued that learning cannot be designed per se, but it can be 'designed for' and that 'there are few more urgent tasks than to design social infrastructures that foster learning' (1998: 225).

So where does that leave the manager or HRD practitioner who may be required to engage in 'acts of design', the likely aim of which is to influence, manage or attempt to control informal as well as formal learning processes in organizations? One of the most crucial aspects of the HRD practitioner's role is to create contexts in which learning can take place. In a social system, such as the workplace, learning cannot be guaranteed, but sets of conditions can be created which increase the probability of learning taking place; moreover by creating conditions that foster learning there may be at least two additional outcomes: first, unintentional, incidental or implicit learning may occur and, second, employees' opportunities for, and motivations to engage in learning may be enhanced on an ongoing, and perhaps even a career- or life-long, basis.

Wenger (1998) offered some general guidelines for the design or building of learning communities based upon the precept that training in any new task or skill (but especially the training of newcomers) engenders a process of reflection that serves both the trainees and the community more widely. For this to occur it is important that learning be construed as a process of participation in practice in which the emphasis is placed upon learning rather than teaching, and that the design of practice is as a place of learning in which resources are made accessible to negotiate connections with other practices (Wenger, 1998: 249). In terms of how this might occur, Wenger argued that is likely to rely upon a number of factors including the following:

RESOURCES

The resources (which often are modest) to create a 'rhythm of engagement', imagination and alignment, for example by means of a period of intensified reflection away from the workplace and the comings-together of individuals who are geographically disparate. From an HRD perspective this may involve some shift in the purpose of HRD, for example from an instructional and knowledge dissemination purpose to the creation of opportunities for knowledge sharing and interpretation, by building a strong continuity between classroom-based activities and the workplace (through partnerships between HRD practitioners and line managers), and the application of specific tools and techniques that may help intensify and 'oil the wheels' of mutual engagement (for example, action learning sets, technology-based knowledge sharing systems and so forth).

DIMENSIONS OF DESIGN

Wenger suggested that there are four dimensions of the learning situation which need to be recognised:

1   Negotiation of meaning through participation in which action calls upon a wealth of past interpretation and negotiation. In terms of planning HRD this calls for newcomers to be exposed to and interact with experienced members of the community in a structured way.
2   Preservation and creation of knowledge through living practices, as well as through books and databases. In HRD this calls for the recognition of the 'softer' and more tacit forms of corporate memory which are embedded in practice.
3   The pursuit of a joint enterprise with mutual accountability makes the spreading and sharing of information absolutely necessary in communities of practice. These communities are nodes for dissemination,

interpretation and application of information. In HRD this calls for the recognition of practice in community as the focal point of learning.

4   The creation and reinforcement of individual identity through participation, and a contribution to the community that has shaped and continues to shape those identities (1998: 253). From an HRD standpoint this calls for conscious attempts to develop and reinforce identities which have mutual interests and mutual accountabilities (for example through team building and leadership development).

Arguably there are parallels between Wenger's assertions regarding the issue of 'identity' and Colbert's complexity-based view in which he called for the eradication of arbitrary borders and the building of a broad-based identity. The practice of HRD might therefore concern itself with the ways in which organizational and work design may contribute to the building of individual and collective identity, for example by cross-functional working, job re-design, and project teams.

BOUNDARIES

Shared practice and generation of meaning gives, according to Wenger, a deepening of the differences between being 'inside' and 'outside' the community. In this respect boundaries can be 'productive discontinuities' (1998: 254) and need to be recognised and understood in this way since they may enable a better appreciation of potential problems of miscommunication, poor coordination, oversight and lack of integration of newcomers. Induction training, coaching and mentoring are all means by which the extant boundaries may become apparent and made explicit to newcomers. Team building activities are ways by which longer-serving employees may reflect upon their own collective identity (and the associated boundaries) and the ways in which this relates to the rest of the organization.

MEANING RATHER THAN MECHANICS

Thus far in our discussion we have used the term 'learner', but Wenger argued (1998: 266) that this itself may be problematic in the sense that in using the term we are reifying participants as learners and also reifying learning as a process. Reifying is the act of treating (materializing) an abstraction as substantially existing or as a 'thing' or concrete material object. Seeing learning as a product of meaningful activities and the learner as a participant in action avoids some of the difficulties of reification. But what does this mean for HRD practice? In our view it involves asking questions based upon Wenger (1998: 266) regarding:

1   The extent to which practice (and the associated knowledge and skills) actually needs to be reified for HRD's purposes;

2   What kinds of practice and participation are required in an HRD which aspires towards facilitating meaningful learning?
3   How far should the reification proceed, or indeed is it required in the first place, before it becomes counter to the aims of HRD, learning and participation in action?

As we have discussed in preceding chapters, for the practitioner these questions translate into flexible responses that are concerned with:

1   the extent to which learning is best conducted at-job, that is *in situ*, rather than in the classroom (and whether it is an either/or question);
2   how at-job learning may be designed in such a way to be as efficient and effective as possible by the creation of a context for learning practice (rather than its being left to chance);
3   how at-job and off-job learning may be successfully integrated in order that they reinforce each other.

This endeavour subsumes many of the issues already alluded to above. The situating of learning in the local context is by definition unique, organization-specific and causally ambiguous. When this causal ambiguity is perceived and interpreted in a less reductive way than technical rationality models of HRD practice (see below) might suggest, the learning that takes place and the capacity to learn may present themselves as potentially valuable and difficult to imitate. In Chapter 8 we have provided some tools that help in the development of flexible responses that are suited to context and learner.

Reflection and HRD practice

As the occupational structure of many western economies and the structure of individual organizations have each evolved there has, within management, been a general rise in the significance of professional work and of managerial professional groups. Within the field of HRD there is the group to whom we have referred as 'practitioners' (this being less contentious than the term 'professional') and whilst the label is not ideal, it is a useful blanket term intended to encompass those individuals whose role engages them in the formal planning, implementation, evaluation or management of activities which are intended to enable and assist (Sadler-Smith, 2006):

1   employees in acquiring new knowledge, skills or attitudes (for example, by providing planned HRD);
2   the collective learning process in organizations (for example, by facilitating or supporting organizational development and change).

The term 'HRD practitioner' is not intended to encompass other groups of stakeholders such as line managers since for these groups, although they may have some key HRD responsibilities, this is not the main part of their job role.

There are ongoing debates about the professional status of the HR practitioner. It has been argued that for the HRD practitioners' role to be sustained, grow and gain continued recognition practitioners must take learning seriously and strategically in an organizational context in which learning is inclusive and built into the ethos of practice (Gold, Rodgers and Smith, 2003: 447). The enhanced esteem and professional status to which Gold *et al.* allude is important if planned interventions are to be successful in supporting organizational strategy and enhancing business performance by getting the 'buy-in' of senior managers especially in turbulent business environments and where resources may be scarce.

One of the issues that professionals in general face is that of matching professional knowledge to the changing characteristics of the problematic situations of practice. The latter are 'inherently unstable' and subject to the forces of uncertainty, instability, uniqueness and value conflicts (Schön, 1983: 14). Against this backcloth each HRD situation, problem or dilemma, with its own unique combination of circumstances (which may be describable in terms of some of the dimensions of diversity we have elucidated in this book) may often present itself to the practitioner as a 'universe of one' (i.e. a unique case) for which 'text book' solutions derived from a technical rationalist approach may serve to reduce complexity and obscure the subtleties of local issues.

Technical rationality was defined by Donald Schön in his seminal work *The Reflective Practitioner: How Professionals Think in Action* as 'instrumental problem solving made rigorous by the application of scientific theory and technique' (1983: 21) based in a positivist epistemology of practice. In HRD the development of a 'technological (i.e. technical rational) HRD' was given an impetus by the Second World War and parallel developments in HRD's base disciplines such as psychology and economics. The origins of many of the principles of modern HRD practice may be traced to the Training Within Industry (TWI) Service of the US Government in the period 1940 to 1945 which had two objectives: to help contractors to the US Government's war effort pursue faster production and to reduce the costs of production of war materials (Ruona, 2001: 121). Rather than training being viewed as an end in itself, it was seen instrumentally as a means to achieving the desired objectives (increased production of resources to support the war effort). The ethos and method of the TWI approach were described by Ruona (2001: 122–5) and included as a central plank of training practice a systematic approach in which training should be based upon the sound analysis of tasks and work processes and be structured to provide opportunity for demonstration, practice and feedback (i.e. training should be based upon assessed needs and implemented in a workplace climate that is conducive to facilitating the transfer of learning from the training situation to the job situation). The various instructional-systems design methodologies (see Patrick, 1992) are further examples of this approach.

A number of authors have pointed out limitations in this systematic approach; for example, according to Pedler *et al.* (1997), the approach to planned learning in organizations in the UK has evolved from a systematic training model (1950s to 1970s), through self-development and action-based approaches (1980s) up to the decades in which the approach in their book (*The Learning Company*) was conceived (the 1980s and 1990s) and the advent of the 'learning organization' movement. They argued that paradoxically we never actually 'get there' (to the ideal approach) because as one problem is solved by the latest method (for example, systematic training) another emerges (for example, lack of transfer of learning from the training room to the work environment) because 'the seeds of [the next problem] were sown by the previous solution' (1997: 12). So for example, the systematic approach (a 'plan–design–do–check' cycle) was limited by its reductionism (the splitting or reducing of jobs into tangible micro-skills was not universally applicable, especially in managerial and creative job roles) which created, amongst other things, problems in relation to describing managerial roles in performance terms with concomitant issues for how to develop managers.

In HRD, therefore, as in other areas of professional practice, the technical rationalist approach has revealed limitations in part born out of the underlying positivistic assumptions. Schön (1983: 40) summarised this general issue succinctly when he argued that:

> From the perspective of Technical Rationality, professional practice is a process of problem solving. Problems of choice or decision are solved through the selection from available means, of the one best suited to established ends. But with this emphasis on problem solving, we ignore problem setting, the process by which we define the decision to be made, the ends to be achieved, the means which may be chosen.

The two key points that Schön makes, and with which we concur in the HRD context, are that:

1 First, in the real-world HRD problems do not present themselves neatly packaged as 'givens', rather they (like solutions) have to be constructed from the puzzling and sometimes messy material of the problematic situation (for example, inadequate workforce performance);
2 Second, problem setting is not itself a technical problem, rather it is an activity by which the practitioner names the things to be attended to and frames the context in which she or he will attend to them.

Clearly, therefore, the way in which the HRD practitioner frames her or his identity and the conjectures whereby problems are named is central to practice. For example, the HRD practice role may manifest itself as one for which the purpose is to be a 'passive provider' of instructional events. Within this conception the naming of problems and framing of solutions is likely to take a particular (perhaps instrumental) form, with convergence towards a set solution (provision of instruction) to meet pre-specified (perhaps behavioural) ends. Contrast this with an HRD role of 'change agent' whereby quite different problems are likely to be perceived and which may be framed in quite different ways. Different thinking and professional skills will be associated with different conceptualizations of the HRD practitioner's role: for example, these may be convergent, technical and analytical in the 'technical rationalist' view of the role; divergent, intuitive and artistic in a 'craft' view of the role.

Of course complex HRD problems rely upon the application of the principles derived from the scientific bases of HRD, but more than this they also call for the craft and artistry which is embodied in HRD expertise which is developed *in situ* through engagement with the 'messiness' of everyday practice and through interaction with the community of HRD practitioners, and with learners and managers. Schön (1983: 49) called for an articulation of the epistemology of practice which is implicit in the intuitive processes that skilled practitioners bring to situations of uncertainty, instability, uniqueness and value conflict. At the core of this epistemology is reflection (reflection-in-action and reflection-on-action) as a legitimate form of professional knowing within a broader context of reflective enquiry which subsumes the expertise conferred by a mere technical rationalist knowledge and skill base.

Conclusion

This book is concerned with how to develop an HRD practice that acknowledges and accommodates a number of dimensions of diversity at the individual and organizational levels. As far as the development of 'professional' HRD is concerned, it is important for practitioners to be trained and developed or to be able to self-develop in order that they may, almost as a matter of course, reflect upon their actions in complex and messy situations. The solving of problems and the setting of problems are linked inextricably; problems are named and framed and solutions emerge through a reflective process of enquiry, that is, by the deceptively simple act of asking questions. But what are the questions that should be asked and what does the knowledge base of the profession have that may contribute to the identification of the questions that might be asked? Our argument in this book has been that effective HRD practice depends upon a consideration of the complex, ambiguous and uncertain nature of the situation in question. Underpinning much of the complexity, ambiguity and uncertainty in HRD are the dimensions of individual and contextual variability (i.e. diversity) that exist and interact in many real-world situations. These are our dimensions of diversity.

Our questions are intended as aids to reflection which may allow problems to be set and solved. The reflective HRD practitioner may ask questions around these and other issues (we do not make any claims of the exhaustiveness of our dimensions) in order that he or she may frame problems and devise solutions that have the potential to be more divergent, holistic, creative and, ultimately, more effective than might be the case if a purely technical rationalist approach were adopted.

From an exclusively reductive point of view, these 'messy' differences may be seen as sources of confusion which complicate practice, and it may be tempting to filter them from our perceptions or assign them to what Schön might refer to as 'junk' categories (1983: 69). On the other hand, they may be seen as potential sources of differentiation which, if reflected on and configured in appropriate ways, may present a source of individual and organizational learning and growth. The capability to accommodate these issues into a blend of HRD policies, plans and practices that work within a particular organizational setting is likely to be a very rare commodity and a valuable source of sustained competitive advantage for individuals and the organizations of which they are a part.

References

Aditya, R.N., House, R.J. and Kerr, S. (2000) 'Theory and practice of leadership: into the new millennium', in C.L. Cooper and A.E. Locke (eds), *Industrial and Organizational Psychology: Linking Theory with Practice*, Oxford: Blackwell.

Alderfer, C. (1972) *Human Needs in Organizational Settings*, New York: Free Press.

Alessi, S.M. and Trollip, S.R. (2001) *Multimedia for Learning: Methods and Development*, Boston, Mass.: Allyn & Bacon.

Alfred, M.V. (2002) 'The promise of socio-cultural theory in democratizing education', in M.V. Alfred (ed.) *Learning and Socio-cultural Contexts: Implications for Adults, Community, and Workplace Education*, San Francisco, Calif.: Jossey-Bass, pp. 3–14.

Allen, P. (2001) 'What is complexity science? Knowledge of the limits to knowledge', *Emergence*, 3(1): 24–42.

Alsagoff, S. (1985) 'Learning styles of Malaysian distance education students', paper presented to the 13th World Conference, International Council of Distance Education, Melbourne.

Anderson, J.R. (1982) 'Acquisition of cognitive skill', *Psychological Review*, 89, 369–406.

Argyris, C. (2002) 'Double loop learning, teaching and research', *Academy of Management Learning and Education*, 1(2): 206–219.

Argyris, C. and Schön, D.A. (1996) *Organizational Learning II: Theory, Method and Practice*, Reading, Mass.: Addison-Wesley.

Arthur, M. (1994) 'The boundaryless career', *Journal of Organizational Behavior*, 15: 295–306.

Australian National Training Authority (2003) *Working and Learning in Vocational Education and Training in the Knowledge Era*, available at <http://flexible learning.net.au/projects/pdfuture.htm> (accessed 29 April 2005).

Ausubel, D.P. (1968) *Educational Psychology: A Cognitive View*, New York: Holt, Rinehart & Winston.

Baker, M. and Wooden, M. (1995) *Small and Medium-sized Enterprises and Vocational Education and Training*, Adelaide: National Centre for Vocational Education Research.

Bandura, A. (1977) *Social Learning Theory*, Englewood Cliffs, NJ: Prentice-Hall.

Barab, S.S. and Duffy, T.M. (2000) 'From practice fields to communities of practice', in D.H. Jonassen and S.M. Land (eds) *Theoretical Foundations of Learning Environments*, London: Lawrence Erlbaum Associates, pp. 25–56.

Barney, J.B. (1991) 'Firm resources and sustained competitive advantage', *Journal of Management*, 17(1): 99–120.

Barney, J.B. (1999) 'Looking inside for competitive advantage', in R.S. Schuler and S.E. Jackson (eds) *Strategic Human Resource Management*, Oxford: Blackwell.

Barry, C. (1996) 'Flexible delivery: some issues and priorities', *Training Agenda*, 4(3): 3–4.

Bartlett, C.A. and Ghosal, S. (1993) 'Beyond the M-form: toward a managerial theory of the firm', *Strategic Management Journal*, 14, 23–46.

Bartlett, K.R. (2001) 'The relationship between training and organizational commitment: a study in the health care field', *Human Resource Development Quarterly*, 12(4): 335–352.

Bassi, L.J., Ludwig, J., McMurrer, D.P. and van Buren, M. (2002) 'Profiting from learning: firm level effects of training investments and market implications', *Singapore Management Review*, 24(3): 61–75.

Bauman, Z. (2001) *The Individualized Society*, Cambridge: Polity Press.

Beamish, N., Armistead, C., Watkinson, M. and Armfield, G. (2002) 'The deployment of e-learning in European corporate organizations', *European Business Review*, 14(3): 105–115.

Becker B. and Gerhart, B. (1996) 'The impact of human resource management on organizational performance', *Academy of Management Journal*, 39: 779–801.

Bennett, R. and Leduchowicz, T. (1983) 'What makes an effective trainer?', *Journal of European Industrial Training* (Special Issue), 7(2).

Berge, Z. (ed.) (2001) *Sustaining Distance Education: Integrating Learning Technologies into the Fabric of the Enterprise*, San Francisco, Calif.: Jossey-Bass.

Berlyne, D.E. (1960) *Conflict, Arousal and Curiosity*, New York: McGraw-Hill.

Berry, M. (1993) 'Changing perspectives on facilitation skills development', *Journal of European Industrial Training*, 17(3): 23–32.

Berryman, S.E. (1991) *Solutions*, Washington DC: National Council on Vocational Education.

Berryman, S. (1993) 'Learning for the workplace', *Review of Research in Education*, 63: 343–401.

Bersin, J. (2002) 'Measuring e-learning's effectiveness', *e-learning*, 3(3): 36–38.

Bhawuk, D.P.S. and Brislin, R.W. (2000) 'Cross cultural training: a review', *Applied Psychology: An International Review*, 49(1): 162–191.

Biggs, J.B. (1994) 'Approaches to learning: nature and measurement of', *International Encyclopaedia of Education*, Vol. 1 (2nd edn), Oxford: Pergamon Press, pp. 319–322.

Biggs, J.B. and Moore, P.J. (1993) *The Process of Learning*, Sydney: Prentice Hall.

Billett, S.R. (1993) 'Authenticity and a culture of practice', *Australian and New Zealand Journal of Vocational Education Research*, 2: 1–29.

Billett, S.R. (1994) 'Situated learning – a workplace experience', *Australian Journal of Adult and Community Education*, 34: 112–130.

Billett, S.R. (1996a) 'Situated learning: bridging socio-cultural and cognitive theorising', *Learning and Instruction*, 6: 263–280.

Billett, S. (1996b) 'Accessing and engaging vocational knowledge: instructional media versus everyday practice', *Education and Training*, 38: 18–25.

Billett, S. (1998) 'Appropriation and ontogeny: identifying compatibility between cognitive and socio-cultural contributions to adult learning and development', *International Journal of Lifelong Education*, 17: 21–34.

Billett, S. (2001) *Learning in the Workplace: Strategies for Effective Practice*, Crows Nest, NSW: Allen & Unwin.

Billett, S.R. and Rose, J. (1996) 'Developing conceptual knowledge in the workplace', in J. Stevenson (ed.), *Learning in the Workplace: Tourism and Hospitality*, Griffith University, Centre for Learning and Work Research, pp. 204–228.

Blanchard, P.N. and Thacker, J.W. (2004) *Effective Training: Systems, Strategies and Practices*, Upper Saddle River, NJ: Pearson Prentice Hall.

Bloomer, M. and Hodkinson, P. (2000) 'The complexity and unpredictability of young people's learning careers', *Education and Training*, 42(2): 68–74.

Boote, J. (1998) 'Learning to learn in vocational education and training: are students and teachers ready for it?', *Australian and New Zealand Journal of Vocational Education Research*, 6: 59–86.

Borthick, A.F., Jones, D.R. and Wakai, S. (2003) 'Designing learning experiences within learners' Zone of Proximal Development (ZPDs): enabling collaborative learning on-site and on-line', *Journal of Information Systems*, 17(1): 107–134.

Boxall, P. (1996) 'The strategic HRM debate and the resource-based view of the firm', *Human Resource Management Journal*, 6(3): 59–75.

Boxall, P. and Purcell, J. (2003) *Strategy and Human Resource Management*, Basingstoke: Palgrave Macmillan.

Boyle, G.J. (1989) 'Breadth-depth or state-trait curiosity? A factor analysis of state-trait curiosity and state anxiety scales', *Personality and Individual Differences*, 10(2): 175–183.

Bransford, J. and Vye, N. (1989) 'Cognitive research and its implications for instruction', in L. Resnick and L. Klopfer (eds), *Toward the Thinking Curriculum: Current Cognitive Research*, Alexandria, Va.: Association for Supervision and Curriculum Development, pp. 171–205.

Brooker, R. and Butler, J. (1997) 'The learning context within the workplace: as perceived by apprentices and their workplace trainers', *Journal of Vocational Education and Training*, 49: 487–510.

Brookfield, S. (1985) 'Self-directed learning: a critical review of research', in S. Brookfield (ed.), *Self-directed Learning: From Theory to Practice*, San Francisco, Calif.: Jossey-Bass, pp. 5–16.

Brookfield, S. (1986) *Understanding and Facilitating Adult Learning*, San Francisco, Calif.: Jossey-Bass.

Brooking, A. (1996) *Intellectual Capital*, London: International Thomson Business Press.

Brown, A. (1987) 'Meta-cognition, executive control, self-regulation, and other more mysterious mechanisms', in F.E. Weinert and R.H. Kluwe (eds), *Meta-cognition, Motivation, and Understanding*, Hillsdale, NJ: Lawrence Erlbaum Associates, pp. 65–116.

Brown, J.S., Collins, A. and Duguid, P. (1989) 'Situated cognition and the culture of learning', *Educational Researcher*, 18(1): 32–42.

Buckley, J.W. (1967) 'Programmed instruction in industrial training,' *California Management Review*, 10(2): 71–79.

Buckley, R. and Caple, J. (1992) *The Theory and Practice of Training*, London: Kogan Page.

Burke, L. and Sadler-Smith, E. (2005) 'The intuitive HRD practitioner', paper presented at the Sixth International Conference on HRD Research and Practice across Europe, Leeds, May.

Burns, W., Williams, H. and Barnett, K. (1997) *Flexible Delivery and Women in TAFE*, Adelaide: Department of Employment, Education and Youth Affairs.

Caine, R. and Caine, G. (1991) *Making Connections: Teaching and the Human Brain*, Alexandria, Va.: Association for Supervision and Curriculum Development.

Calder, J. and McCollum, A. (1998) *Open and Flexible Learning in Vocational Education and Training*, London: Kogan Page.

Calder, J., McCollum, A., Morgan, A. and Thorpe, M. (1995) *Learning Effectiveness of Open and Flexible Learning in Vocational Education*, Sheffield, Research Series No. 58: Department for Education and Employment.

Candy, P. (1991) *Self-direction for Lifelong Learning*, San Francisco, Calif.: Jossey-Bass.

Candy, P., Crebert, G. and O'Leary, J. (1994) *Developing Lifelong Learners through Undergraduate Education*, National Board of Employment, Education and Training (Commissioned Report No 28), Canberra: Australian Government Printing Service.

Canfield, A.A. (1980) *Learning Styles Inventory Manual*, Ann Arbor, Mich.: Humanics Media.

Cannon-Bowers, J.A., Salas, E., Tannenbaum, S.I. and Mathieu, J.E. (1993) 'Toward theoretically-based principles of training effectiveness: a model and initial empirical investigation', *Military Psychology*, 7: 141–164.

Case, R. (1985) *Cognitive Development*, New York: Academic Press.

Chalofsky, N. (2003) 'Meaningful work', *Training and Development*, December: 52–58.

Chivers, G. (1999) 'Open, distance and flexible learning', in J.P. Wilson (ed.), *Human Resource Development: Learning and Training for Individuals and Organizations*, London: Kogan Page.

CIPD (2004) *Coaching Fact Sheet*, November. <http://www.cipd.co.uk/research/_coaching.htm> (accessed Nov. 2004).

Clardy, A. (2000) 'Learning on their own: vocationally-oriented self-directed learning projects', *Human Resource Development Quarterly*, 11(2): 105–126.

Cleverly, D. (1994) 'Learning styles of students: development of an eclectic model', *International Journal of Nursing Studies*, 31: 437–450.

Coffield, F., Moseley, D., Hall, E. and Ecclestone, K. (2004) *Should We Be Using Learning Styles? What Research Has to Say about Practice*, London: Learning and Skills Development Agency.

Cohen, D. and Prusack, L. (2001) *In Good Company*, Boston, Mass.: Harvard Business School Press.

Colarelli, S.M. and Bishop, R.C. (1990) 'Career commitment: functions, correlates, and management', *Group and Organization Studies*, 15: 158–176.

Colbert, B.A. (2004) 'The complex resource based view: implications for theory and practice in strategic human resource management', *Academy of Management Review*, 29(3): 341–358.

Cole, M., Gay, J., Glick, J. and Sharp, D.W. (1971) *The Cultural Context of Learning and Thinking*, New York: Basic Books.

Collins, A. (1991) 'Cognitive apprenticeship and educational technology', in L. Idol and B.F. Jones (eds), *Educational Values and Cognitive Instruction: Implications for Reform*, Hillsdale, NJ: Lawrence Erlbaum Associates, pp. 121–138.

Collins, A. (1997) 'Cognitive apprenticeship and the changing workplace', keynote address to the 5th Annual International Conference on Post-compulsory

Education and Training, Centre for Learning and Work Research, Griffith University, Queensland.

Collins, A., Brown, J.S. and Newman, S. (1989) 'Cognitive apprenticeship: teaching the crafts of reading, writing, and mathematics', in L.B. Resnick (ed.), *Knowing, Learning, and Instruction: Essays in Honor of Robert Glaser*, Hillsdale, NJ: Lawrence Erlbaum Associates, pp. 453–494.

Collins, A., Hawkins, J. and Carver, S.M. (1991) 'A cognitive apprenticeship for disadvantaged students', in B. Means, C. Chelmer and M.S. Knapps (eds), *Teaching Advanced Skills to At-risk Students*, San Francisco, Calif.: Jossey-Bass, pp. 216–243.

Collis, D. (1996) 'Organizational capability as a source of profit', in B. Moingeon and A. Edmondson (eds), *Organizational Learning and Competitive Advantage*, London: Sage.

Compeau, D.R. and Higgins, C.A. (1995) 'Computer self-efficacy: development of a measure and initial test', *MIS Quarterly*, 19(2): 189–211.

Cooper, A. (2004) '21st century tribes, *Sunday Life*, 7 March, 24–26.

Cornford, I.R. and Beven, F.A. (1999) 'Workplace learning: differential learning needs of novice and more experienced workers', *Australian and New Zealand Journal of Vocational Education Research*, 7(2): 25–54.

Cornford, I. and Gunn, D. (1998) 'Work-based learning of commercial cookery apprentices in the New South Wales hospitalities industry', *Journal of Vocational Education and Training*, 50: 549–568.

Costa, P.T. and McCrae, R.R. (1988) 'Personality in adulthood: a six year longitudinal study of self-report and spouse ratings on the NEO Personality Inventory', *Journal of Personality and Social Psychology*, 54: 853–863.

Cross, J. (2003) 'Informal learning: a sound investment', *Chief Learning Officer*, 2(6): 19.

Csikszentmihalyi, M. (2003) *Good Business: Leadership, Flow and the Making of Meaning*, London: Hodder and Stoughton.

Cunningham, J. (1998) 'The workplace: a learning environment', paper presented at the First Annual AVETRA Conference, Sydney, February.

Curry, L. (1983) 'An organization of learning styles theory and constructs', ERIC Document Retrieval Service, TM 830 554.

Davis, H. (1996) 'A review of open and distance learning within management development', *Journal of Management Development*, 15(4): 20–34.

Davis, L.N. and Mink, O.G. (1992) 'Human resource development: an emerging profession – an emerging purpose', *Studies in Continuing Education*, 14(2): 187–202.

Day, H.I. (1971) 'The measurement of specific curiosity', in H.I. Day, D.E. Berlyne and D.E. Hunt (eds), *Intrinsic Motivation*, Toronto: Holt, Rinehart & Winston.

Delahoussaye, M. (2002) 'The perfect learner', *Training*, 39(5): 28–35.

Despres, C. and Chauvel, D. (2000) 'A thematic analysis of the thinking in knowledge management' in C. Despres and D. Chauvel (eds) *Knowledge Horizons: The Present and the Promise of Knowledge Management*, Boston, Mass.: Butterworth Heinemann.

Dobbs, K. (2000) 'Simple moments of learning', *Training*, 37(1): 52–56.

Doktor, R.H. (1978) 'Problem solving styles of executives and management scientists', *TIMS Studies in Management Sciences*, 8: 123–134.

Doktor, R.H. and Bloom, D.M. (1977) 'Selective lateralisation of cognitive style related to occupation as determined by EEG alpha symmetry', *Psychophysiology*, 14: 385–387.

Dowling, P. and Schuler, R. (1990) 'Human resource management', in R. Blanpian (ed.), *Comparative Labor Law and Industrial Relations in Industrialized Market Economies*, Vol. 2, Deventer and Boston, Mass.: Kluwer Law and Taxation Publishers, pp. 125–149.

Doyle, D. and Brown, F.W. (2000) 'Using a business simulation to teach applied skills – the benefits and challenges of using student teams from multiple countries', *Journal of European Industrial Training*, 24(6and7): 330–336.

Dreyfus, S.E. (1982) 'Formal models vs human situational understanding. Inherent limitations on the modelling of business expertise', *Office: Technology and People*, 1: 133–165.

Dwyer, P. and Wyn, J. (2001) *Youth, Education and Risk*, London: Routledge Falmer.

Ellington, H. (1997) 'Flexible learning – your flexible friend', in C. Bell, M. Bowden and A. Trott (eds), *Implementing Flexible Learning*, London: Kogan Page, pp. 3–13.

Eraut, M. (2002) 'Conceptual analysis and research questions: do the concepts of "Learning Community" and "Community of Practice" provide added value?', paper presented at the Annual Meeting of the American Educational Research Association, New Orleans, La., 1–5 April.

Ericsson, K.A. and Charness, N. (1994) 'Expert performance: its structure and acquisition', *American Psychologist*, 49: 725–747.

Ester, D.P. (1995) 'CAI, lecture, and student learning style: the differential effects of instructional method', *Journal of Research in Technology in Education*, 27(2): 141–153.

Evans, G. (1994) 'Learning in apprenticeship courses', in J. Stevenson (ed.), *Cognition at Work: The Development of Vocational Expertise*, Adelaide: National Centre for Vocational Education Research.

Evans, K. (2002) 'Taking control of their lives? Agency in young adult transitions in England and the new Germany', *Journal of Youth Studies*, 5(3): 245–269.

Evans, K. and Furlong, A. (1997) 'Metaphors of youth transitions: niches, pathways, trajectories or navigations', in J. Brynner, K. Evans and A. Furlong (eds), *Youth, Citizenship and Social Change in a European Context*, Aldershot: Ashgate.

Evans, T.D. (2001) 'Two approaches to workplace flexible delivery and assessment in a rural community', *Australian and New Zealand Journal of Vocational Education Research*, 9(2): 1–22.

Fagenson, E.A. (1989) 'The mentor advantage: perceived career/job experiences of protégés versus non-protégés', *Journal of Organizational Behavior*, 10: 309–320.

Farmer, J.A., Jr., Buckmaster, A. and LeGrand, B. (1992) 'Cognitive apprenticeship', *New Directions in Adult and Continuing Education*, 55: 41–49.

Fernald, P.S. and Jordan, E.A. (1991) 'Programmed learning versus standard text in introductory psychology', *Teaching of Psychology*, 18(4): 205–211.

Fincham, R. and Rhodes, P. (1999) *Principles of Organizational Behaviour*, Oxford: Oxford University Press.

Fletcher, C. and Baldry, C. (1999) 'Multi-source feedback systems: a research perspective', in C.L. Cooper and I.T. Robertson (eds), *International Review of Industrial and Organizational Psychology*, 14: 130–165.

Flexible Delivery Working Party (1992) *Flexible Delivery: A National Framework for Implementation in TAFE*, Brisbane: Flexible Delivery Working Party.

Floodgate, J.F. and Nixon, A.E. (1994) 'Personal development plans: the challenge of implementation – a case study', *Journal of European Industrial Training*, 18(11): 43–47.

François, P. (2002) *Social Capital and Economic Development*, London: Routledge.

Fuller, A. (1996) 'Modern apprenticeship, process and learning: some emerging issues', *Journal of Vocational Education and Training*, 48: 229–248.

Gagne, R.M. and Briggs, L.J. (1974) *Principles of Instructional Design*, New York: Holt, Rinehart & Winston.

Gagne, R.M., Briggs, L.J. and Wager, W.W. (1992) *Principles of Instructional Design*, Fort Worth, Tex.: Harcourt Brace Jovanovich College Publishers.

Galagan, P.A. (2001) 'Mission e-possible', *Training and Development*, 55(2): 46–56.

Garavan, T.N., Costine, P. and Heraty, N. (1995) 'The emergence of strategic human resource management', *Journal of European Industrial Training*, 19(10): 4–10.

Garavan, T.N., Morley, M., Gunnigle, P. and Collins, E. (2001) 'Human capital accumulation: the role of human resource development', *Journal of European Industrial Training*, 25(2/3/4): 48–68.

Garcia, M.U. and Vano, F.L. (2002) 'Organizational learning in a global market', *Human Systems Management*, 21(3): 169–181.

Gardner, H. (1983) *Frames of Mind: The Theory of Multiple Intelligences*, New York: Basic Books.

Gardner, H. (1993) *Multiple Intelligences: The Theory in Practice*, New York: Basic Books.

Garrison, D.R. (1995) 'Constructivism and the role of self-instructional course material: A reply', *Distance Education*, 16: 136–140.

Gee, J.P., Hull, G. and Lankshear, C. (1996) *The New Work Order: Behind the Language of the New Capitalism*, St Leonards, NSW: Allen & Unwin.

Gibb, J. (1999) 'The relevance of a training culture to small business in Australia', in C. Robinson and K. Arthy (eds), *Lifelong Learning: Developing a Training Culture*, Adelaide: National Centre for Vocational Education Research, pp. 39–61.

Gibbs, G., Morgan, A.R. and Taylor, E. (1984) 'The world of the learner', in F. Marton, N. Entwistle and D. Hounsell (eds), *The Experience of Learning*, Edinburgh: Scottish Academic Press, pp. 165–188.

Gilman, S. (1946) 'Correspondence courses in the accounting education programme', *The Accounting Review*, 21: 396–404.

Gist, M.E. and McDonald-Mann, D. (2000) 'Leadership training and development', in C.L. Cooper and E.A. Locke (eds), *Industrial and Organizational Psychology*, Oxford: Blackwell, pp. 62–63.

Gist, M.E. and Mitchell, T.B. (1992) 'Self-efficacy: a theoretical analysis of its determinants and malleability', *Academy of Management Review*, 17(2): 183–211.

Glaser, R. (1984) 'Education and thinking: the role of knowledge', *American Psychologist*, 39: 93–104.

Glaser, R., Lesgold, A., Lajoie, S., Eastman, R., Greenberg, L., Logan, D., Magone, M., Weiner, A., Wolf, R. and Yengo, L. (1985) *Cognitive Task Analysis to Enhance Technical Skills Training and Assessment* (Contract No. F41689-83-C-0029), Brooks AFB, TX: AFHRL, cited in Gott, S. (1989) 'Apprenticeship instruction for real world tasks', *Review of Research in Education*, 15: 101.

Glass, A. and Riding, R.J. (2000) 'EEG differences and cognitive style', *Biological Psychology*, 51(1): 23–41.

Goddard, H.H. (1917) 'Mental tests and immigrants', *Journal of Delinquency*, 2: 243–277.

Gold, J., Rodgers, H. and Smith, V. (2003) 'What is the future of the human resource development professional? A UK perspective', *Human Resource Development International*, 6(4): 437–456.

Goldstein, I.L. (1993) *Training in Organizations: Needs Assessment, Development and Evaluation*, Pacific Grove, Calif.: Brooks/Cole Publishing.

Goleman, D. (1995) *Emotional Intelligence*, New York: Bantam.

Gott, S. (1989) 'Apprenticeship instruction for real world tasks', *Review of Research in Education*, 15: 97–169.

Greeno, J.G. (1989) 'A perspective on thinking', *American Psychologist*, 44: 134–141.

Gregorc, A. (1979) 'Learning/teaching styles: their nature and effects', in NASSP (National Association of Secondary School Principals) (eds), *Students Learning Styles: Diagnosing and Prescribing Programmes*, Reston, Va.: National Association of Secondary School Principals.

Gruber, C.P. and Carriuolo, N. (1991) 'Construction and preliminary validation of a learner typology for the Canfield Learning Styles Inventory', *Educational and Psychological Measurement*, 51: 839–855.

Guglielmino, T. (2001) 'From formal training to communities of practice via network-based learning', *Educational Technology*, March/April, 5–14.

Hager, P., Athanasou, J. and Gonzci, A. (1994) 'Assessment in the context of CBT', in *Assessment Technical Manual*, Canberra: Australian Government Publishing Service.

Halford, S. and Leonard, P. (2001) *Gender, Power, and Organizations: An Introduction*, Basingstoke: Palgrave.

Handy, C. (1995) *Beyond Certainty: The Changing Worlds of Organizations*, London: Hutchinson.

Hardré, P.L. (2003) 'Beyond two decades of motivation: a review of the research and practice in instructional design and human performance technology', *Human Resource Development Review*, 2(1): 54–81.

Harris, R. and Volet, S. (1996) 'Developing competence through work-based learning processes and practices: a case studies approach', paper presented at the Third Annual ANTARAC Conference, 31 October–1 November, Melbourne.

Harris, R., Simons, M. and Bone, J. (2000) *More Than Meets the Eye? Rethinking the Role of the Workplace Trainer*, Adelaide: National Centre for Vocational Education Research.

Harris, R., Willis, P., Simons, M. and Underwood, F. (1998) *Learning the Job*, Adelaide: National Centre for Vocational Education Research.

Harrison, R. (2002) *Learning and Development*, London: Chartered Institute of Personnel and Development.

Harvey, M.G. and Lusch, R.F. (1999) 'Balancing the intellectual capital books: intangible liabilities', *European Management Journal*, 17(1): 85–72.

Hayton, G. (1993) 'Skill formation in the construction industry', paper presented to the Conference on Vocational Education and Training Research, Griffith University, 1–2 July.

Healy, A.F., Fendrich, D.W., Crutcher, R.J., Wittman, W.T., Gesi, A.T., Ericsson,

K.A. and Bourne, L.E. (1992) 'The long-term retention of skills', *Cognitive Processes: Essays in Honor of William K. Estes*. Vol. II, Hillsdale, NJ: Lawrence Erlbaum Associates, pp. 87–118.

Heikkinen, M., Pettigrew, F. and Zakrajsek, D. (1985) 'Learning styles vs teaching styles', *NASSP Bulletin*, 69: 80–85.

Hofstede, G. (1984) *Culture's Consequences: International Differences in Work-related Values*, Beverly Hills, Calif.: Sage Publications.

Hofstede, G. (1986) 'Cultural differences in teaching and learning', *International Journal of Intercultural Relations*, 10: 301–319.

Hofstede, G. (2001) *Culture's Consequences: Comparing Values, Behaviours, Institutions and Organizations Across Nations*, London: Sage Publications.

Holland, R. (1980) 'Learner characteristics and learner performance: implications for instructional placement decisions', *Journal of Special Education*, 16: 7–20.

Honey, P. and Mumford, A. (1992) *The Manual of Learning Styles*, Maidenhead: Peter Honey.

Houle, C.O. (1961) *The Inquiring Mind*, Madison, Wisc.: University of Wisconsin Press.

Huczynski, A. and Buchanan, D. (2001) *Organizational Behaviour: An Introductory Text*, Harlow: Financial Times Prentice Hall.

Hudson, F.M. (1999) *The Handbook of Coaching*, San Francisco, Calif.: Jossey-Bass.

Industry Task Force on Leadership and Management Skills (1995) *Enterprising Nation: Renewing Australia's Managers to Meet the Challenges of the Asia-Pacific Century: Report of the Industry Task Force on Leadership and Management Skills*, Canberra: Australian Government Publishing Service.

Jaju, A., Kwak, H. and Zinkhan, G.M. (2002) 'Learning styles of undergraduate business students: a cross cultural comparison between the US, India and Korea', *Marketing Education Review*, 12(2): 49–60.

Jarvis, J. (2004) 'Get the right coach', *People Management*, 10(13) June: 49.

Jayne, V. (2003) 'Coaches, mentors and you', *New Zealand Management*, 50(1): 34–39.

Johnes, G. (1993) *The Economics of Education*, New York: St Martin's Press.

Johnson, L.D. (2001) 'Coaching and mentoring', *Manage*, 52(4) May: 10–12.

Jurie, J.D. (2000) 'Building capacity: organizational competence and critical theory', *Journal of Organization Change Management*, 13(3): 264–274.

Keegan D. (1980) 'On defining distance education', *Distance Education*, 1(1): 13–36.

Keeling, D., Jones, E., Botterill, D. and Gray, C. (1998) 'Work-based learning, motivation and employer–employee interaction: implications for lifelong learning', *Innovations in Education and Training International*, 35: 282–291.

Kember, D. (1995) *Open Learning Courses for Adults: A Model of Student Progress*, Englewood Cliffs, NJ: Educational Technology Publications.

Keys, B.J., Fulmer, R.M. and Stumpf, S.A. (1996) 'Microworlds and simuworlds: practice fields for the learning organization', *Organizational Dynamics*, 24(4): 36–49.

Kirby, J.R. (1988) 'Style, strategy and skill in reading', in R.R. Schmeck (ed.), *Learning Style and Learning Strategies*, New York: Plenum.

Kirkpatrick, D.L. (1998) *Evaluating Training Programmes: The Four Levels*, San Francisco, Calif.: Berrett-Koehler.

Knowles, M.S. (1990) *The Adult Learner: A Neglected Species*, Houston, Tex.: Gulf Publishing Company.

Knowles, M.S., Holton, E.F. and Swanson, R.A. (1998) *The Adult Learner: The Definitive Classic in Adult Education and Human Resource Development*, Woburn, Mass.: Butterworth-Heinemann.

Kolb, D.A. (1976) *Learning Styles Inventory: Technical Manual*, Boston, Mass.: McBer & Company.

Kornbluh, H. and Greene, R. (1989) 'Learning, empowerment and participative work processes: the educative work environment', in H. Leymann and H. Kornbluh (eds), *Socialization and Learning at Work: A New Approach to the Learning Process in the Workplace and Society*, Brookfield, VT: Gower.

Kram, K.E. (1985) *Mentoring at Work: Developmental Relationships in Organizational Life*, Glenview, Ill.: Scott, Foresman & Co.

Kuper, A. (1999) *Culture: The Anthropologists' Account*, Cambridge, Mass.: Harvard University Press.

Latham, G.P. (2004) 'The motivational benefits of goal-setting', *Academy of Management Executive*, 18(4): 126–129.

Laurillard, D. (2002) *Rethinking University Teaching*, 2nd edn, London: Kogan Page.

Lave, J. and Wenger, E. (1991) *Situated Learning: Legitimate Peripheral Participation*, Cambridge: Cambridge University Press.

Lee, M.M. (2003) 'The complex roots of HRD', in M.M. Lee (ed.) *Human Resource Development in a Complex World*, London: Routledge.

Lim, G.S. and Chan, A. (2003) 'Individual and situational correlates of motivation for skills upgrading: an empirical study', *Human Resource Development International*, 6(2): 219–242.

Lindeman, E. (1926) *The Meaning of Adult Education*, New York: New Republic.

Locke, E.A. and Latham, G.P. (1990a) 'Work motivation and satisfaction: light at the end of the tunnel', *Psychological Science*, 1: 240–246.

Locke, E.A. and Latham, G.P. (1990b) *A Theory of Goal Setting and Task Performance*, Englewood Cliffs, NJ: Prentice-Hall.

Long, H.B. (1989) *Theoretical Foundations of Self-Directed Learning*, Norman, Okla.: Oklahoma University.

McCracken, M. and Wallace, M. (2000) 'Towards a redefinition of strategic HRD', *Journal of European Industrial Training*, 24(5): 281–290.

McCrindle, M. (2003) 'Understanding Generation Y', *Principal Matters*, vol. 55: 28–31.

MacDonald, R. (1999) 'Research and a training culture: implications for large and small businesses', in C. Robinson and K. Arthy (eds), *Lifelong Learning: Developing a Training Culture*, Adelaide: National Centre for Vocational Education Research, pp. 63–71.

McGregor, D. (1967) *The Professional Manager*, New York: McGraw-Hill.

McKavanagh, C.W. (1996) 'Comparison of classroom and workplace learning environments', in J. Stevenson (ed.), *Learning in the Workplace: Tourism and Hospitality*, Brisbane: Griffith University, pp. 188–203.

McKenna, E. (1994) *Business Psychology and Organizational Behaviour: A Student's Handbook*, Hove: Lawrence Erlbaum Associates.

McLean, G.N. and McLean, L. (2001) 'If we can't define HRD in one country how can we define it in an international context?', *Human Resource Development International*, 4(3): 313–326.

Maclennan, N. (1995) *Coaching and Mentoring*, Aldershot: Gower.

McLoughlin, C. (2002) 'Learner support in distance and networked learning environments: ten dimensions for successful design', *Distance Education*, 23(2): 149–162.

Manning, B.H. and Payne, B.D. (1996) *Self-talk for Teachers and Students: Metacognitive Strategies for Personal and Classroom Use*, Boston, Mass.: Allyn & Bacon.

Mansfield, R. (1991) 'Deriving standards of competence', in E. Fennel (ed.), *Development of Assessable Standards for National Certification*, London: Department for Education and Employment.

Marland, P., Patching, W. and Putt, I. (1992a) *Learning from Text: Glimpses inside the Minds of Distance Learners*, Townsville: James Cook University of North Queensland.

Marland, P., Patching, W. and Putt, I. (1992b) 'Thinking while studying: a process tracing study of distance learners', *Distance Education*, 13: 193–217.

Martin, C.A. (1965) 'Programmed learning and the teaching of accounting', *Abacus*, 65(1): 92–96.

Maslow, A.H. (1954) *Motivation and Personality*, New York: Harper & Row.

Maurer, T.J. (2002) 'Employee learning and development orientation: toward an integrative model of involvement in continuous learning', *Human Resource Development Review*, 1(1): 9–44.

Mayo, A. (2000) 'The role of employee development in the growth of intellectual capital', *Personnel Review*, 29(4): 521–533.

Mezirow, J. (1991) *Transformative Dimensions of Adult Learning*, San Francisco, Calif.: Jossey-Bass.

Mintzberg, H. (1989) *Mintzberg on Management: Inside our Strange World of Organizations*, New York: Free Press.

Misko, J. (1994) *Flexible Delivery: Will a Client Focused System Mean Better Learning?* Adelaide: National Centre for Vocational Education Research.

Mitchell, C. and Sackney, L. (2000) *Profound Improvement: Building Capacity for a Learning Community*, Lisse, Netherlands: Swets & Zeitlinger.

Mitchell, J. (1999) 'Effective professional development in flexible delivery: findings from two national projects', paper presented to the Biennial Forum of the Open and Distance Learning Association of Australia, Deakin University, Geelong, Victoria, September.

Molina, J.A. and Ortega, R. (2003) 'Effects of employee training on the performance of North American firms', *Applied Economics Letters*, 10: 549–552.

Morgan, A.R. (1993) *Improving Your Students' Learning: Reflections on the Experience of Study*, London: Kogan Page.

Morgan, R.R., Ponticell, J.A. and Gordon, E.E. (1998) *Enhancing Learning in Training and Adult Education*, Westport, Conn.: Praeger.

Mumford, A. (1995) 'Four approaches to learning from experience', *Industrial and Commercial Training*, 27(8): 12–19.

Nahapiet, J. and Ghosal, S. (1998) 'Social capital, intellectual capital, and the organizational advantage', *Academy of Management Review*, 23(2): 242–266.

Naquin, S.S. and Holton, E.F. (2003) 'Motivation to improve work through learning in human resource development', *Human Resource Development International*, 6(3): 355–370.

Nelson, R. and Winter, S. (1982) *An Evolutional Theory of Economic Change*, Cambridge, Mass.: Belknap Press.

New, G.E. (1996) 'A three-tier model of organizational competencies', *Journal of Managerial Psychology*, 11(8): 44–51.

Nisbett, R., Fong, G., Lehman, D. and Cheng, P. (1987) 'Teaching reasoning', *Science*, 238 (October): 625–631.

Noe, R.A. (1986) 'Trainee attributes and attitudes: neglected influences on training effectiveness', *Academy of Management Review*, 4: 736–749.

Noe, R.A. and Schmitt, N. (1986) 'The influence of trainee attitudes on training effectiveness: a test of a model', *Personnel Psychology*, 39: 497–523.

Noe, R.A. and Wilk, S.L. (1993) 'Investigation of the factors that influence employees' participation in development activities', *Journal of Applied Psychology*, 78(2): 291–302.

O'Malley, J.M. and Chamot, A.U. (1990) *Learning Strategies in Second Language Acquisition*, Cambridge: Cambridge University Press.

O'Regan, N. and Ghobadian, A. (2004) 'Testing the homogeneity of SMEs: the impact of size on managerial and organizational processes', *European Business Review*, 16(1): 64–79.

Parsloe, E. and Wray, M. (2000) *Coaching and Mentoring*, Kogan Page: London.

Parsons, T. (1951) *The Social System*, London: Routledge & Kegan Paul.

Patrick, J. (1992) *Training Research and Practice*, London: Academic Press.

Pea, R.D. (1993) 'Learning scientific concepts through material and social activities: conversational analysis meets conceptual change', *Educational Psychologist*, 28: 165–177.

Pedersen, J.S. and Sorensen, J.S. (1989) *Organizational Culture in Theory and Practice*, Oxford: Blackwell.

Pedler, M., Burgoyne, J. and Boydell, T. (1997) *The Learning Company: A Strategy for Sustainable Development*, London: McGraw-Hill.

Peoples, K., Robinson, P. and Calvert, J. (1997) *From Desk to Disk: Staff Development for VET Staff in Flexible Delivery*, Brisbane: Australian National Training Authority.

Peteraf, M.A. (1993) 'The cornerstones of competitive advantage: a resource-based view', *Strategic Management Journal*, 14: 179–191.

Pettigrew, A., Jones, E. and Reason, P. (1982) *Training and Development Roles in their Organizational Setting*, Sheffield: Manpower Services Commission.

Phillips, J.J. (1996) 'ROI: the search for best practice', *Training and Development*, 10 (February): 42–47.

Pillay, H., Boulton-Lewis, G. and Lankshear, C. (2002) 'Understanding changing conceptions of work: implications for development of training initiatives', *Australian and New Zealand Journal of Vocational Education Research*, 10(2): 27–44.

Pittenger, K.K.S. and Heimann, B.A. (2000) 'Building effective mentoring relationships', *Review of Business*, 21(1/2): 38–42.

Plaskoff, J. (2003) 'Creating a community culture at Eli Lilly', *Knowledge Management Review*, 5(6): 16–19.

Poell, R.F. and Van der Krogt, F.J. (2002) 'Using social networks in organizations to facilitate individual development', in M. Pearn (ed.), *Individual Differences and Development in Organizations*, Chichester: John Wiley & Sons, pp. 285–304.

Poell, R.F., Chivers, G.E., Van der Krogt, F.J. and Wildemeersch, D.A. (2000) 'Learning-network theory', *Management Learning*, 31(1): 25–49.

Prahalad, C.K. and Hamel, G. (1990) 'The core competence of the corporation', *Harvard Business Review*, 68(3): 79–91.

Raelin, J.A. (2000) *Work-based Learning: The New Frontier of Management Development*, Upper Saddle River, NJ: Prentice Hall.

Raffe, D. (2003) 'Pathways linking education and work: a review of concepts, research, and policy debates', *Journal of Youth Studies*, 6(1): 3–19.

Ragins, B.R., Cotton, J.L. and Miller, J.S. (2000) 'Marginal mentoring: the effects of type of mentor, quality of relationship, and programme design on work and career attitudes', *Academy of Management Journal*, 43(6): 1177–1194.

Reddy, A. (2002) 'E-learning ROI calculations: is a cost/benefit analysis a better approach?', *e-learning*, 3(1): 30–32.

Reece, I. and Walker, S. (1994) *A Practical Guide to Teaching, Training and Learning*, Sunderland: Business Education Publishers.

Reed, R. and DeFillippi, R.J. (1990) 'Causal ambiguity, barriers to imitation and sustainable competitive advantage', *Academy of Management Review*, 15(1): 88–102.

Reeve, F., Gallacher, J. and Mayes, T. (1998) 'Can new technology remove barriers to work-based learning?', *Open Learning*, 13: 18–26.

Reio, T.G. and Wiswell, A. (2000) 'Field investigation of the relationship among curiosity, workplace learning and job performance', *Human Resource Development Quarterly*, 11(1): 5–30.

Resnick, L.B. (1987) 'Learning in school and out', *Educational Researcher*, 16(9): 13–20.

Revans, R.W. (1982) *The Origins and Growth of Action Learning*, Bromley: Chartwell-Bratt.

Revans, R.W. (1983) *The ABC of Action Learning*, Bromley: Chartwell-Bratt.

Reynolds, M. (1998) 'Bright lights and the pastoral idyll: social learning theories underlying management education methodologies', paper presented at the conference *Emergent Fields in Management: Connecting Learning and Critique*, University of Leeds, July.

Riding, R.J. (1991) *Cognitive Styles Analysis*, Birmingham: Learning and Training Technology.

Riding, R.J. (1997) 'On the nature of cognitive style', *Educational Psychology*, 17(1–2): 29–50.

Riding, R.J. and Cheema, I. (1991) 'Cognitive styles: an overview and integration', *Educational Psychology*, 11: 193–215.

Riding, R.J. and Douglas, G. (1993) 'The effect of cognitive style and mode of presentation on learning performance', *British Journal of Educational Psychology*, 63: 297–307.

Riding, R.J. and Rayner, S. (1998) *Cognitive Styles and Learning Strategies: Understanding Style and Differences in Learning and Behaviour*, London: David Fulton Publishers.

Riding, R.J. and Sadler-Smith, E. (1992) 'Type of instructional material, cognitive style and learning performance', *Educational Studies*, 18: 323–340.

Riding, R.J. and Sadler-Smith, E. (1997) 'Cognitive style and learning strategies: some implications for training design', *International Journal of Training and Development*, 1(3): 199–208.

Robertson, I. (1996) 'Workplace based training in small business enterprises: employers' views of factors which contribute to a successful programme', Melbourne: Office of Training and Further Education.

Robins, A. (1998) 'Transfer in cognition', in S. Thrun and L. Pratt (eds), *Learning to Learn*, Boston, Mass.: Kluwer Academic Publishers, pp. 45–67.

Roebuck, M. (1987) 'Flexible learning: developments and implications in education', in F. Percival, D. Craig and D. Buglass (eds), *Aspects of Educational Technology* vol. 20, London: Kogan Page, pp. 326–332.

Rogoff, B. (1984) 'Introduction: thinking and learning in social context', in B. Rogoff and J. Lave (eds), *Everyday Cognition: Its Development in Social Context*, Cambridge, Mass.: Harvard University Press, pp. 1–8.

Rogoff, B. (1995) 'Observing socio-cultural activity on three planes: participatory appropriation, guided participation, apprenticeship', in J.W. Wertsch, A. Alvarez and P. del Rio (eds), *Socio-cultural Studies of Mind*, Cambridge: Cambridge University Press, pp. 139–164.

Rogoff, B. and Lave, J. (eds) (1984) *Everyday Cognition: Its Development in Social Context*, Cambridge, Mass.: Harvard University Press.

Rojewski, J.W. and Schell, J.W. (1994) 'Cognitive apprenticeship for learners with special needs: an alternate framework for teaching and learning', *Remedial and Special Education*, 15: 234–243.

Romme, A.G.L. (2003) 'Learning outcomes of micro-worlds for management education', *Management Learning*, 34(1): 51–61.

Rosenshine, B.V. and Meister, C. (1992) 'The use of scaffolds for teaching less-structured cognitive tasks', *Educational Leadership*, 49(7): 26–33.

Roth, W.M. (1998) *Designing Communities*, Dordrecht: Kluwer Academic Publishers.

Rothwell, W. and Wellins, R. (2004) 'Mapping your future: putting new competencies to work for you', *Training and Development*, 58(5): 1–8.

Rouillier, J.Z. and Goldstein, I.L. (1997) 'The relationship between organizational transfer climate and positive transfer of training'. in D. Russ-Eft, H. Preskill and C. Sleezer (eds) *Human Resource Development Review: Research Implications*, Thousand Oaks, Calif.: Sage Publications.

Rowe, C. (1994) 'Assessing the effectiveness of open learning: the British Aerospace experience', *Industrial and Commercial Training*, 26(4): 22–27.

Rowntree, D. (1990) *Teaching through Self-instruction: How to Develop Open Learning Materials*, London: Kogan Page.

Ruona, W.E.A. (2001) 'The foundational impact of the Training Within Industry project on the HRD profession', *Advances in Developing Human Resources*, 3(2): 119–126.

Ruona, W.E.A., Leimbach, M., Holton, E.F. and Bates R. (2002) 'The relationship between learner utility reactions and predicted learning transfer among trainees', *International Journal of Training and Development*, 6(4): 218–228.

Sadler-Smith, E. (1996a) '"Learning styles" and instructional design', *Innovations in Education and Training International*, 33: 185–193.

Sadler-Smith, E. (1996b) 'Approaches to studying: age, gender and academic performance', *Educational Studies*, 22: 367–380.

Sadler-Smith, E. (2006) *Learning and Development For Managers: Perspectives from Research and Practice*, Oxford: Blackwell.

Sadler-Smith, E. and Lean, J. (2003) 'The practice of human resource development (HRD) in smaller firms', in J. Stewart and G. Beaver (eds), *Human Resource Development in Small Organizations: Research and Practice*, London: Routledge.

Sadler-Smith, E. and Riding, R. (1999) 'Cognitive style and instructional preferences', *Instructional Science*, 27: 355–371.

Sadler-Smith, E. and Smith, P.J. (2001) 'Work-based learning: some perspectives from Australia and the UK', paper presented at the 2nd conference on HRD Research and Practice in Europe, University of Twente, The Netherlands, 26–27 January.

Sadler-Smith, E., Down, S. and Lean, J. (2000) '"Modern" learning methods: rhetoric and reality', *Personnel Review*, 29(4): 474–490.

Sadler-Smith, E., Gardiner, P., Badger, B., Chaston, I. and Stubberfield, J. (2000) 'Using collaborative learning to develop small firms', *Human Resource Development International*, 3(3): 285–306.

Saffold, G.S. (1988) 'Culture, traits, strength and organizational performance: moving beyond "strong" culture', *Academy of Management Review*, 13: 514–558.

Salas, E. and Cannon-Bowers, J.A. (2001) 'The science of training: a decade of progress', *Annual Review of Psychology*, 52(1): 471–499.

Salas, E., Kosarzycki, M.P., Burke, C.S., Fiore S.M. and Stone, D.L. (2002) 'Emerging themes in distance learning research and practice: some food for thought', *International Journal of Management Reviews*, 4(2): 135–153.

Sayer, D. (1983) *Marx's Method: Ideology, Science and Critique in Capital*, Hassocks, Sussex: Harvester Press.

Scandura, T.A. (1992) 'Mentorship and career mobility: an empirical investigation', *Journal of Organizational Behavior*, 13(2): 169–174.

Schmidt, F.L. and Hunter, J.E. (1998) 'The validity and utility of selection methods in personnel psychology: practical and theoretical implications of 85 years of research findings', *Psychological Bulletin*, 124: 262–274.

Schön, D.A. (1983) *The Reflective Practitioner: How Professionals Think in Action*, Aldershot: Ashgate.

Senge, P.M. (1990) *The Fifth Discipline: The Art and Practice of the Learning Organization*, London: Doubleday.

Shim, I. and Paprock, K.E. (2002) 'A study focusing on American expatriates learning in host countries', *International Journal of Training and Development*, 6(1): 13–24.

Short, E.J. and Weisberg-Benchell, J.A. (1989) 'The triple alliance for learning: cognition, metacognition, and motivation', in C.B. McCormick, G.E. Miller and M. Pressley (eds), *Cognitive Strategy Research: From Basic Research to Educational Applications*, New York: Springer, pp. 33–63.

Sloman, M. (2003) 'E-learning: the final frontier', *e-learning age*, April: 32–34.

Sloman, M. and Reynolds, J. (2003) 'Developing the e-learning community', *Human Resource Development International*, 6(2): 259–272.

Smith, A. and Dowling, P.J. (2001) 'Analyzing firm training: five propositions for future research', *Human Resource Development Quarterly*, 12(2): 147–167.

Smith, P.J. (1997) 'Flexible delivery and industry training: learning styles and learning contexts', in J. Osborne, D. Roberts and J. Walker (eds), *Open, Flexible and Distance Learning: Education in the 21st Century*, Launceston: University of Tasmania, pp. 421–427.

Smith, P.J. (2000a) 'Flexible delivery and apprentice training: preferences, problems and challenges', *Journal of Vocational Education and Training*, 52(3): 483–502.

Smith, P.J. (2000b), 'Preparedness for flexible delivery among vocational learners', *Distance Education*, 21(1): 29–48.

Smith, P.J. (2000c) *Preparing for Flexible Delivery in Industry: Learners and Their Workplaces*, Doctoral Dissertation, Deakin University, Victoria, Australia.

Smith, P.J. (2001a) 'Using learner preferences to assist in training design', *Training and Management Development Methods*, 15(4): 7.13–7.21.

Smith, P.J. (2001b) 'Learners and their workplaces: towards a strategic model of flexible delivery in the workplace', *Journal of Vocational Education and Training*, 53(4): 609–628.

Smith, P.J. (2002) '"Modern" learning methods: rhetoric and reality – further to Sadler-Smith *et al.*', *Personnel Review*, 31(1): 103–113.

Smith, P.J. (2003a) 'Learning strategies used by apprentices in flexible delivery', *Journal of Vocational Education and Training*, 55(3): 369–383.

Smith, P.J. (2003b) 'Workplace learning and flexible delivery', *Review of Educational Research*, 73(1): 53–88.

Smith, P.J. and Dalton, J. (2005) *Accommodating Learning Styles: Relevance and Good Practice in VET*, Adelaide: National Centre for Vocational Education Research.

Smith, P.J. and Stacey, E. (2003) 'Quality practice in computer supported collaborative learning: identifying research gaps and opportunities', in G. Davies and E. Stacey (eds), *Quality Education @ A Distance*, Dordrecht: Kluwer Academic Publishers, pp. 119–128.

Smith, P.J., Murphy, K.L. and Mahoney, S.E. (2003) 'Towards identifying factors underlying readiness for online learning: an exploratory study', *Distance Education*, 24(1): 57–68.

Smith, P.J., Robertson, I. and Wakefield, L. (2002) 'Developing preparedness for flexible delivery of training in enterprises', *Journal of Workplace Learning*, 14(6): 222–232.

Smith, P.J., Wakefield, L. and Robertson, I. (2001) *Preparing for Flexible Delivery: Learners and Their Workplaces*, Adelaide: National Centre for Vocational Education Research.

Snell, S. and Dean, J. (1992) 'Integrated manufacturing and human resource management: a human capital perspective', *Academy of Management Journal*, 35(3): 467–504.

Snow, C.C. and Snell, S.A. (1993) 'Staffing as a strategy', in N. Schmitt and W.C. Borman (eds), *Personnel Selection in Organizations*, San Francisco, Calif.: Jossey-Bass, pp. 448–478.

Soloway, E.M. (1986) 'Learning to programme = learning to construct mechanisms and explanations', *CACM*, 29, 850–858, cited in Gott, S. (1989) 'Apprenticeship instruction for real world tasks', *Review of Research in Education*, 15: 101.

Southern, R. (1996) 'Business Impact Project', Melbourne: Office of Training and Further Education.

Spearman, C. (1927) *The Abilities of Man*, New York: Macmillan.

Spender, J.-C. (2000) 'Managing knowledge systems', in C. Despres and D. Chauvel (eds), *Knowledge Horizons: The Present and the Promise of Knowledge Management*, Boston, Mass.: Butterworth Heinemann.

Stacey, E., Smith, P.J. and Barty, K. (2004) 'Adult learners in the workplace: online learning and communities of practice', *Distance Education*, 25(1): 107–124.

Stacey, R.D., Griffin, D. and Shaw, P. (2000) *Complexity and Management: Fad or Radical Challenge to Systems Thinking?* London: Routledge.

Stebbins, M.W. and Shani, A.B. (1995) 'Organization design and the knowledge worker', *Leadership and Organization Development Journal*, 16(1): 23–30.

Sternberg, R.J. (1985) *Beyond IQ: A Triarchic Theory of Human Intelligence*, New York: Cambridge University Press.

Sternberg, R.J. (1988) *The Triarchic Mind*, New York: Viking.

Sternberg, R.J. and Grigorenko, E.L. (1997) 'Are cognitive styles still in style?', *American Psychologist*, 52: 700–712.

Sternberg, R.J. and Hedlund, J. (2002) 'Practical intelligence, g, and work psychology', *Human Performance*, 15(1/2): 143–160.

Stewart, J. and Winter, R. (1995) 'Open and distance learning', in S. Truelove (ed.), *Handbook of Training and Development*, Oxford: Blackwell.

Stewart, T.A. (1997) *Intellectual Capital*, New York: Doubleday.

Sue-Chan, C. and Latham, G.P. (2004) 'The relative effectiveness of external, peer and self-coaches', *Applied Psychology: An International Review*, 53(2): 260–278.

Sveiby, K.E. (1997) *The New Organizational Wealth: Managing and Measuring Knowledge-based Assets*, San Francisco, Calif.: Berrett-Koehler.

Taylor, M. (1996) 'Learning in the workplace: a study of three enterprises', Paper presented at the ANTARAC third annual conference, *Researching and Learning Together*, Melbourne, October–November.

Tharenou, P. (1997) 'Organizational, job and personal predictors of employee participation in training and development', *Applied Psychology: An International Review*, 46(2): 111–134.

Thornhill, A.R. (1993) 'Management training across cultures: the challenge for trainers', *Journal of European Industrial Training*, 17(10): 43–51.

Thurstone, L.L. (1938) *Primary Mental Abilities*, Chicago, Ill.: University of Chicago Press.

Tomporowski, P.D. (2003) *The Psychology of Skill: A Life-span Approach*, Westport, Conn.: Praeger.

Torrington, D., Hall, L. and Taylor, S. (2002) *Human Resource Management*, Harlow: Financial Times Prentice Hall.

Tosey, P. (1999) 'The peer learning community: a contextual design for learning?', *Management Decision*, 37(5): 403–410.

Tracey, J.B., Hinkin, T.R., Tannenbaum, S. and Mathieu, J.E. (2001) 'The influence of individual characteristics and the work environment on varying levels of training outcomes', *Human Resource Development Quarterly*, 15(1): 5–24.

Traut, C.A., Larsen, R. and Feimer, S.H. (2000) 'Hanging on or fading out? Job satisfaction and the long-term worker', *Public Personnel Management*, 29(3): 343–351.

Trompenaars, F. and Hampden-Turner, C. (1997) *Riding the Waves of Culture: Understanding Cultural Diversity in Business* (2nd edn), London: Nicholas Brealey.

Twyford, K. (1999) 'Supporting students in a flexible learning environment: can it be managed better?', in *Quality and Diversity in VET Research*, proceedings of the second national conference of the Australian Vocational Education and Training Research Association, pp. 347–352.

Tymon, W.G. and Stumpf, S.A. (2003) 'Social capital in the success of knowledge workers', *Career Development International*, 8(1): 12–20.

Unwin, L. and Wellington, J. (1995) 'Reconstructing the work-based route: lessons from the modern apprenticeship', *The Vocational Aspect of Education*, 47: 337–352.

Van der Krogt, F.J. (1998) 'Learning network theory: the tension between learning systems and work systems in organizations', *Human Resource Development Quarterly*, 9(2): 157–177.

van Merriënboer, J.J.G., Kirschner, P.A. and Kester, L. (2003) 'Taking the load off a learner's mind: instructional design for complex learning', *Educational Psychologist*, 38(1): 5–13.

Veale, D.J. and Wachtel, J.M. (1996) 'Mentoring and coaching as part of a human resource development strategy: an example at Coca Cola Foods', *Management Development Review*, 9(6): 19–24.

Vermunt, J.D. (1989) 'The interplay between internal and external regulation of learning, and the design of process-oriented instruction', paper presented at the Third Conference of the European Association for Research on Learning and Instruction, Madrid, Spain, September.

Vermunt, J.D. (1992). *Leerstijlen en sturen van leerprocessen in het hoger: naar procesgeriche instructe in zelfstandig denken.* (Learning styles and regulation of learning in higher education: towards process-oriented instruction in autonomous thinking), Amsterdam/Lisse: Swets & Zeitlinger, cited in Vermunt, J.D. (1996) 'Metacognitive, cognitive and affective aspects of learning styles and strategies: a phenomenographic analysis', *Higher Education*, 31: 25–50.

Vermunt, J.D. (1996) 'Meta-cognitive, cognitive and affective aspects of learning styles and strategies: a phenomenographic analysis', *Higher Education*, 31: 25–50.

Verner, C. and Davidson, C.V. (1982) 'Physiological factors in adult learning and instruction', in F. Adam and G. Aker (eds), *Factors in Adult Learning and Instruction*. Tallahassee, Fla.: Florida State University.

Viljoen, J. and Dann, S. (2000) *Strategic Management: Planning and Implementing Successful Corporate Strategies*, French's Forest, NSW: Pearson Education Australia.

Vince, R. (2003) 'The future practice of HRD', *Human Resource Development International*, 6(4): 559–563.

von Glaserfield, E. (1987) 'Learning as a constructive activity', in C. Janvier (ed.), *Problems of Representation in the Teaching and Learning of Mathematics*, Hillsdale, NJ: Lawrence Erlbaum Associates.

Vroom, V.H. (1964) *Work and Motivation*, New York: Wiley.

Vygotsky, L.S. (1978) *Mind in Society – The Development of Higher Psychological Processes*, Cambridge, Mass.: Harvard University Press.

Waldman, E. and de Lange, P. (1996) 'Performance of business undergraduates studying through open learning: a comparative analysis', *Accounting Education*, 5(1): 25–33.

Wales, S. (2003) 'Why coaching?', *Journal of Change Management*, 3(3): 275–282.

Warner, D., Christie, G. and Choy, S. (1998) *The Readiness of the VET Sector for Flexible Delivery Including On-line Learning*, Brisbane: Australian National Training Authority.

Weick, K.E. and Westley, F. (1999) 'Organizational learning: affirming an oxymoron', in S.R. Clegg, C. Hardy and W.R. Nord (eds), *Managing Organizations: Current Issues*, London: Sage.

Welton, M. (1991) *Toward Development Work: The Workplace as a Learning Environment*, Geelong, Victoria: Deakin University Press.

Wenger, E. (1998) *Communities of Practice: Learning, Meaning and Identity*, Cambridge: Cambridge University Press.

Wenger, E. (2000) 'Communities of practice: stewarding knowledge', in C. Despres and D. Chauvel, D. (eds), *Knowledge Horizons: The Present and the Promise of Knowledge Management*, Boston, Mass.: Butterworth-Heinemann.

Wenger, E., McDermott, R. and Snyder, W.M. (2002) *Cultivating Communities of Practice*, Boston, Mass.: Harvard Business School Press.

White, C. (1997) 'Eliciting and analysing expectations of novice distance learners', *Journal of Distance Learning*, 3: 3–11.

Whittaker, G. (1995) 'The BA in Post Qualifying Social Work: Preliminary Evaluation Report', Glasgow: Glasgow Caledonian University, cited in F. Reeve, J. Gallacher and T. Mayes (1998) 'Can new technology remove barriers to work-based learning?', *Open Learning*, 13 (November), 18–26: 19.

Whittaker, M. and Cartwright, A. (2000) *The Mentoring Manual*, Aldershot: Gower.

Willis, H. and Dodgson, J. (1986) 'Mentoring of Canadian women in educational administration', *The Canadian Administrator*, 25(2): 1–6.

Wlodowski, R.J. (1985) *Enhancing Motivation to Learn*, San Francisco, Calif.: Jossey-Bass.

Woodall, J. and Winstanley, D. (1998) *Management Development: Strategy and Practice*, Oxford: Blackwell.

Woodley, A. and McIntosh, N.E. (1979) 'Age as a factor in performance at the Open University', paper presented at the 5th International Conference on Improving University Teaching, London, City University.

Wright, T. (1987) 'Putting independent learning in its place', in A. Tait (ed.) (1993) *Key Issues in Open Learning*, Harlow: Longmans.

Yamauchi, L.A. (1998) 'Individualism, collectivism and cultural compatibility: implications for counsellor and teachers', *Journal of Humanistic Education and Development*, 36(4): 189–197.

Yinger, J. and Eckland, R. (1975) *Problem Solving with Children*, San Francisco, Calif., Far West Laboratory for Educational Research and Development. Cited in H. Ellington (1997) 'Flexible learning – your flexible friend', in C. Bell, M. Bowden and A. Trott (eds), *Implementing Flexible Learning*, London: Kogan Page, p. 4.

Young, M.F. (1993) 'Instructional design for situated learning', *Educational Technology Research and Development*, 41(1): 43–58.

Zemsky, R. and Massy, W.F. (2004) *Thwarted Innovation: What Happened to E-learning and Why*, University of Pennsylvania: The Learning Alliance.

Index

Delahoussaye, M. 103–4
demography 3, 16
Despres, C. 15
development 2, 9, 25–6, 145, 204;
  career 112; constraints 183;
  flexibility 190–1; identifying areas
  for 173; novice to expert 45–6, 147;
  personal development plan 69–70,
  82; processes of 184–6; proximal
  zone of 143–4; development
  methods 136
development orientation 59
developmental coaching 112, 138
dialogic learning 36
didacticism: advantages and
  disadvantages 116; degree of 115
dispositional knowledge 35
dispositional skills 15
distance education 176–7; tension from
  177
distance learning 109, 117–22, 140;
  characteristics of 117; definition of
  118; evaluation of 120; and physical
  separation 120–1; programme
  design 121; and support 136; and
  technology 118; variations in 120–1
Dobbs, K. 135
Dodgson, J. 44
domain knowledge *see* declarative
  knowledge
Dowling, P.J. 70–1
Down, S. 48, 176–7
Doyle, D. 130
Dreyfus, S.E. 37–8, 45, 147, 159
Duffy, T.M. 33
Duguid, P. 160
Dwyer, P. 90

e-learning 109, 121, 122–9, 141;
  communities 127, 128–9; definition
  of 122; informal 127; measuring
  outcomes of 126–7
Eli Lilly and Company 48–9
Ellington, H. 175
employee groups 27
employees: agendas of 2–3; confidence
  40; individual capability 29;
  interests of 2–3; management of
  61–2; needs 75; pro forma 184
entrepreneurial work 13, 22
environmental analysis 178–9, 181–2,
  190
environmental dynamism 193

environmental skills 36
Eraut, M. 39, 42
ERG theory 63
Ester, D.P. 124
Evans, G. 38
Evans, K. 90
Evans, T.D. 46, 180

Farmer, J.A., Jr 45
feedback 38, 40, 110, 130, 152, 156,
  187; and adjustment 186
Feimer, S.H. 74–5
Fernald, P.S. 119
Fiore, S.M. 120
flexible delivery 175–6; key features
  175–6
Flexible Delivery Working Party
  (1992), Australia 175
flexible learning 175–9; concept of 175;
  developing individual learners
  179–86; planning 177–9, 190
François, P. 17
Fuller, A. 147, 158

Gagne, R.M. 37
Gallacher, J. 156
games 109, 123, 129–32, 141
Gardiner, P. 26, 158
Gardner, H. 92
Garrison, D.R. 143
Gay, J. 91
Ghobadian, A. 26, 28
Ghosal, S. 15, 16, 17, 18
Gibb, J. 25
Gibbs, C. 156
Gilman, S. 118
Glick, J. 91
goal based learning 35, 45
goal orientation 59
goal setting 64, 68–9, 156; high
  performance cycle model 156
goals 76, 81
Goddard, H.H. 91
Gold, J. 203
Goldstein, I.L. 119–20, 153
Gonzci, A. 164
Gott, S. 36–7, 38
Gray, C. 47
Greene, R. 159
Gruber, C.P. 95
Guglielmino, T. 48

Hadré, P.L. 71

see also computer-based learning;
participative methods
Learning Network Theory 22, 27, 41,
46, 84
learning networks 12, 22–4, 30, 186;
external 23; horizontal 23, 39, 84;
vertical 23; *see also* liberal learning
networks; learning organization,
definition 19
learning orientation 7–8, 52–77;
identification of 76; situational
dependence 57–8
learning outcomes 78, 172, 189; and
motivation 61
learning practitioner 1, 8; flexibility of
9–10; identifying issues 2; judgement
of 9–10; roles of 5; *see also* coach;
HRD practitioner; mentor
learning preferences 8, 78, 93–101,
105, 115, 186–7, 188; context 96;
non-verbal/verbal 95–6; observation
of 96; self-directed/dependent 95–6
learning process 32–3, 78
learning process advantage 13–14
learning room 172
learning schedule 172
learning strategies 100–1, 106, 155–62,
173; cognitive 100, 102; meta-
cognitive 100, 102; non-preferred
150; selection of 173; social/affective
100, 103
learning styles 78, 86, 93–101, 105,
186–7, 188; abstract 124;
accommodators 86, 97; activist 97;
assimilators 86, 97; concept of
186–7; concrete 124; convergers 86,
97; divergers 86, 97; pragmatist 97;
reflector 97; theorist 97; theory 189;
utility and assessment of 101–4
Learning Styles Inventory 97
Learning Styles Questionnaire 98
learning support 9, 126, 143–73;
development of 171–2; policies
163–5; resources for 144; structures
165–7; workplace model 145–55
learning transfer system 153
Leduchowicz, T 73–4, 169
LeGrand, B. 45
liberal learning networks 23, 39, 84;
barriers to 183
Lim, G.S. 58
Lindeman, E. 89
Locke, E.A. 156

London Business School 130

McCollum, A. 15, 46, 152
McCracken, M. 56
McDermott, R. 41, 42
MacDonald, R. 27
McGregor, D. 61
machine bureaucratic work 22
McKavanagh, C.W. 47
McLean, G.N. 20
McLean, L. 20
Maclennan, N. 109–10, 114
McLoughlin, C. 144
Mahoney, S.E. 124
management 12, 18–22; competencies
20–1; culture 30; development 131;
formulas 60; views and value on
HRD 18–19
management games, categories 131
managers 8, 61, 76–7; action approach
132; attitude 14, 71; defensive
routines 133; and incidental learning
135; incompetence of 133; and
intuitive learning 135; and
prospective learning 135; roles of
77; and training matters 152
managers, orientation of 70–2; and
hierarchy 70–1; short-termism 70
Manning, B.H. 149
Mansfield, R. 35–6
market 24; deregulation of 3;
globalisation 3; requirements 25;
value 12
Marland, P. 100
Martin, C.A. 119
Maslow, A.H. 62
Massachusetts Institute of Technology
130
Massy, W.F. 125
Maurer, T.J. 59
Mayes, T. 156
Mayo, A. 12, 28
mentor 40–1, 152; and coach 110;
definition of 44–5; formal and
informal 44; identifying 44; and
protégé 113–14; roles 165–6
mentoring 7, 34, 35, 43–6, 75, 108,
113–15, 139; and coaching 113–14;
definition of 113–15; informal 114;
and self-efficacy 114
Mezirow, J. 36
micro-worlds 130
Mintzberg, H. 22

Lightning Source UK Ltd.
Milton Keynes UK
UKOW06f0213120416